ONE WEEK IN MARCH

MARK SHERWIN, and

One Week

FOUNDED 1838

GPPS

CHARLES LAM MARKMANN

In March,

G. P. Putnam's Sons **NEW YORK**

to our children and grandchildren,
who ought to know

CONTENTS

ONE WEEK IN MARCH

The Money Simply Stopped

THE week of March 1 to March 7, 1933, moved in massive paradoxes its historic wonders to unfold. The richest country in the world was penny-poor. A financial panic was averted by shutting off the supply of money. They called it a bank holiday. Farmers were going broke producing more food than a hungry America could afford to consume. A people impatient with breadlines, unemployment and cloying promises of prosperity stood by with muted excitement as the government changed hands.

The whole world was trembling with disaster, political upheaval, social unrest, revolution, militarism and fear, but this did not seem to bother the well-dressed man kneeling intently over a subway grating, trying to fish a nickel through the opening with the aid of a moist and masticated piece of chewing gum at the end of a stick. This man, like so many others all over the country, was unconsciously dramatizing a situation. He had in his wallet a $500 bill and three $100 bills. He needed the nickel for his subway fare.

In another part of town a mink-coated dowager strode into an Automat, placed a dollar bill on the counter and received 20 nickels. She was unable to suppress a smug smile as she walked out clutching her precious coins. She did not make a purchase. She had just given up her last dollar, literally. All she had left in her purse was several $100 bills.

In thousands of drugstores throughout the startled land a timely vignette from life was being acted out amid comic solemnity. With minor variations, it went something like this:

A man would walk in and casually ask for some shaving cream (large); three dozen razor blades; shaving lotion (the biggest bottle); tooth paste and some aspirins. The charge would be around $2.53. The man would give the clerk a $50 bill or a bigger one. The clerk would either sneer or smile sympathetically, depending upon how frequently he had been a participant in this kind of transaction, and push the bill back to the dismayed customer. While laboriously restoring the goods to the shelves, he might say: "I'll give you change of five dollars, but no more." The customer would plead: "But I need this stuff. What am I going to do?" The clerk would shake his head and say: "Grow a beard. We need the change more than we need this sale." The customer would stalk out, muttering something about an upside-down world where a man could have lots of money in his pocket and still be poor.

In Elgin, Illinois, a large crowd had beaten a path to the door of a 16-year-old boy. He had something far better (for this week only) than a better mousetrap. With the help of wise parents he had been saving pennies toward his college education, and by this day he had accumulated 11,357 of them. Storekeepers, taxi drivers, newspaper vendors and housewives had heard of this young man, and they were making friendly overtures for his precious holdings. History will never know whether he made a profit on the deal, but he did give up his pennies to enable his community's commerce to function effectively for a day or so.

Even John D. Rockefeller didn't have a dime. Are you old

enough to remember the kindly old gentleman with the silver-gray toupé, who in the later years of his life made himself beloved of the newsreels by giving away shiny new dimes to bright-eyed children? He had spent half his life amassing billions and the second half giving them away to foundations and universities. But billions were not easy for the common people to understand, so John D. had yielded to the clever suggestions of his public-relations man, Ivy Lee, and had translated his give-away into understandable dimes. During this week, Rockefeller made no newsreel appearances. He even gave his golf caddy a dollar instead of the usual dime.

A salesman of ladies' undergarments, whose home office was in St. Louis, found himself stranded in Seattle with nothing more than a checkbook that was supported by an impeccable balance in a closed bank. But the checks were only nicely printed pieces of paper now. No one would cash a check for any amount. The salesman, who dealt in wholesale quantities, selling his items to large stores and chains by the thousands of dozens, took his sample satchel and sold his wares singly, door to door, to get enough money for bus fare home. He sold these items well below their regular retail cost, and housewives could not resist the prices, raiding their cookie jars, teapots and other hiding places for the ready cash.

Was there much of this kind of money in the homes? A newspaper survey in Massachusetts showed that the average family had $18.23 in purses, coffeepots, piggy banks and trouser pockets. With the exception of farm areas, this held true for the rest of the country. The problem was not big money. There was lots of it in spotted areas all over the land. Small change and small bills, the legal tender for a bus ride, a pack of cigarettes, a telephone call from a pay station, a shoeshine, a newspaper and a haircut, were in short supply. Commuters throughout the land went to railroad stations to redeem their monthly tickets in order to get coins. In New York, crowds flourishing bills in denominations of $100 and more stormed into Pennsylvania Station to purchase tickets for Newark, which is ten miles away. The railroad rendered heroic service until its small-change supply was exhausted. One man presented a $1,500 certified check at the Hotel Astor and asked for a night's lodging and change. He was turned away with polite regrets.

This was truly a time when in the small areas of daily commerce the rich were as needy as the poor.

It was the week of the great bank holiday—the week when the money stopped and a bewildered America, hanging on desperately to its good humor, sought to maintain a steadfast calm, deeply aware that the slightest movement toward panic would bring the ultimate disaster.

On a material basis, this was America's bravest hour.

What were the causes of this strange holiday that saw the creeping fear of financial catastrophe envelop an already stifled economy? They began in the fabulous, if irresponsible, prosperity of the twenties that ended with the Stock Market débâcle in 1929. The debilitating Depression that followed had left the lower and middle classes economically and spiritually exhausted and frightened, despite the chimeric promises of a reluctant prosperity that was shyly hiding around the corner.

The banks of the country had managed to fight off the encroaching deflation for three years. Even the strongest banking houses held securities and mortgages that had plummeted to a fraction of their former values. The financially wise who were not in the banking business were aware of this dangerous condition. There were 18,569 banks in the United States, possessing ready cash of $6 billion to cover $41 billion in deposits.

It was a strategic opportunity for the pessimists, professional and emotional, to sing their dirge of doom. Businessmen who had failed, workers who were jobless, spoke freely of the end of capitalism. These were the desperate and downhearted Americans who felt the Government should not have let them down. There were also the Communists who declaimed on street corners and in labor meetings that this "never-ending Depression" was perfect proof of the inability of the democratic system to cope with a real financial crisis. They predicted it was only a matter of months before there would be barricades in the streets.

But among the real leaders in America there were many vigorous optimists.

Charles Edison, son of the inventor, a moral power in New Jersey and later its governor, gave assurance that "the country is not going to hell." He preached patience and co-operation and promised that "out of this chaos and confusion will come organization and method that will forever banish want and desperation."

If Franklin D. Roosevelt was listening, he got a number of good suggestions from another optimist, Frank A. Vanderlip, banker and former Assistant Secretary of the Treasury. Vanderlip proposed a national financial plan that included an embargo of gold, a limited U.S. guarantee of bank deposits, legislation for the complete separation of investment and commercial banking and the devaluation of the dollar by reducing its gold content. His proposal was signed by James H. Rand Jr., president of Remington-Rand; John H. Hammond, chairman of the Bangor & Aroostook Railroad; Robert E. Wood, president, and Lessing J. Rosenwald, chairman, of Sears Roebuck; Vincent Bendix, Samuel Fels, Philip Wrigley, the chewing gum tycoon; Howard E. Coffin and E. L. Cord, automobile manufacturers; Edward A. O'Neill 3d, of the American Farm Bureau Federation; Louis J. Taber, master of the National Grange; Farney R. Wurlitzer, the organ manufacturer; William J. McAneeny of the Hudson Motor Car Co. and William A. Wirt, educator. . . .

CHAPTER 2

Boom and Bust

To ALL Americans except a handful of astute students of the economy, the explosion of the boom of the 1920's was an incomprehensible shock. For years the cost of living had remained almost static in the face of rising wages and a phenomenal rate of improvement in the general standard of living. More and more of everything—food, clothing, durable goods, automobiles, appliances, services—was being produced and consumed almost before it was available, and fluctuations in the price index were almost microscopic. On the surface of things, it was the utopian's dream of an ever richer economy from which inflation had been banished.

The boom had begun, of course, at the end of the First World War in late 1918, when all countries were hungry for so many of the things they had had to go without and governments could at last wipe out wartime curbs on production and spending. The United States, the least damaged of all the belligerents and the richest in manpower, in money, in natural resources and in technical development, was naturally the quickest to turn back to a civilian economy. But it went so fast and so far in the first few years after the war that a minor depression set in, in 1921, and tapered off

16

gradually until in 1923 all the curves on the graph were once more pointing upward.

The stability of price levels obscured much that was happening in the nation's economy. Technological progress was accelerating the output of all kinds of goods, and to move them into the hands of consumers, installment purchasing was making tremendous strides in all strata of society. Taxes were negligible and people had plenty of money to spend or to commit for future spending. Owning one's own home was the goal of even the unskilled worker, and Herbert Hoover's 1928 campaign slogan, A CHICKEN IN EVERY POT AND TWO CARS IN EVERY GARAGE, was already well on the way to becoming reality before the election. But the garages were built on mortgages and both cars were being paid for out of income. So, very often, were the furniture, the lamps, the clothes and virtually every other purchase of any consequence.

Corporate earnings rose steadily during the years from 1923 to 1929, and ahead of them raced the prices of stocks. Speculating in common stocks, the issue of which was virtually unregulated except by such policing as the Stock Exchange itself could manage, was ahead even of baseball as the national sport; no longer the exclusive province of the financially knowledgeable and shrewd, it was the great game of bootblacks and maiden aunts, taxi drivers and housewives. The secret lay in the fact that virtually no one paid for the shares he bought, for *margin* was the universal catchword.

What *margin* meant was simply that the stockbroker, borrowing from the bank, lent the buyer 90 per cent of the purchase price of his stock and, as long as it held steady or continued to rise, forgot about the debt save for collecting the interest on the loan, usually out of dividends. Every margin agreement bound the stock buyer to put up, in cash, more margin if the stock fell below the price at which he had bought it; but for six years virtually nothing dropped. People sold at a profit the stocks for which they had paid 10 per cent of the price and used the proceeds as the 10 per cent basis for much bigger purchases, pyramiding these transactions to astronomical heights. Using the already mortgaged profits as security, they borrowed still further to raise their levels of living in a literal spree of buying. It was "the American way" that was making private enterprise and unregulated capitalism the envy of the world and providing a new cliché for the politician of every stripe.

What no one—except a few Cassandras—recognized was a credit inflation whose very subtlety made it so dangerous. Ostensibly, the economy could not have been sounder: more and more of everything was being made and bought at no increase in cost to the consumer; but he was mortgaging more and more of his income in order to consume even further. How was this possible?

Basically, the ultimate source of credit was the banks, those archetypes of conservative caution. There were county banks—chartered by the county in which they were run; state banks—chartered by the state in which they operated; and national banks, chartered by the United States Government. Each had the power to issue not only bank notes but credit against the security of its reserves and deposits; in practice, few county banks exercised this power to issue currency and, by 1929, not many state banks availed themselves of it. In addition, the Government itself issued currency: gold certificates, payable in gold on demand; silver certificates, payable in silver on demand; ordinary paper money backed only by the credit of the Government; and Federal Reserve notes.

These last were the creation of the Federal Reserve System, a kind of hydra-headed analogue to the Bank of England established just before the First World War. The system embraces twelve banks in as many geographical areas, wholly owned but not controlled by member banks. All national banks were required to be members of the Federal Reserve System and some state banks were allowed to join under specified conditions. The Federal Reserve banks were designed to prevent such money panics as that of 1907; they were empowered to issue currency and to advance money or credit to member banks on the security of the latter's loans and other assets—to "rediscount" and to establish their own rate of interest, which in turn governed the rates charged by member banks to their customers. The Federal Reserve banks were required to maintain a gold reserve equal to at least 40 per cent of their currency issues plus sound short-term commercial loans whose face value equaled 100 per cent of the bank notes issued. Not all the country's banks were required or even permitted to be members of the Federal Reserve System; but those that were accepted were required to maintain on deposit with the System specified percentages of their total deposits as reserves. These percentages varied with economic conditions, types of deposits (time or savings deposits as against demand or checking accounts) and the classification of the member bank itself. It was also permitted to maintain on deposit an excess reserve —that is, more money than the regulations required. All this was intended to assure a certain stability to the banking system of the nation.

A member bank was permitted to borrow from the Federal Reserve in stipulated proportion to its required and excess reserve and, in turn, to lend this money to its customers, who might be entrepreneurs, consumers, manufacturing corporations or finance companies that re-lent the money at still higher rates, with or without collateral, and generally to borrowers who for one reason or another could not command bank credit. Hence the actual cash in circulation and on deposit in banks of all kinds could never equal the face amount of the outstanding credit.

In 1926, three years before the Stock Market's Black Thursday, there had been a rather frightening collapse of real-estate and mortgage values, which had been vigorously inflated beyond all realistic limits by a rush of investors competing for land, buildings and mortgages. These investors constituted a very small percentage of the public, however, and what happened to them in the minor crash of their dream—except for the much-publicized Florida land boom and bust—taught nothing to the nation at large. It was a freak, an accident that could never happen again. The survivors joined their fellow citizens in a fresh gold rush among the concrete precipices of Wall Street, sending stock prices up even farther until they reached the 1929 peaks of 381.17 for the Dow-Jones industrial average, 189.11 for the railroad average and 144.61 for the utility average.

Some weeks before October's débâcle there was a sharp break in the entire stock market. The general public, faithful to the old adage, was buying at the top and the professionals began to sense that it was time to get out. The vast amounts of stock that they unloaded forced prices down precipitately and for the first time in years, brokers began en masse to demand that their customers produce cash for their margin purchases. But then the market rallied, seducing even many of the professional investors and speculators, and, with varying degrees of timorousness, the public began to buy again.

By fall the prices of stocks had been forced up to levels at which no intelligent person would buy them; brokers, lacking ready cash to meet their notes at their banks, began again to call on stockholders to post more margin; and these, already pressed for cash because of overcommitment of their incomes, had no choice but to start to sell. The shrewd, detached students knew that the market had reached its peak because the credit economy was overstrained; those who had not already put themselves in a liquid cash position after the earlier break lost no time now in stripping themselves of the beautifully engraved share certificates in return for smaller, less impressive but far more valuable bank balances.

The collapse of the stock market was only a warning of what was to come in the economy as a whole, which, like the market, had been strained beyond its capacity to endure. Credit had been expanded and expanded again until there was no basis left for more, and debtors lacked the assets and the income to meet their obligations. Millions of people found without warning that they were penniless, sold out of their securities with mounting losses and saddled with notes they could no longer pay. The worst sufferers were those whose hopes were strongest and who refused as long as they could to rid themselves of their stocks: as the pressure grew, prices tumbled still farther and panic selling set the pace. Foreign capital that in the preceding years had sought refuge in Wall Street's seemingly topless escalator from the uncertainties of Europe shriveled before it could muster its resources to flee.

Overnight the United States was plunged into a major depression. Creditors, frightened, demanded immediate payment; debtors, stunned and hamstrung, had no ready money. Mortgagees began to foreclose, collection lawyers grew busy; people who had cash savings began to draw on them. Above all, people suddenly stopped buying and the merchant and manufacturer listened longingly for the music of the cash register. As it regressed from *andantino* to *andante* to *adagio,* they could no longer pay all their employees or all their bills; workers and creditors were thrown little by little on their own resources. If there were no buyers there was obviously no reason for sellers; and if sellers could not pay their staffs, there could be no buyers. It was impossible to determine which was the chicken, which the egg.

Within a year of the explosion the rolls of the unemployed had swollen, augmented by the thousands of small business people whose size had made it certain that they would be the first of the capitalists to be struck down. The slums that had never been erased from the country's cities and rural areas began to spread. Panic was subsiding into unremitting fear, which in turn began to breed anger. People wanted something done; for the first time in a decade they remembered they had a government and they demanded that it do something or join the jobless.

Political awareness on any broad scale was a new phenomenon. Since 1920, when the voters had enthusiastically cast off the Democratic Party under whose aegis the United States had become a belligerent, there had been an unbroken Republican hegemony of contentment and complacency. Warren G. Harding had been swept into the Presidency on a tide of postwar inflation, promising to keep the nation within its borders and to pay absolutely no attention to the rest of the world; he had died in office, just as the 1921–23 recession was ending, and had been succeeded by Calvin Coolidge, whose sagacious refusal to express any views on any subject was exploited as New England shrewdness, and, by the time Coolidge came up for election, the slump was already a memory. During the next four years the apparently infinite prosperity of the country made it harder than ever for the Democrats to persuade the nation to change horses in midstream, even though they promised to repeal the hated Prohibition Amendment. Against the appealing image of Herbert Hoover, the Great Engineer—a designation that was magic to a nation devoted to efficiency—the Democrats made the mistake of running a Roman Catholic, underestimating the strength of bigotry in their stronghold, the Bible Belt of the South, despite its unmistakable revulsion at the nomination of Governor Al Smith of New York.

During those years the isolated political independents— Fiorello LaGuardia, Representative from New York, and Senators George Norris of Wyoming and Robert LaFollette of Minnesota were outstanding exemplars—had been almost ignored by the nation at large when they strove to bestir the Government from its pleasant indolence to active effort on behalf of the unions, the consumers, the backward areas to which the new civilization had not yet extended its boons. But in the fall of 1930, when one-third of the Senate and the full House of Representatitves was to be elected, people were hungry and frightened; unable to help themselves or to win succor from the captains of industry who had for so long seemed the high priests dispensing the divine will, they demanded new vicars of God to help them out of the morass. Hoover, the Great Administrator, had proved unable to do more than promise, whenever he spoke, that "prosperity is just around the corner." But the depression was a long straight road where one never came to the corner. The people could not turn the President out of office before the fulfillment of his term, but they could replace a Congress as unwilling as the President to take action—any action, even if it were mistaken, as long as it was an effort to make things better.

The Republican candidates ran on the record of the receding past; the Democrats, who had nothing to lose, began to make promises. The Republicans tried to reassure the owning class and the high-income groups that everything would once more be as it had been; the Democrats pledged themselves not to restore the *status quo ante* but to create new rights and interests and to vest them in those who had always had nothing. They would create jobs, they would restore the value of the dollar, they would save the homes of the "little people." The appeal was irresistible—the majority of the electorate, like the Democrats, had nothing more to lose and everything to gain—and for the final two years of his tenure Hoover, the stand-pat Republican, found himself confronted with a Democratic Congress.

That Congress tried mightily to enact legislation that would do something to stem the deepening depression; but virtually every bill it passed was vetoed by the President, generally out of conviction, often out of purely political motivation. And in turn, on the rare occasions when the Republican President genuinely sought to win the adoption of remedial legislation, the Democratic Congress, its eye on the 1932 Presidential election, refused to listen. But in the various states the Democrats were capturing governorships and legislatures and some among them were planning already for the nominating convention of 1932.

Undoubtedly the shrewdest politician of the lot was Franklin Delano Roosevelt, crippled heir of the less wealthy branch of the family that had already produced one President, whose name still carried much emotional weight in all parts of the country. Assistant Secretary of the Navy during the war, Franklin Roosevelt had turned to politics after an unsuccessful legal and business career and had made a reputation in New York State as a forward-looking and vigorous friend of the underdog in the Legislature and in the Governorship.

As the convention neared, he exploited Hoover's tendency to seek to revive the economy by letting crumbs fall from the top; Roosevelt proclaimed his determination to start rebuilding at the bottom by bettering the lot of the common man first and striving to protect him against any recurrence of the catastrophe through which he was still living. In the murky climate of bank failures as resources proved insufficient to meet the demands of jobless depositors, of evidence of manipulation and outright dishonesty among financiers and industrial magnates, Roosevelt declared war on the "money-changers in the temple" and the "malefactors of great wealth" and vowed a "new deal" for all the people that would begin with the elimination of fear.

He had at hand, after his nomination and as the election campaign progressed, new legislation, some of it forced through over Hoover's veto, that the Democratic Congress had devised in order to vastly implement the power of the Executive, even though Hoover refused to utilize it. Roose-

velt had also a dual advantage: whenever Hoover spoke publicly his ineptitude and his timidity of policy made people
forget his good faith, and his natural reserve tended to
alienate people by the millions. Roosevelt offered a bold
policy of constant dynamism, devoid of caution; and he had
an almost irresistible warmth and charm that won and held
the devoted loyalty of men and women of all backgrounds.
His impartial constant search for the best brains of the nation gained him the support of the independents and the
intellectuals, who had never shared Hoover's dictum that
the ability to run a big corporation or a major engineering
project was the sole qualification for a governmental official
or adviser.

Roosevelt came to the polls after three years of constantly
mounting economic misery throughout the country. Against
the fatigued bewilderment of leaders who had no followers he pitted audacity and experiment and, above all, the
will to act, without delay. Americans as a whole felt they had
reached bottom; their only choice was whether to stay there
and await a new natural law of levitation or to adopt a course
and a leader who would try to anticipate the miracle. For
the first time since the depression began they were offered
concrete hope; they seized it with thanks. Too fear-beset
and too exhausted to seek any longer to shape their own
destinies, they wanted now to be led out of the Slough of
Despond and, for the first time since the war, they had a
leader.

CHAPTER 3

Figures and Facts, and Two Fancies

WHEN the closing bell rang on the floor of the New York Stock Exchange at 3 P.M. on Friday, March 3, the economic barometer still pointed, as it had almost since the preceding July 8, when stock averages reached their lowest point in the Exchange's history, to fair weather ahead. Students of the Dow Theory, whose major thesis holds that stock prices forecast tomorrow's economic climate, rather than reflect today's or yesterday's, noted that the Dow-Jones average of thirty industrial issues stood at 53.84, against its July low of 41.22; the average of twenty railroad stocks was 24.76, almost double the July figure of 13.23; and the fifteen utilities averaged 21.95, against July's 16.53. The barometer had signaled the Depression's end eight months earlier, when unemployment, according to the American Federation of Labor, stood at 12.3 million; by now the rolls of the jobless had risen to 13.7 million in the United States. In almost every other major country, including Germany, the first and worst victim of the Depression, unemployment was decreasing slightly but steadily.

Despite the general drop in the American working population, manufacturing jobs had actually increased since the preceding summer; it was in the white-collar fields and the professions that the blow struck. Though the steel mills were operating at only 19 per cent of their capacity, industry was beginning to see an upturn. "Big Steel"—the United States Steel Corp.—had finished 1932 with a deficit of $91.9 million, but it paid all its dividends nonetheless, an example followed by General Motors with a 1932 deficit of $63 million.

Those banks that had not already been closed were selling government securities heavily, for these represented the most liquid of their assets. Some of these were bought up by the Federal Reserve System. As a result of the heavy withdrawals by bank depositors, money in circulation stood at the record peak of just under $6 billion. In the first days of March, those who were using their cash or credit for investments were almost unanimously deserting such fixed-income securities as bonds and preferred stocks, with the result that in some cases the returns on these represented a yield as high as 17 per cent of the price that they fetched in the open market. The investors who were unloading these issues were shifting to common stocks, obviously the best hedge available if inflation was to come. But a great deal of the money in circulation was leaving the country, and its goal was chiefly London, though much of it went also to Switzerland. In New York City alone, banks lost $444 million of deposits in the week ended Thursday, March 2; to raise this cash, they had had to sell $100 million in Government bonds and $200 million in short-term Treasury bills, as well as borrowing $180 million from the Federal Reserve Bank. Its reserve had fallen by the end of February to 45.8 per cent of actual deposit credits to member banks, and by March 7, according to *The Economist* of London, the cash reserve was barely 25 per cent.

The Economist predicted on Inauguration Day that the United States would be compelled to guarantee bank deposits in order to prevent a general collapse. The various state bank holidays, in the view of British experts, were leading to a national closing of the banks, and this was deplored as a political maneuver that would slow the reviving economy, encourage hoarding and only put off the inevitable day when some banks would simply have to go out of business. At the same time, financial experts in Britain and most of Europe were confident that the United States would hold to the gold standard. Nonetheless, caution ruled in London on Inauguration Day—it would seem that the shrewder investors and speculators had some advance inkling of Roosevelt's plans, or at any rate of the true state of the American banking system—and all foreign-exchange operations in the City were suspended for the day.

Even as Roosevelt was drafting his holiday proclamation on Sunday, the Reverend Charles E. Coughlin was making his weekly nationwide radio appeal for a 100 per cent inflation of the currency. The Michigan priest, already the trusted shepherd of an innumerable flock of listeners whose contributions paid the $4,000 weekly cost of his broadcasts, was eyed with some distaste by his clerical superiors whenever he took to the microphone to urge the Government to double the face value of every coin and bank note in circulation; he was still too cautious to take overt political action or to attack Jewish financiers specifically. What Father Coughlin did not mention—perhaps he did not know it, or perhaps its significance eluded him—was the fact that the assets and liabilities of member banks of the Federal Reserve System were actually in sounder condition than in the roseate July of 1929; liabilities of $22 million in 1929 had shrunk to $19 million in 1933, whereas assets of $39 million had risen to $41 million.

The trouble was, of course, that the average depositor did

not read the weekly Federal Reserve reports and might very likely have been unable to understand them in the light of his own steadily shrinking cash. It was not easy to explain to a penniless bank depositor that his bank's assets were largely long-term holdings that could not be liquidated overnight without causing tremendous hardship to everyone, including perhaps the exigent depositor; he was quite often a debtor of the bank as well as its creditor, and in order to satisfy him in the one guise it might have to destroy him in the other. It is not only at the race track that scared money never wins.

Big scared money flowed into London in such quantities that by March 4 the loan rate was down to one-quarter of one per cent, and no one was interested in lending. While continental rates were higher, they were still relatively low, and, since the flight of capital bypassed Europe, they were unaffected. In contrast, New York rates for short-term loans had risen from 1 per cent at the end of February to 4 per cent by March 3, and again—though for a different reason from that of London—there was no business; no one could afford to borrow.

The same contrast prevailed in long-term financing and bank rates. The Federal Reserve Bank raised its interest rate to 3.5 per cent from 2.5 per cent; at the same time the national banks of other countries were lowering theirs. British bankers, unlike the detached observers in the offices of *The Economist,* were on the whole pleased by America's bank holiday; they were sure it marked the end of what they called the dream of their American competitors to transfer the world's financial center from London to New York.

Otherwise the closing of the banks in the United States had little effect abroad. When foreign-exchange trading was resumed in London on March 6, the dollar was not included; but in Germany it was still quoted and held almost firm; valued at 4.213 marks on March 4, it was traded at 4.180 marks three days later. Foreign stock exchanges—all the

American exchanges remained closed throughout the holiday—were normally active and the general trend was a rising one, even for those American issues traded abroad. In Germany, where Hjalmar Schacht succeeded to the presidency of the Reichsbank and immediately declared a moratorium on all local, municipal, provincial and national bonds, the stock market opened vigorously on March 6, the day after the Reichstag election, in anticipation of big governmental expenditures for unemployment relief and public-works projects.

A pressing problem for every country was foreign trade. In the United States, the latest monthly export figure was $120 million, the latest for imports was $96 million; both sums were the smallest since the preceding summer. Britain, which had only recently abandoned its historic free-trade principle for a protective tariff, was beginning to be sharply divided on the question; most bankers, guided by a self-interest that was not afflicted with myopia, firmly advocated the end of the high tariff. France and Germany had begun talks intended to establish a customs union, but after the March 5 election in Germany realists held little hope of their continuance. Some solace was found, however, in the conclusion of a mutually favorable trade pact with Sweden. As aware of Germany's probable trend as the French, the Dutch nevertheless began commercial negotiations with the Germans on the day after the latter's election. Meanwhile all Europe was watching and waiting to see what would happen in the United States, whose new Secretary of State, Cordell Hull, was regarded abroad as a staunch free-trader. In violent contrast to the hopes and actions of the Europeans, Chile simply raised all its customs duties by 50 per cent.

Internally, virtually every country faced the same problems: continuing unemployment, too slow in declining; inadequate production and insufficient income; increased spending and deficit financing. The mortgage moratorium, already accepted in some American states, was a favorite medicine of the agricultural nations, which imposed a cessation of payments of interest or of both interest and principal. It was especially popular in Cuba, Argentina and Hungary; the last also pioneered in the imposition of currency restrictions. Japan was looking into similar action.

Hungary exemplified the cruel paradox that depression worked the greatest hardship on those nations that had benefited least from the boom that preceded it. Primarily an agricultural country almost untouched by the Industrial Revolution, Hungary tried to help its farmers by raising the price of bread when strikes for basic safety in the primitive factories were aggravating the already overwhelming unemployment. During this first week of March there were five to eight suicides daily among the Magyars; except when the motive was believed to be a crossed love, the press gave no reasons for the deaths. One of the most touching of the suicides was a double one: Imre Zsoke, 23, and Julianna Maikus, 21, forbidden by their parents to marry, hanged themselves with the one rope.

The personal advertisements in the *Pesti Hirlap* of March 4—the day when all America was looking with hope toward Washington and a large part of Germany was anticipating the next day's election triumph—were indicative of the desperation of the Hungarians of all classes:

Will pay reward to anyone who finds me a job.

Wife of invalid officer, mother of two children, can take any job, day or night.

Gentlewoman offers plain needlework and darning at good houses for one pengö per day. (The pengö was worth a few cents.)

Teacher gives French, English or piano lessons in return for lunch.

What well-to-do gentleman will marry tall, slender young lady who can offer only a lonely soul longing for kindness?

Those who could not afford to advertise went by the thousands to root out fuel and whatever else might prove useful from municipal dumping grounds. The others, who still owned land or enjoyed earned or unearned incomes, suffered somewhat less; the government limited the rate of taxation on both sources and made due allowance for large families. Bachelors, however, faced the imposition of a special tax.

In violent contrast to Hungary, a country in which feudalism had not yet really given way to mercantile and industrial capitalism, Russia was plunging fanatically into the Second Five-Year Plan. Trotskyist internationalism had been extirpated; Stalinist devotion to completing the Communist revolution at home was making tremendous strides. While the Russians, like the Hungarians, had never known the economic and technological advances of capitalism, they were determined to achieve these not by evolution from feudalism through capitalism but by an incredible leap across a chasm of centuries. One of the weapons of Russia's internal economic war was education; in three years, illiteracy had been reduced from 33 per cent to less than 20 per cent of the population. The small shopkeeper had been eliminated, and the *kulak,* or private-enterprise agriculturist, was almost gone, lost in the growth of collectives and state farms if he had survived ordinary massacre.

In this first week of March, when all the rest of the world was watching the United States and Germany for signs of the immediate future and looking toward Russia only with dread, if indeed at all, the dictatorship of the proletariat smelted 108,000 tons of pig iron and 107,000 tons of steel; it brought out of the earth 1,308,000 tons of coal and 361,000 tons of oil. Automobile output exceeded 135 units daily and tractors came off the line at the rate of 180 a day. The Moscow subway was under construction; new blast furnaces were being blown in as others were begun. While Roosevelt was taking the oath of office in Washington, the Academy of

Sciences and the State Planning Commission of the USSR were opening the industrial-economic-political-scientific Conference on the Greater Dnieper in Kiev. Even then the Soviet ruling class was co-opting the best scientific minds of the country to work with the managers and the political leaders in projecting the development of industry far into the future.

While western governments were studying makeshifts and modifications that might preserve capitalism, and Marxists were damning it out of hand, one non-Marxist substitute for the profit system was expiring and another was gathering naïve recruits throughout the capitalist world.

Technocracy hated politics as much as profits. Howard Scott, an engineer who was the father, mother and midwife of this technologists' fascism, viewed his profession as the destroyer-lifegiver of ancient legend brought back to earth.

Starting with the thesis that social phenomena can be measured and that these measurements can provide the source of the laws of control of society, Scott went on to announce as dogma that the engineer had already destroyed the price system because the use of the machine to produce goods and services had made it impossible to measure the value of production in terms of any single commodity or means of exchange: thus he ruled out not only barter but the gold or any other standard.

Hence, according to Scott, money no longer meant anything. Furthermore, he argued, the expansion of credit under capitalism—or, to view it from the other side, the creation of debt—had already so seriously deranged the relative claims of capital and labor to their joint production that, as any fool could see, capitalism had already collapsed. For him this was certainly true, because for months his rent, food, carfare and tailor bills had been the charge of his friends. From this vantage point above the battle he saw quite clearly that the economics of the modern social order were far too complicated to be understood and controlled by politicians, and that only engineers were competent to produce and distribute goods and services and to govern the whole of society. While the election of Roosevelt in November, 1932, had pierced the heart of Technocracy, it proved one of history's most reluctant corpses. On Inauguration Day, Howard Scott was declared a bankrupt in a Federal Court in New York.

Technocracy, which got little enough serious attention in the United States, was virtually ignored elsewhere except by a Scots major in the British Army, Clifford Hugh Douglas, who was as anti-profit as Scott but by no means anti-politics. A man of sound classical education, Douglas was also far more articulate than Scott, and by the spring of 1933 his Social Credit movement could claim clamorous advocates throughout the United Kingdom, Europe, South Africa, Australia, Canada (in one province of which it was later to be tried, disastrously) and the United States, where Gorham B. Munson, a literary critic of the self-styled neohumanist school, adopted it enthusiastically. In general, Social Credit made much more sense than Technocracy to those intellectuals who were equally repelled by Adam Smith, Karl Marx and straight thinking.

What concerned Douglas was the fact that the sum of all wages and salaries in any given period did not equal the retail price of the goods produced in the same period. To him, the only reason for the discrepancy was the profits taken by producers and distributors; hence he agreed with Scott that production must be taken out of the hands of profit seekers and put wholly in the control of engineers. The primary criterion of what and how much should be produced was to be the needs and the buying power of the consuming public. But Douglas did not envisage the elimination of money— perhaps because, unlike Scott, he still had some.

Douglas proposed to overhaul the entire monetary system.

There was to be one central bank—the Government's—which would lend money without charging interest to manufacturers and sellers so that they could produce and distribute more goods at lower prices. Private banks would be allowed to stay in business as individual lenders, but they would no longer be able to create or expand credit; that is, they could lend only from actual cash physically in the vaults, and only when the proposed loan had received the unanimous consent of the depositors. That this would soon enough mean the elimination of the private bank without specific legislation could hardly have escaped the major's vision.

Furthermore, Douglas declared, all currency standards—gold, silver or any other metal—would have to be abandoned forthwith. The Government would issue national dividends —Social Credits—to consumers at various intervals; these would constitute a currency based on the supply of goods and services available at the time of issuance. The supply of credits (or money) would not be increased unless the supply of needed goods and services increased; conversely, every such rise in available goods and services would be accompanied by an equal expansion of the currency. How the costs of administering this highly complicated system could be met without recreating the disparity between total wages and salaries on the one hand and the retail prices of goods on the other was not explained.

But none of this meant much to the man and woman on Broadway or Main Street, if indeed it ever came to his attention. If he was working, there was still the problem of making his income cover his living costs—having a surplus to save was hard to imagine. At.this time, when $5,000 a year was considered an upper-middle-class income and the income tax started from a realistic basis, the average American had no tax problem unless he owned his home. The income tax began at 4 per cent, but a married couple was allowed an exemption of $2,500 a year, plus $400 for each child. The number of couples with two children who earned over $3,300 and thus paid income tax was negligible. And the number of Americans who paid the highest rate was microscopic. The maximum normal tax was 8 per cent on all amounts above $8,000; surtax began at 1 per cent of a $6,000 taxable income and ranged to 55 per cent of all above $1,000,000.

While people were grasping nickels and dimes, wondering where the larger amounts would come from for ordinary living expenses and payment of debts, the Bureau of Internal Revenue announced its unalterable position that income taxes were due by March 15. But, for once, the tax man proved to be human. The Treasury Department agreed to accept checks and hold them until they could be cashed.

This realistic example was swiftly followed by life insurance companies and utilities. Payments had to be made, but the checks would be held. In several states emergency laws were passed prohibiting utilities from shutting off their services for nonpayment of bills. Local governments throughout the nation also agreed to accept payment under these conditions.

In New York City one could ride the length of the subway system—38 miles—for five cents. This was the lowest rate in the country; in Philadelphia, whose public transport was far less modern and covered much less ground, the fare was seven and a half cents, or two rides for fifteen cents (tokens were sold in the fractional values), and a ride beyond a given fare zone cost more. A package of twenty top-brand cigarettes cost ten to fifteen cents (including five to seven cents federal tax) in any chain store; the average office worker who lunched in a restaurant paid fifty cents for a full-course meal. If the March wind blew his hat into a sewer, he could buy a new Stetson for five dollars. If he had a car, he could buy five or six gallons of 70-octane gasoline—the best available—for a dollar; if he felt that he had already hit bottom and things could become only better, he could buy a new six-cylinder Pontiac business coupé for $585 f.o.b. Detroit or a five-passenger coach for $50 more. A Chevrolet coupé was $445; or, with a rumble seat, $475. Reading his two-cent newspaper after dinner, he could tease himself with the thought of a weekend in the chic Hotel Ambassador in New York at $5 per day for himself or, since he might as well dream comfortably, a suite at $10. Cunard-White Star would carry him tourist class to Europe for $98.50, or he could have a 30-day trip through six countries, all expenses paid, for $260 to $979 and, on his return, buy a luxurious Cadillac-engined La Salle or a straight-eight Packard for a little over $2,000 with the knowledge that it would run indefinitely. His wife, peering over his shoulder, could see that a first-class General Electric refrigerator would end the nuisance of the old-fashioned icebox for only $99.50.

Houses with one-car garages—the typical six-room structure—were offered at $3,500; for $6,000 one could buy an excellent residence in a good middle-class area with a respectable lawn and garden; big fieldstone houses built at the very twilight of the boom in eminently desirable neighborhoods, on plots 200 feet square, were offered at $10,000. Such establishments of course required servants living on the premises; the best couple—cook-housemaid and butler-chauffeur—were glad to work for $100 a month and their keep. A maid of all work who "lived in" could be hired at $35 to $50 a month.

A three-room apartment on Riverside Drive in New York —it was still a good middle- and upper-middle-class street then—could be had for $67 a month; a similar apartment in an outlying borough was available generally at half that figure, and the landlord would allow six weeks' occupancy rent-free. For the stenographer who was looking for work at $10 a week—$15 if she were that aristocrat of her calling, the first-rate legal stenographer—unfurnished one-room apartments were available at $10 or $11 a month. The furniture buyer could get a complete dining-room set in mahogany veneer at Macy's for $69.95 (in maple it was $3 more); Gimbel's had a five-piece maple dinette set at $17.95; Wanamaker's offered an excellent dinner service for 12 for $23.95. A 9 x 12 Axminster rug cost $17.95. John David, a typical retailer of good ready-made clothes for men, was having a sale: only $16.50 for a suit that regularly cost $23; the ordinary shirt cost 98 cents and the best was just $2 more. Women's shoes ran from $1.98 to a specialty-shop peak of $18. Women's suits of top quality were advertised at $65 by exclusive Fifth Avenue shops; men's custom tailors would make a suit for $100. Silk stockings cost a woman 39 cents a pair, but more people bought rayon at 23 cents. A good cotton print dress cost $1.58. All the merchants advertised during the bank holiday that they would be more than delighted to extend credit for any purchase. Even an impressive funeral could be had, for credit or cash, at $150.

Few people were buying the Knabe baby grand piano at $650; but even in this strange economic limbo some were buying table radios at $8.44. Coal, when bought in lots of five to ten tons, was $7.25 a ton for the pea size, $7.75 in smaller lots; egg coal was $8. A 16-ounce loaf of bread was five cents; a quart of milk was nine or ten; eggs were 25 cents a dozen, and in many stores a dozen meant thirteen. Butter was 25 cents a pound, as was the best coffee; ham cost five cents less. Popular cigars sold in packages of ten for 35 cents or, in a better grade, five for 25 cents. A round trip, New York to Buffalo, in a lower berth cost $6.95.

On Broadway, Fred Astaire and Claire Luce were starring in *The Gay Divorcée,* seats for which ranged from $1 to $3, and Ethel Merman was in *Take A Chance,* which had a $2 top. A Shakespeare repertory season was playing to an audience that paid from 25 cents to $1.10 a ticket. A couple could dine and dance before the theatre for $2.50 in the Paramount Grill on Broadway, or have after-the-show supper, again with dancing, for $3. The biggest movie houses, including the new Music Hall, charged 35 cents until 1 P.M., 55 cents until 6 P.M. and 75 cents thereafter; and the Music Hall urged cashless customers to pay by check. This convenience was not available in the neighborhood houses, which charged, on the average, 15 cents during the afternoon and 25 cents at night.

Hence there is little surprise in the results of the question put by a New York newspaper to ordinary office, shop and other workers: "What do you consider the minimum income required to enable you to live decently?" A childless couple in Manhattan estimated rock-bottom at $25 a week; a suburban father of six declared he could manage quite well, and even run a car, on an assurance of $50 a week.

The workingman, regardless whether he belonged to a union—most did not—was remarkably hopeful. Somehow he had managed to preserve his dignity and integrity through three years of depression. If he was one of the 13 million jobless during the week—the total working force was approximately 50 million—he was determinedly trying to get whatever kind of work he could find or create; if he was employed, he was very likely receiving a substandard wage in a sweatshop but nonetheless giving an honest day's work for considerably less than an honest day's pay. Of planned financial security he knew nothing. He knew only that he could be fired at the caprice of a straw boss or laid off without notice. He knew that if he or his family became ill they would wind up in the charity ward of a hospital (if there was room). He had just about reached the limit of his patience and endurance. Yet he was hopeful because of the promises made by Roosevelt.

William Green, the $30,000-a-year president of the American Federation of Labor, which had a little more than 2,000,000 members, was taking Roosevelt's promises literally. Shortly before the inauguration, he had ordered his assistants to draw blueprints for legislation to help labor. He declared openly that labor was to have its say in Congress, that organized labor planned to expand and that it was prepared to use the strike as its ultimate weapon where negotiation failed. He uttered such new phrases as "insurance for the unemployed" and "compulsory federal and state old-age pensions." In this he was joined by the United Mine Workers and the few other independent unions.

The workingman listened to these words and remembered the speeches made by Roosevelt and Senator Robert F. Wagner of New York. These were encouraging and they strengthened his faith in the future, but in the meantime he had to exist under conditions that were heartbreaking. He had to overcome the feeling that he was not wanted by industry. If he was an ordinary laborer, or unskilled, or a member of the white-collar class, he shuddered at the published statistic that 26 per cent of the skilled trade-union members were out of work this week.

He had only to look at New York State, always in the past a high-wage area, to get a good portrait of the rest of the country. In a special message to the Legislature, Governor Herbert H. Lehman spoke out against "the sweating of women and children." In New York City many working women slept regularly in the subways because they earned too little to pay rent; the charity wards of hospitals in that city and Chicago reported numerous cases of women who had to be treated for sheer exhaustion because they were regularly working seven 14-hour days for a weekly wage of $5. In calling for a minimum-wage law, Lehman said the "evidence is overwhelming that the Depression has been exploited by shortsighted and selfish employers who pay wages unreasonably low and not at all commensurate with the service rendered. Instances have come to my attention of payment to women of wages as low as $4 for a full week."

New York City was described as the worst sweatshop locale in the state; the garment industry, employing more than 50,000 women, was called "the most sweated" trade. The Scripps-Howard newspapers made a survey with the help of welfare workers and discovered that a liner of slippers got 21 cents to line 72 pairs. If she lined one slipper every 45 seconds, she could make $1.05 in a nine-hour day. Two sisters and their mother were paid 80 cents a gross to make decorations for men's pajamas. Their combined weekly income was $4. Thirteen-year-old packing girls in a food factory got one cent for filling a dozen jars, putting them in wooden boxes and lugging the boxes to another room. Their maximum daily pay was 50 cents.

The employers replied that they had to pay this kind of wage to keep their firms going in a highly competitive market. They were partly supported in their contention by a record number of bankruptcies.

The Stock Market's last day of trading, until the banks were reopened, was March 3. Inauguration Day newspapers carried such representative quotations as these:

	INDUSTRIAL STOCKS
Allied Chemical	74½
American Can	52½
American Telephone	
and Telegraph	97⅞
American Tobacco	50
Anaconda Copper	5¾
Bethlehem Steel	11½
Du Pont	35⅞
General Electric	11⅞
General Foods	24⅛
General Motors	10¾
Goodyear	30
International Harvester	15
International Nickel	7
Johns Manville	13¼

INDUSTRIAL STOCKS

Owens-Illinois Glass	32
Proctor & Gamble	21½
Sears Roebuck	13¾
Standard Oil (Calif.)	20½
Standard Oil (N.J.)	23
Texas Co.	11⅞
Union Carbide	22
U.S. Steel	25
Westinghouse	21
Woolworth	28½

RAILROAD ISSUES

Atlantic Coast Line	18⅞
Baltimore & Ohio	9⅛
Canadian Pacific	8¾
Chesapeake & Ohio	26½
New York Central	15½

UTILITY SHARES

Columbia Gas & Electric	11⅝
Detroit Edison	56
Electric Bond & Share	12¾
People's Gas	51
Public Service Electric & Gas	98

But none of these fascinating figures mattered to the millions of unemployed receiving public relief. For the most part they did not receive cash; the state or the county—there was no federal relief system in 1933—paid their rent directly to the landlord, their gas and electric bills directly to the utility company, their fuel bills directly to the coal dealer. Before one could be eligible for relief, one had to dispose of all salable assets except essential clothing and furniture; the public authorities would not pay a telephone bill. Food was supplied through the issuance of food orders to the relief recipients, and food dealers were forbidden to redeem these for cash, though such occurrences were not unknown. The size of the food order varied, of course, with the size of the family, but it was never large enough to allow more than the essential nutriment. In some areas, where it was found that relief recipients tended to redeem the whole order in luxury foods for one grand spree and then had to cadge where they could until the next order was due, the food draft was made payable only in specified items.

In Pennsylvania, on Inauguration weekend, 500 unemployed from all parts of the state converged on Harrisburg, the state capital—some came by bus, some crowded into borrowed automobiles, some simply walked—to stage a march demanding that the Legislature appropriate $100 million immediately for public relief. But the legislators, like those of many other states, were preoccupied with drawing bills for state control of the liquor industry in eager anticipation of the repeal of Prohibition, which by now was taken for granted.

It did not matter to the Pennsylvania legislators, or to those in other states, that such public assistance as there was took no account of clothing needs. These were supplied, sometimes, by church groups, the Salvation Army and similar organizations. Often, the unemployed were compelled to beg on the streets or from door to door for castoff clothing, extra food or the money to buy either. There was not a "good neighborhood" in the country where it was not a daily occurrence to see an exhausted young mother, trailing one or more bedraggled children because she had no one with whom to leave them, rap timidly at a back door to ask for whatever could be spared. But during those first days of March the reluctant supplicant could expect to be helped only in kind—the closing of the banks reached directly into the lives even of those who had no property, no money and no incomes.

CHAPTER **4**

The Crime of the Week

MARCH 1, 1933, was the first anniversary of a kidnaping that had shocked the whole world—the abduction of the eldest son of Col. Charles A. Lindbergh. March 1, 1933, was also the date on which an almost equally sensational kidnaping ended with the release of the victim—no infant, but the 31-year-old son of a multimillionaire Denver investment banker.

Charles B. Boettcher 2nd had gone to a party on Lincoln's Birthday—February 12—with his seven-months-pregnant wife, leaving their 5-year-old daughter, Anna Lou, in the care of their servants. The Boettchers came home before midnight and stopped their car in the driveway while Boettcher got out to open the garage doors. Another car pulled in behind his; according to Mrs. Boettcher, there were four men in it. "Come here, Charlie," one of them said, pointing a revolver, "and throw up your hands." Rigid with fear, Mrs. Boettcher sat still in her husband's car and watched him obey the order. One of the abductors came up to her, taking great pains not to touch her car, and gave her a note in his gloved hand. Then he got back into the gang's car, in which Boettcher was already held in the rear, and the gang left. Mrs. Boettcher could not describe the car or give its registration number.

She opened the note and read: *Don't notify the police. Tell Claude Boettcher* [the victim's father] *he had better get $60,000 ransom. Follow instructions. Remember the Lindbergh baby would still be alive if ransom had been paid. Notify us through a personal ad stating: "Please write. I am ready to return. Mabel."* Mrs. Boettcher pulled herself together, ran into the house and telephoned her father-in-law, who at once informed the police but also placed the advertisement requested by the kidnapers.

During the next 24 hours Charles Boettcher sat blindfolded in the gang's sedan—a small one, he said later, to judge by its riding qualities. There were three stops for gasoline; sandwiches, coffee and milk were given to the victim at each stop. But he had no idea in what direction he was being taken. The blindfold was not removed when the destination was reached; he was led down some stairs into what he inferred was a basement, where he was to spend the next 15 days, blindfolded the whole time. The kidnapers, he said later, were "as gentlemanly as could be expected under the circumstances," but they threatened him quite often and said that if he did anything to frustrate their plan, it would be "unfortunate" for him. During his captivity he was allowed to shave only once (though without removing the blindfold); he was also instructed to write several notes, which the gang mailed to his father, saying that he was alive and well.

During the next week several contacts were made between the abductors and the elder Boettcher, who told the press on February 19 that he was trying to scale down the ransom demand and had promised that there would be no police intervention if the kidnapers would communicate with the intermediary he had designated. But they either refused or could not make contact with him, and Claude Boettcher released an announcement to the newspapers saying that his offer to pay the entire $60,000 would remain good only through midnight of February 25, a Saturday. Meanwhile 4,000 volunteers from the American Legion and other groups were making a house-to-house search for the victim in the Denver area, while sheriffs' posses scoured the badlands of northern Colorado.

They had no means of knowing that Charles was being held on a ranch in Mitchell, South Dakota, far from any other habitation. Here Carl W. Pearce, who posed as an insurance broker, took care of the correspondence with the Boettchers; it was his activity at a typewriter while an ostensible stenographer sat idle that aroused the suspicions of a woman client and ultimately led to his arrest. The "stenographer" was his mistress, 39-year-old Mrs. Ruth Kohler, who had her 16-year-old daughter, Merelyn, with her, as well as her sister Mrs. Verne Sankey, whose husband, a society bootlegger, owned the ranch.

Whether the ransom was actually paid was never established. A brother-in-law of the victim's mother said his wife, Charles's aunt, told him it had been paid; Dr. John Foster, a friend of the family, was believed to have tossed the packet of bills across a culvert ten miles west of Denver, as directed by the kidnapers, two hours before the release.

What was known definitively was that on the night of February 27–28 young Boettcher was marched back into the abductors' car for another 24-hour journey. This time he managed occasionally to slip the blindfold and to note at one point that they were passing through the town of Torrington, Wyoming. Nothing in his story corroborated the report of a stop outside Denver to collect the ransom package. Instead, he said he was put out of the car, still blindfolded, and instructed to walk 150 paces forward and then turn right. But the moment he heard the car move off, he turned around and tried to rip off the blindfold. By the time he succeeded, the car was a speck of red light far down a dark road.

Boettcher found he was in a lower-middle-class residential neighborhood and looked for a drugstore. From there he telephoned his father and a friend, Sidney Sinsheimer, who sent a car for him. The car took him directly to his father's home, and the elder Boettcher telephoned Police Chief Albert T. Clark to announce that Charles was free and unharmed. But the father would say no more; he would not even allow Clark to talk to his son. When reporters swarmed over the lawn, demanding information, Claude Boettcher drove them off with a pistol. However, he did say he had never promised immunity in return for his son's freedom, and he pledged himself to press the hunt for the abductors as long as he lived. He posted a $25,000 reward for their capture and conviction.

At 10 o'clock that night of March 1, sheriffs' deputies in Brighton, Colorado, twenty miles north of Denver, opened fire on a car that they believed was the kidnapers'; its occupants returned the fire and got away. Relieved of the risk that pursuit might endanger the victim, the police plunged almost fanatically into a search for the criminals. Their initial theory was that the crime was the well-organized work of a first-rank gang, and they went looking for Louis (Diamond Jack) Alterie of Chicago. The possibility of a grudge was also weighed, and the WANTED list added the name of Tommy Coleman, an escaped convict who had shared a cell in the Colorado State Prison with one Weimer Nutt, sentenced for forging the elder Boettcher's name to a number of checks.

Five days after Charles Boettcher's release the first arrests were made: Pearce and the three women. Later the same day, in Chamberlain, South Dakota, Arthur Youngberg was seized and accused of having actually held the gun on Boettcher and forced him into the kidnap automobile. That night Youngberg cut his wrists and throat with a razor blade, but he botched the job. (Ultimately Youngberg was sentenced to 16 years in Leavenworth under the Lindbergh Law, and

Pearce got 26 years; each was also fined $1,000 for using the mails to defraud. Sankey, when finally captured, confessed, but he hanged himself in his cell before his trial. The women were freed. Mrs. Charles Boettcher, delivered of a son two months after her husband's release, killed herself with a revolver in 1941 because of poor health.)

Otherwise, it was a slack season for crime, which rather accurately reflects the curves of the economic graph. Petty thefts born of desperate need were still commonplace and, in general, courts did try to temper justice with whatever mercy they could muster in such cases; but the sort of crime that is conceived from a profit-making motive was in a grave decline. Ironically, it was the panic of the banking situation that brought about one of the few large robberies of the week, if not the largest.

An immigrant woman in Brooklyn, alarmed by the stories of bank closings and unable to distinguish between those ordered by various state governments and those forced by sheer lack of funds, went to her savings bank on Friday, March 3, to withdraw the $10,180 that she and her husband had amassed in their joint lifetimes. She was going to take the money home, where it would be safe and accessible, whatever happened. When the teller gave her the bills, she stuffed them into her purse, put it in her pocketbook and started homeward. Two strangers drew up alongside her, threatened her and seized her pocketbook. Almost hysterical, she told her story to the nearest policeman and went home to await the arrival of her husband, dreading to have to tell him they were penniless.

Four days later the two robbers were arrested in South Carolina. They had spent less than $2,000 of the frightened woman's savings; they still had $8,200 in their pockets. The South Carolina police notified Brooklyn headquarters, which in turn called the local precinct, and a kindly desk sergeant informed the old woman that almost all her money had been recovered and would be returned to her. Tearfully, she asked him how soon the banks would reopen so that she could put her savings back in a really safe place.

Aside from such things, courts had little before them but routine proceedings, civil and criminal, whose monotonous nature concealed the individual tragedy that underlay each case: mortgage foreclosures, loan defaults, alimony arrearages. In New York City, Supreme Court Justice Paul Bonynge, whose wittily disillusioned opinions in actions brought under the state's Catholic-dominated divorce laws had won him a nationwide reputation ("Here we have," he had written in one of the thousands of uniform adultery complaints, "the same unidentified blonde in the same black undergarments"), found at last a way of defeating what he called the "petticoat justice" that was holding hundreds of men in jail on charges of contempt of court because they had not made alimony payments stipulated in a more prosperous era.

Bonynge had before him the case of one Umberto Politanto, who had spent the past 31 months in a cell because he could not meet his alimony obligations. Previously, the courts in New York had set no limit on such imprisonments for contempt, stating only that the defendant could be released solely when he had purged himself of the contempt: i.e., when he had paid the money. The illogic of the situation, however manifest, had made no impression on jurists who ignored the blatant fact that a man in jail has no way of acquiring the cash to meet his obligations. Bonynge, however, wanted more than logic to ground his action: he wanted a legal precedent that would be upheld on appeal, and he found it. First of all, he noted in his decision, the state had established a maximum penalty of 30 days in jail and a $250 fine for criminal contempt, a far worse offense than civil contempt; in addition, both the state and the federal constitutions expressly forbade the imposition of excessive bail and/or cruel and unusual punishment. To hold a man in prison for nonpayment of a debt or for violation of a court order without a specific term, he found, was both cruel and unusual and hence clearly in defiance of both constitutions. He ordered the unfortunate Politanto sent back to the freedom of a world in which, for the moment, there was no money at all. More important, Bonynge knocked the keystone out of the walls of New York's Alimony Jail, and it collapsed soon afterward.

At the same time manful blows were being struck at that mainstay of the gold digger, the so-called heart-balm suit, which empowered a jury of twelve good men and true to establish to the last cent the monetary value of the wounds inflicted on the soul by either the breach of a promise of marriage or the enticement of a loved one from the empty arms of the plaintiff. New York's Legislature, two days after the inauguration, received two bills to take unrequited love off the market; but it was to be two years before they would become law.

Much more onerous statutes were crumbling all across the country. Roosevelt had been elected on a platform that included the repeal of Prohibition. When the 18th Amendment had been enacted, each of the states had adopted a law of its own to cover intrastate violations and implement the federal law; and now, in the same week when the new President closed the banks, state after state announced that it would no longer prosecute alleged violators of its liquor laws or even make arrests. Though Prohibition was still nominally the law of the land, the speakeasy attained overnight a kind of *de facto* legality, and the bootlegger became respectable.

CHAPTER 5

"Sound as a Bank"

. . . It was not only the individual or the corporation that could not meet obligations. Most governmental
units paid salaries monthly or semimonthly; but on March 1
the city of Newark, New Jersey, did not issue the $1,160,000
worth of checks that its employees were counting on. For
days before, the city's newspapers had openly predicted the
default even while they reported the efforts being made to
avert it. At the last minute, the Public Service Electric & Gas
Company, whose annual tax bill of $1 million was ordinarily
payable in installments, paid in full in order to help the city
—and, incidentally, to take advantage of the 3 per cent discount offered to any taxpayer who settled his account in a
lump. But even with this windfall of $970,000, the city was
still several hundred thousand dollars short of its needs; and
the banks that had been advancing money to the municipal
government for months previously refused to lend more. The
first of the month passed and the employees remained un-
paid; so, in turn, did those to whom they owed money. For
the next two days the city continued its efforts to find the
money somewhere; so did its workers.

Then it was Inauguration Day—Saturday—and nothing

could be done. There was still hope that, after the Sunday hiatus, a solution might be found. But the proclamation of the bank holiday made it impossible, and neither the city nor the individual men and women on its payroll knew when money would be seen again. Detroit, where that arch-foe of banks, Henry Ford, had found himself forced to come to their aid, had managed to issue the customary first-of-the-month checks to its workers, but of 1,400 men employed as laborers, more than 1,000 had been unable to find any means of cashing the checks. Literally too hungry to stand, many of them fainted on the job until the city hurriedly issued food cards that it prevailed on local merchants to honor.

Long before the moment of crisis, bank depositors had withdrawn heavily. During the first days of March more than 15 per cent of the nation's cash had been taken out of circulation by hoarders, to be held indefinitely.

There were other compelling reasons for the withdrawals. Men who lost their jobs began to fall back on their savings. Business firms seeking to maintain themselves during the deadly doldrums drew on their reserves in banks, holding on with dramatically daring optimism. There was, however, the third and sinister reason: hoarding. There were those frightened individuals and conditioned pessimists who admittedly had more money than their immediate needs called for. But they lined up in front of banks and withdrew cash and gold to be secreted in vaults, iron boxes or nooks and corners of their homes.

The banks were finding themselves in an untenable situation. In order to meet demands from depositors they were forced to sell mortgages and securities at dangerously deflated prices, suffering as well as inflicting heavy losses. Not daring to stop the withdrawals, they turned to the Government for help. President Hoover did his ineffective best against a hostile Congress. The Reconstruction Finance Corporation made loans to banks. A general debtor-relief policy was fostered. Industries got some protection with higher tariffs on rubber goods and shoes from Czechoslovakia and sneakers from Japan. There were other ludicrous tariff regulations, which managed merely to stave off the crisis for a moment or two.

As the country became more aware of the financial crisis, the hoarders increased their activities. The Federal Reserve Bank reported that during the week $226 million in gold had been withdrawn. Many of the rich were moving swiftly and decisively. The French liner *Paris* was at her berth in the Hudson River. She had aboard all the regular cargo she was expected to carry. However, a special part of her hold was reserved for a shipment of $9 million in escaping gold.

These were the final signs. The stopping of the money had actually begun much earlier in the year.

In February, the Union Guardian Trust Company of Detroit found itself dangerously short of cash. It could not withstand a heavy rush of withdrawals. If it were to fail, experts predicted, it would drag every other bank in the city into oblivion. An urgent appeal was made to William A. Comstock, Michigan's Democratic governor, who agreed to discuss the matter on St. Valentine's Day. He met the bankers in downtown Detroit at 3 P.M. and by midnight he was persuaded to declare a bank moratorium. The next day he issued a proclamation closing the state's 550 banks.

At this point, one should pause to ponder on the fortunate flash of genius that must have enveloped Governor Comstock and his assistants during the trying hours from midnight to morning as they composed the text of the proclamation. *Moratorium,* without a doubt, was a fine word. Its connotation was in the esoteric language of high finance. What it would mean to the average citizen was that the institution that was holding his savings was slamming its doors in his face. Perhaps, during the dark hours, Comstock was searching for some semantic magic that would dull the shock. Did he and his advisers pore over the thesaurus and the dictionary for a word or a phrase that would make the closing of the banks palatable? Or did some divine inspiration thrust the word into their minds? It will never be known. What is known, and the country must be forever grateful for it, is that Governor Comstock referred to the closings as a *holiday* in order to let the banks bring order out of chaos.

The entire country was shocked and startled, but this was as nothing to the astonishment and annoyance shown by the people of Detroit and the rest of Michigan. Comstock, his state police, local police and the bankers waited apprehensively. But nothing sensational happened.

There was no manifestation of panic, hysteria or even anger. There were no gatherings in front of closed banks. There was good-natured bantering. The general attitude was one of relieved pressure. All the banks were closed. All the people of the state were in the same predicament. Order must follow chaos. As long as the money was in the banks no one could take it out. The situation had an equalizing effect on the populace that astounded and relieved the bankers and the government.

A year before, there had been two small bank holidays. One was in Nevada, with a population of 91,000, passing almost unnoticed amid the general groans of a nationwide shortage of jobs and money. The other was in Louisiana, where the banks were closed during one weekend. But the holiday in Michigan was big news. The rest of the nation followed the travails of Michigan workingmen and housewives in the newspapers with a lively but detached curiosity. There were some editorial suggestions that, if the Michigan experiment succeeded, it might well be considered for the rest of the country.

The people of Detroit set a fine example and delivered a foretaste of life under a bank holiday to the nation. The very newspapers that announced the moratorium were hard to buy because of the sudden shortage of coins. People on their way to work discovered that they had been cut off from all small purchases with only the cash they had on hand. Newsboys sold their papers to regular customers on credit. Merchants, waving bills, roamed their neighborhoods in search of shoeshine boys or news vendors, pleading for change. Some, dealing with transient trade, were forced to close. The earlier Judgment Day gaiety of the crowds was being replaced by chagrin and short tempers, but that was as far as emotions were displayed. There were no signs of real fury or departure from order.

While milk companies promised to continue deliveries, and merchants combined to set up a change bureau, the people watched and waited. They felt the holiday could not last more than a day or so. Then the United States Government stepped in with action that bolstered the morale of all. Before noon of the first day, $20 million in gold was shipped from the Federal Reserve vaults in Chicago, and in the evening, $5 million more in gold arrived from Washington to meet requests for postal money orders and Postal Savings withdrawals. This had the effect of a balm. It informed all and sundry that Uncle Sam was having no holiday on his obligations and that the country was sound.

The doors did not open in Michigan's banks the next day or the next. Detroit's Colonial Department Store resorted to open barters, offering dresses and suits for salted Saginaw herring. The store accepted livestock, eggs, honey, cheese and potatoes for any of its manufactured goods. Other merchants, large and small, went along with this temporary solution. The accepted attitude was that business must go on if the banks were ever to reopen. When it was found that pawnshops kept large amounts of cash in small bills, many well-to-do people pawned watches, rings and jewelry to obtain the money for their daily needs. The pawnshops, however, refused to act as change depots.

The plight that brought Michigan to the bank holiday was not exceptional. It was typical of a nation that had been thrashing in the pernicious grasp of the Depression for more than three years. During that time real estate values had hurtled to the bottom; 5,500 banks had closed permanently; widespread unemployment was increasing the relief rolls, and farmers were losing their land and their hope. By the beginning of March hoarding was taking $20 million a day from the Government.

The people of the rest of the country, alternately bewildered and frightened by the events in Michigan, began to be edgy. Humorists noted that Hoover had made his final official speech before the Republican National Committee over a nationwide radio network on the eve of the Michigan bank closing. His repeated and ill-advised remark that prosperity was just around the corner had become a household jest. It seemed, the humorists remarked, that every time he uttered another optimistic statement, the country plunged deeper into the economic abyss.

Several days after Hoover's speech, government observers began to notice a definite pattern in the behavior of many bank depositors. On February 20, long lines started to form in front of the Baltimore Trust Company. Before the end of the day, the bank had paid out $13 million. Late that night, Governor Albert Ritchie of Maryland declared a three-day shutdown. He, too, called it a *bank holiday*. On Sunday, February 26, banks in Indianapolis and Akron announced that withdrawals would be limited to 5 per cent of balance. The next day more than 100 banks in Ohio and 5 in Covington, Kentucky, adopted similar restraints.

Older people who had experienced financial panics in 1907 and 1921 were the first to feel real fear for their money. They had known what it meant for banks to crash, for savings to be wiped out. Intentionally or not, they passed this fear on to the younger generation. Soon in areas that had no banking restrictions lines started to form in front of banks. There were some deposits, but these were light. Withdrawals were heavy. By the first week of March the bank queues were part of the national tableau.

It seemed as if everybody wanted money and many were willing to make every effort, short of robbery, to get it. The lines grew longer and the footsore people more impatient. The end of the line always seemed miles from the door and some people started to figure out short cuts.

In New York's Bronx, for example, a softhearted policeman saw a woman carrying a baby at the end of the line. With the general consent of those in front of her, he allowed her to get out of line and go into the bank first. He did this several times as other mothers appeared holding their infants. After a while, despite his preoccupation with keeping the line cheerful and orderly, the babies getting preference for their mothers began to look alike. The puzzled policeman blamed it on fatigue and continued to labor at his post, thinking of his own wife, who probably was queued up in another part of town. But the babies continued to look alike. At one point someone in the line gave the baby a lollipop—a bright yellow one. A few minutes later the cop recognized the lollipop and the baby in the arms of another woman. Confronted with this evidence, the woman confessed she had borrowed the baby from a young mother around the corner who was renting it out at 25 cents a trip.

By March 1, seventeen states had declared bank holidays. Governor Henry Horner of Illinois was told that in two weeks Chicago banks had paid out $350 million. Governor Gifford Pinchot of Pennsylvania signed a bill allowing individual banks to close if they wished. At Hyde Park, President-elect Franklin Delano Roosevelt received a phone call from Thomas W. Lamont stating that "in the view of J. P. Morgan & Co., the emergency could not be greater."

CHAPTER 6

Hail to the Chief!

. . . THE DAY on which Franklin Delano Roosevelt became the thirty-second President of the United States dawned with dull, formless clouds hanging oppressively over Washington. The mercury was climbing from a low of 36 toward a high of 43 while streaks of sunlight sought to thrust through the heavy mist. March 4, 1933, was one of those rare days in history when the entire civilized world paused in the midst of its own travail to watch.

Some two weeks before, the League of Nations had unanimously condemned Japan's invasion of Manchuria, making a generous offer for a peaceful solution. Japan's reply was to withdraw her delegation from the assembly, though she continued her membership. Several days later, Great Britain banned all arms exports to Japan and China. The Reichstag fire of February 27 was giving Hitler the impetus he needed to win a majority in the Reichstag elections scheduled for March 5. Anti-Machado terrorists were attacking trains and sacking villages in Cuba. The OGPU announced the arrest of 70 persons on charges of conspiring to wreck the Soviet system of collective farming. Even the elements contributed to the tragic pattern. Storms were rampaging through the

United States. Gales and mountainous waves were raging in the Atlantic. Quakes and tidal waves in northeastern Japan killed 2,500, wrecked 2,000 fishing boats and destroyed 4,500 homes.

Roosevelt and every other citizen in the United States awoke that morning in the middle of the almost nationwide bank moratorium that had been accumulating state by state for a month. During that time the people, eager to see the end of three years of stress and misery, had urged him to assume power at once. They sang "Happy Days Are Here Again," and took cheer in the expected fulfillment of his campaign promises that "something would be done" to bring back better times. Responsible men, editorialists and countless citizens had urged him to start the country on the road to recovery even before the inauguration. Hoover himself had invited Roosevelt to confer during the lame-duck hiatus.

But Roosevelt made it clear that he intended to move in the normal channels of law and tradition. Those closest to him explained that he was a *democrat* as well as a Democrat. It was known that he had labored with his advisers to form the New Deal program from the day he had been elected. On Wednesday, March 1, he came down from Albany to his Manhattan home at 49 East 65th St. and went into conference with William Woodin, his Secretary-designate of the Treasury.

They did not emerge until Thursday afternoon, weary, but evidently exhilarated. Roosevelt sparkled as he entered his limousine, surrounded by Secret Service men who admonished him that henceforth he would never travel without them. Roosevelt made a mock grimace at their reminder, which was grim and firmly respectful. The whole country had shuddered at the close call Roosevelt had had only a fortnight earlier—February 15—when the crazed Zangara had tried to assassinate him as he rode through Miami in an open car. The bullet had struck Mayor Anton Cermak of Chicago, who died a few days after the inauguration. It was ironic that Cermak, who had escaped assassination in his battle against Chicago gang lords, stopped the fatal bullet meant for Roosevelt.

A light morning snow covered Fifth Avenue as the motorcade turned south and then west toward the Hudson River. There is always a crowd in New York, and the motorcycle sirens caused people to stop and gape. Those few who recognized the President-elect cheered and waved. On the New Jersey side of the big river stood a special B & O train. Roosevelt and his party boarded it and, as it thundered on to Washington through a freezing fog, Roosevelt continued to talk finances with Woodin, breaking off only long enough to joke with James A. Farley about politics. Toward the end of the trip, participants recalled, the conversation turned to religion, morals, and the way of life in Washington. Sleet, snow and slush covered the capital city when the train arrived.

That night in his suite at the Mayflower Hotel—the Presidential suite—Roosevelt surrounded himself with his advisers, who sought to create form and posture out of the financial chaos. He spent most of Friday with Woodin, who was about to become the master of the greatest treasury in the world, and Raymond Moley, the first of the army of professors who were to populate Washington for years to come. They staged a run-through of the New Deal legislation that Roosevelt was to present to Congress during the first days of his administration. (During the first 100 days, Congress passed every proposal made by Roosevelt.)

At four in the afternoon, Roosevelt made the traditional courtesy call upon President Hoover. But protocol was swiftly thrust into the discard when the two men examined the following statistics:

On Thursday and Friday $500 million had been drained from the Federal Reserve banks. An all-time record of $116 million in gold had been taken from the Federal Reserve System in one day, mostly by the withdrawal of foreign balances.

Hoover sent for Ogden L. Mills, his Secretary of the Treasury; Roosevelt sent for Moley. In the ensuing conflict both men agreed that something had to be done. They disagreed on how it should be done. Roosevelt urged Hoover to proclaim a national bank holiday. Hoover refused. Roosevelt suggested, according to one report, that the Government guarantee 50 per cent of all bank deposits. Hoover felt that this should be done through an emergency message to Congress by the new President. Roosevelt declined. When the coolness between the two leaders had reached the freezing point, Roosevelt went back to his hotel. There was no solution.

Roosevelt stayed up late the night before the inauguration in conference with Cordell Hull, his Secretary of State-designate, and Jesse Jones of Texas, head of the Reconstruction Finance Corporation. Woodin joined them later, making the kind of sacrifice that only an artist could appreciate. His composition, "On the Prairie," was being played for the first time by the National Symphony Orchestra. Among those attending were Sara Delano Roosevelt, the President's mother, and her grandchildren. Woodin had to wait for the morning papers to find out that his music had been well received by the critics and had brought enthusiastic and warm applause from the audience.

As he worked with the men who later were to be called his brain trust, Roosevelt was jovial and optimistic. The bank crisis was the uppermost matter discussed. Time was taken out for final polishing of the inaugural address, the legislative program, and the entire concept of government-in-business that was to become known as the New Deal.

When Roosevelt was finally persuaded to retire, Woodin and Moley rushed to a meeting of the Federal Reserve Board for some discussions and long-distance telephone conversations with George Leslie Harrison, governor of the Federal Reserve Bank in New York, and Eugene Morgan Stevens, governor of the Federal Reserve Bank in Chicago.

Despite his crippling polio, Roosevelt was in glowing health, and he faced the long and tiring ceremonials of the day with a verve that gladdened those close to him. Accompanied by his family, his Cabinet-to-be and a few close friends, he went to services at St. John's Episcopal Church near the White House. *Time* magazine reported the proceedings:

> His face cupped in his hands, Franklin Delano Roosevelt began the biggest day in his life with this prayer ringing in his ears: "O Lord, our Heavenly Father, the high and mighty ruler of the Universe, Who dost from Thy throne behold all the dwellers upon earth; most heartily we beseech Thee with Thy favor to behold and bless Thy servant, Franklin, chosen to be the President of the United States." At the altar in cassock and surplice stood his old schoolmaster, Groton's Dr. Endicott (Peabo) Peabody, who had married him to Anna Eleanor Roosevelt. From his heart, from the hearts of his little band of worshipers, from the heart of a stricken nation, rose a wordless appeal for divine strength to right the great ills. . . . The President-elect stood up in his pew, squared his shoulders. As he walked out of St. John's, a brief streak of sunlight shot down upon him through gray wintry clouds.

As he left the church more than 500,000 were waiting in the streets for America's grand quadrennial pageant to begin. At first the throng was strangely quiet, depressed by the flags at half-staff over the Senate and House Office Buildings in mourning for Montana's Senator Thomas J. Walsh, Attorney-General-designate, who had died two days earlier after a brief marriage to a Cuban sugar planter's widow.

The lowering clouds and chill, moist blasts that are so characteristic of Washington in March did nothing to lift the spirit of the people beset by personal economic woes. They had come from all parts of the nation—50,000 from New York alone—on special trains, planes and buses; by automobile and on foot. They had come, however, with hope, heartened by the promise of a new deal for the little man and the even greater promise of action—any kind of action, but action.

In front of the White House portico a small crowd had gathered to watch Hoover and Roosevelt. The latter, smiling and wearing a silk hat that was a Christmas gift from Thomas M. Lynch of Poughkeepsie, president of the New York State Tax Commission, waited in his car. Hoover came out. Both men lifted their hats, Roosevelt grinning, Hoover straight-faced. Richard Jervis, gray-haired chief of the White House Secret Service, slipped into the front seat, keeping the door slightly open with one hand while the other gripped something in his coat pocket. He signaled and the motorcade proceeded.

Even inaugural arrangements go astray sometimes. The car whizzed up Pennsylvania Avenue, missing its cavalry escort, and had to pull up before the Post Office building for the horsemen to catch up. During the one-and-a-quarter-mile ride, reporters noted that Roosevelt kept up an amiable conversation with Hoover, who seemed to reply in monosyllables. His face drawn and downcast, Hoover left to Roosevelt the task of acknowledging the friendly cheers and applause. As the day warmed, the crowds warmed. They stood ten deep, some on soapboxes, chairs or ladders; others hung from branches of the trees lining the historic thoroughfare. Contractors demolishing buildings at the lower end of the avenue stopped the hammering and rented observation space in the gaping fronts of the empty houses.

More than 100,000 were gathered on the forty acres of park and pavement in front of the Capitol. They filled the bare trees, perched on rooftops and just stood on the ground, stretching and gaping. The car took Hoover and Roosevelt to the Capitol, where they separated.

Roosevelt went to the Military Affairs Committee room to wait. Huey Long of Louisiana walked toward Roosevelt, halted at the threshold, then suddenly turned about and tiptoed away. Ten minutes later Roosevelt started out of the room toward the Senate chamber but was stopped and told it was not yet time. He laughed and said: "All right, we'll go back and wait some more."

Hoover went into the President's room to sign some bills. Four years of turmoil and travail, heartbreak and frustration were ending for him. The black oval table in the room just off the Senate lobby was piled high with bills looking even more formidable in the reflection of an enormous wall mirror that also doubled the features of President McKinley in a bronze bust in the corner, stern and glowering. Hoover, his term of office coming closer to the end with every tick of the clock, had to decide whether to sign or reject. Carefully he parted the tails of his cutaway coat, laid his silk hat upon the table and picked up a pen. Helping the thirty-first President conclude an era were his official friends and associates, watching and whispering. As senators, representatives, Cabinet members, military aides, clerks and bodyguards stood by, Hoover swiftly and silently signed bill after bill, the scratch of his pen sounding strident and raucous over the murmur.

The 72d Congress had left behind the following unfinished legislation:

It failed to pass a beer bill; it failed to give the RFC more money for the relief of unemployment; it failed to increase taxes for a balanced budget; it failed to provide for adequate mortgage relief; it failed to act on the St. Lawrence Seaway Treaty; it failed to draw a protocol for the World Court; it failed to create a debt moratorium for municipal-

Hoover and Roosevelt on the way to the inauguration

Roosevelt holds his first press conference, March 8

Hitler, in civilian clothes, bows and scrapes before President Hindenburg shortly before the election

The new Hitler reviews his Storm Troopers a few days after the election that made him absolute dictator of Germany

Wearing white camouflage, Japanese cavalry advances across the snow-swept frontier of Manchuria

A Japanese sniper waits and watches from a promontory near Chinchow

Charles Evans Hughes
Chief Justice

Ignace Paderewski
Pianist-Statesman

Will Rogers
Humorist

Norman Vincent Peale
Fashionable Preacher

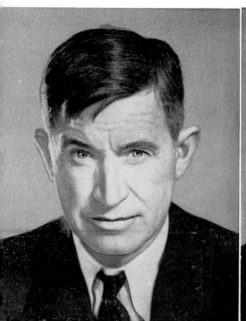

Carl Hubbell

He won for the Giants

The Day the Money Stopped. The lines of depositors were long. The people were frightened, bewildered and hopeful.

There was some cheer for the needy. Food for the hungry family and an encouraging word.

The poor got poorer . . .

. . . and squalor was widespread

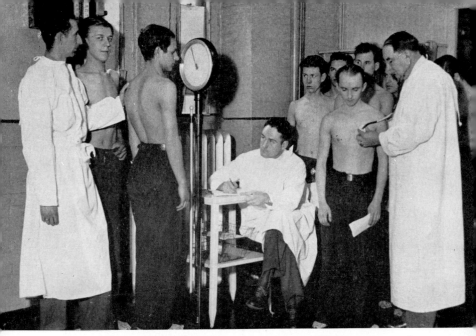

Work for strong and willing young men. Here a group is examined for jobs in the reforestation program (CCC)

Off the street corners to a comfortable place to sleep, three square meals a day, money in your pocket and a job to do

ities; and it failed to approve 2,000 nominations for various offices submitted by Hoover.

It did approve the submission to the states of a resolution to repeal Prohibition; it approved independence for the Philippines; it revised the bankruptcy laws; and it gave great reorganization powers to the new President.

Suddenly Hoover came to a last-minute measure proposed by Cotton Ed Smith of South Carolina, providing for a government cotton pool in return for a reduction in acreage. Hoover frowned and tossed it aside. There were more signatures and more rejections. Each action brought sounds of approval or dismay, but the President seemed unaware of his surroundings.

When he had finished, he arose and nodded somberly to those around him. Then, grim and gray, utter weariness lining his normally cherubic features, he marched into the Senate chamber, where he heard Vice-President Curtis swear in his successor, John Nance Garner. Curtis made a short but emotional farewell address that concluded the final "lame duck" session in U.S. history. There was none of the traditional singing or sentimental swearing of undying friendships among those departing. The nearest thing to humor was expressed by Republican Senate Leader Watson, who had been soundly defeated for re-election. He declaimed that he was "going home with the almost unanimous consent of the people of Indiana."

Roosevelt, a happy twinkle in his eye, watched the swearing in and shook hands with his Vice-President warmly, chatting with those about him and chuckling at some private joke. But he kept glancing toward the doors as if impatient for the rest of the ceremonies to begin.

Meanwhile, before the towering dome of the Capitol, the good-natured crowd observed the activities on the temporary platform, which was hung with laurel and draped with shields and medallions of the Great Seal of the United States. The roof of the extended portico was supported by ponderous Corinthian pillars to harmonize with the great stone columns of the Capitol. On this platform the more than 90 members of the official party crowded, pushed, milled and smiled.

The New York Times reported:

> At the edge of the platform stood three well-known New Yorkers, Mayor John P. O'Brien, John F. Curry, leader of Tammany Hall, and John H. McCooey, Brooklyn's Democratic leader, all with tall silk hats, which were outdone in elegance by the topper of Sergeant James Brannigan, the Mayor's bodyguard.

These were not the only representatives from the clubhouse level. In evidence were the professional gentlemen from Jersey City, Chicago, Memphis, Kansas City, Boston, and other well-oiled political machines who, after 12 years of hope and faith, were looking forward to some personal charity.

On the platform, the mighty men of the nation, those coming in and those going out, were acting like people. They waved, they grimaced, they shook hands in all directions. Genial Jim Farley, the biggest political boss in all Democratic history, shouldered his way about, nodding, grinning, making friends and remembering names. Mrs. Roosevelt, wearing a blue ensemble, and her mother-in-law, in rustling silks, managed to squeeze through to their places, retaining their dignity despite the crush. Garner, a muffler around his throat, already the Vice-President while Roosevelt was still not President, stood stiff and glum. Hoover had a front-row seat on the platform and stared at his shoes. Mrs. Hoover, her brown suit covered by a coat of black Persian lamb, sat next to him chatting brightly. The *Times* said: "Hoover's face was grave and solemn, but Mrs. Hoover had a happy smile."

While everyone was waiting for Roosevelt to appear, radio, which was flexing its muscles as a news medium, gave the crowd several amusing minutes. An announcer described the activities of the moment from a prepared script that bore no relation to what was going on. The crowd laughed when the amplified broadcast described a "hush" that did not then exist; later, during a moment of dead silence, the broadcaster informed the crowd that it had just broken out in "a roar of voices." At the swearing-in ceremony, the loudspeaker blared forth again, and Chief Justice Charles Evans Hughes, his hand poised over the Bible, waited twenty seconds for the sound to cease.

It was a historic occasion for radio, however, 150 stations carrying the ceremony to all parts of the nation and the world. It is not known whether Hitler, Stalin or Mussolini listened in, and it is not likely, since the first two did not know English, but in London the King and Queen listened at Buckingham Palace; the Prince of Wales heard it at Fort Belvedere, his country residence; and Prime Minister Ramsay MacDonald heard it at his country home, Chequers.

A bugler sounded a fanfare and through the great bronze doors that depict the story of Columbus walked Franklin Roosevelt, leaning on the arm of James, his eldest son. They walked up a special ramp carpeted in maroon. The crowd cheered stoutly and waved; the Marine Band struck up "Hail to the Chief," and the air became charged with genuine excitement. As Roosevelt, smiling, walked toward the Chief Justice, there was a hush and the crowd knew it was witnessing history. An assistant held out the old Dutch Bible brought to this country by Klaus Nicholas van Roosevelt some 300 years before. It was open to the 13th Chapter of St. Paul's First Epistle to the Corinthians—faith, hope and charity. Roosevelt did not kiss the Bible as some of his predecessors had done. *Time* magazine reported:

> Mr. Roosevelt rested his hand on the Bible. Chief Justice Hughes recited the oath. In a loud, clear voice, like a bridegroom at the altar, Roosevelt did the extraordinary thing of repeating after him: "I, Franklin Delano Roosevelt, do solemnly swear that I will faithfully execute the office of President of the United States and will, to the best of my ability, preserve, protect and defend the Constitution of the United States. So help me God."

Before the crowd and the radio audience had an opportunity to appreciate this departure from tradition, Roosevelt, hatless and coatless, his tie slightly askew beneath his wing collar, his strong hands gripping the lectern, began his inaugural address. He had dropped his amiable smile, assumed a stern expression and, thrusting out his chin as if in defiance of some invisible and symbolic adversary, declaimed:

> "This is a day of national consecration. . . . The only thing we have to fear is fear itself—nameless, unreasoning, unjustified terror which paralyzes needed efforts to convert retreat into advance. Our common difficulties concern only . . . material things. Values have shrunk to fantastic levels; taxes have risen; our ability to pay has fallen; government of all kinds is faced by serious curtailment of income; the means of exchange are frozen in the currents of trade; the withered leaves of industrial enterprise lie on every side; farmers find no market for their produce; the savings of many years in thousands of families are gone. A host of unemployed citizens face the grim problem of existence. Only a foolish optimist can deny the dark realities of the moment. . . . The money-changers have fled from their high seats in the temple of our civilization. We may now restore that temple to the ancient truths. . . . This nation is asking for action, and action now. Our great primary task is to put people to work. It can be accomplished in part by direct recruiting by the Government

itself, treating the task as we would treat the emergency of a war. . . . There must be strict supervision of all banking and credits and investments; there must be an end to speculation with other people's money, and there must be provisions for an adequate but sound currency."

He said this and much more. In loud, clear tones, his head bobbing amid the cluster of microphones, looking directly at the crowds and yet addressing himself to unseen millions at home and abroad, Roosevelt set forth this line of attack:

"I shall presently urge upon a new Congress in special session detailed measures for their fulfillment. Our international trade relations, though vastly important, are secondary to the establishment of a sound national economy. In the field of world policy I would dedicate this nation to the policy of the good neighbor. If we are to go forward we must move as a trained and loyal army willing to sacrifice for the good of a common discipline. I assume unhesitatingly the leadership of this great army. It is to be hoped that the normal balance of executive and legislative authority may be wholly adequate to meet the unprecedented task before us. But in the event that the Congress shall fail, I shall ask the Congress for the one remaining instrument to meet the crisis— broad executive power to wage a war against the emergency as great as the power that would be given to me if we were in fact invaded by a foreign foe. In this dedication of a nation we humbly ask the blessings of God. May He protect each and every one of us. May He guide me in the days to come."

The stirring points in the address evoked murmurs of approval that grew in a crescendo of applause and cheers from the warmed-up throng. Newspapers of the day, according to party posture, agreed or disagreed with the reports on crowd reaction to the speech. But there was no doubt as to the feelings of the crowds as Roosevelt drove down Pennsylvania Avenue toward the glass-fronted stand—he had prohibited bullet-proof glass—where he took his place with family and friends to review the inaugural parade of 18,000, led by Army Chief of Staff Douglas MacArthur. General John J. Pershing had been designated to lead the parade, but illness had forced him to remain in Arizona.

As the marchers passed the stand for three hours, the dirigible *Akron* sailed smoothly 800 feet overhead while planes in fighting formation scooted across the skies, their distant roar audible to the people below. Jim Farley, benevolent and expansive, rode by in the back of an automobile, getting the most cheers from those professionals who saw him as the omnipotent dispenser of 100,000 political jobs. The biggest cheers of all were for New York's Al Smith, who walked past the reviewing stand with the uncompromising insignia of a Tammany Sachem about his shoulders. Roosevelt, propped on a high stool, seemed to relish every moment, doffing his hat repeatedly until Mrs. Roosevelt suggested that he keep it on his head because of the raw wind. The man who had carried forty-two states in the election, the man who was the undisputed leader of the United States, the man who even then had more power than any peacetime President in our history, did as his lady commanded.

The mercury was at a bone-chilling low at dusk when Roosevelt left for the White House, where a tea was in progress with at least a thousand guests, among them a number of Republicans. Roosevelt went directly to his second-floor study, where his entire Cabinet was waiting; and Supreme Court Justice Benjamin Cardozo, a New Yorker appointed by Hoover, administered the oath to the seven Democrats and three ex-Republicans. Conservatism seemed predominant; most of the new secretaries were more than prosperous and none of them had ever really known hardship.

The Secretary of State was Cordell Hull, a Tennessee senator who, when he was in the House of Representatives, had written the first federal income- and inheritance-tax laws. A former chairman of the Democratic National Committee, he was firmly committed to tariffs for revenue only and believed strongly in the freest possible movement of men and goods.

Woodin, the Secretary of the Treasury, had resigned twenty-one major directorships to accept his appointment. A manufacturer of railroad equipment, he was known as a "hard-money" man who had been won away from Republicanism a decade earlier by Al Smith. Put to work after college at a menial job in his father's western Pennsylvania foundry, he had fled to Europe to study music but returned to industry, retaining his love of the arts and continuing to compose without any illusions about his works. The author of a book on numismatics, he was also a collector of the etchings of George Cruikshank, Dickens' illustrator, and a trustee of Roosevelt's Warm Springs Foundation for polio victims.

An inventor and financier who owned banks, power companies and canneries, Secretary of War George Henry Dern had been Governor of Utah until he learned of his Cabinet appointment just as he was leaving for the inauguration. His wife and Roosevelt's were close friends. Dern made no secret of his innocence of all military knowledge, but he was keenly interested in the Army's engineering projects and Roosevelt's plans for the operation of the Muscle Shoals power complex and the development of the Tennessee River basin.

The new Attorney General, Homer S. Cummings of Connecticut, was a stopgap appointee selected in haste when the original designate, Senator Thomas Walsh, died en route to Washington. Like Hull, he had been chairman of the Democratic National Committee; unlike Hull, he had never succeeded in his various campaigns for the House and Senate. His only political office was the Mayoralty of Stamford, Connecticut.

Postmaster General James A. Farley earned his post as the traditional reward of the President-maker. A super-salesman of gypsum and building materials, a back-slapping Elk and

Red Man, he had set a marketing record in Selling Roosevelt to the country, and he settled comfortably at once into his equally important, if totally unrecognized, role as the Administration's dispenser of patronage.

Senator Claude A. Swanson's background was equally undistinguished when Roosevelt saved his political reputation by rescuing him from the necessity of campaigning for reelection against the much stronger Harry Byrd, who had refused to become Secretary of the Treasury. Swanson, as virgin of martial lore as Dern, was made Secretary of the Navy.

A lawyer whose wife's inheritance freed him for independent politicking, Secretary of the Interior Harold L. Ickes was a nominal progressive Republican whose appointment infuriated the Illinois Democratic organization. Describing himself as a "lone wolf" in politics, Ickes had been backing poor men's candidates since 1912, relaxing among his dahlias and his stamp collection on his Winnetka estate.

Family rancor against Hoover brought Henry A. Wallace his post as Secretary of Agriculture. As President Harding's Secretary of Commerce, Hoover had frustrated the farm-relief dreams of Wallace's father, then Secretary of Agriculture, who nevertheless remained a loyal Republican. The younger Wallace inherited the dreams and the feud and, even before his appointment, trumpeted in the columns of *Wallace's Farmer* for direct government relief to farmers in cash and for massive inflation of the currency to ease farmers' debts. He was by far the most radical member of the new Cabinet, but his vehemently personal campaign against Hoover in the 1932 election was his first venture into politics.

Virtually his diametric opposite was the new Secretary of Commerce, Daniel C. Roper, the owner of two South Carolina cotton plantations and a shrewd Washington income-tax lawyer. As a young congressional secretary he had helped to draft the Underwood Tariff Act of 1913; then he had served three years as Commissioner of Internal Revenue. To avoid taking a stand on the controversial nomination of Al Smith for the Presidency in 1928, Roper had left abruptly on a European vacation and was thus counted as a Hoover man by default. He was an ardent defender of Prohibition.

The first woman ever to hold Cabinet office was Secretary of Labor Frances Perkins, a veteran of many years in social and industrial welfare work whose appointment had no backing from organized labor. Roosevelt, who had known and admired her since his early days in the Albany Legislature, when Miss Perkins served on the State Industrial Commission, considered her the most brilliant woman in American public life. The daughter of a prominent Boston family, she had been fired with the zeal of reform shortly after the turn of the century and abandoned college teaching to devote herself to improving the life of the working class.

Roosevelt presented each member with a signed commission, shook hands and issued a fiat that henceforth Frances Perkins should be addressed as Madame Secretary.

Then he went to the Red Room, where he greeted thirteen polio-crippled children from the institution he had helped to found at Warm Springs, Georgia. Later, seventy-two Roosevelts and friends dined in the White House. They included Republican Alice Roosevelt Longworth, who brought good wishes to her fifth cousin. When the dinner was over, Eleanor Roosevelt took five automobiles filled with relatives to the Inaugural Ball. John, the youngest Roosevelt son, escorted Barbara Cushing, whose sister Betsy was the wife of his eldest brother, James.

Earlier in the day, Mr. and Mrs. Hoover, free at last of the Secret Service guard that had been inescapable for four years, had been driven to Union Station to exchange farewells with a loyal little group. In his pocket Hoover had the $500 check that had been brought to him that morning by Miss Catherine Shea of the Treasury Department, with another for $125, representing his final salary and expenses as President of the

United States. The second check was handed back to Miss Shea by Hoover, as part of the $15,000 reduction he had imposed on himself long before. In any case, this last morning as President was a day of unpaid labor, for his statutory salary period had expired at midnight March 3. Now he was bound for his retreat in the Waldorf Towers, while Mrs. Hoover was going to California to visit members of the family.

Even before Hoover's train left Union Station in Washington, the new President's Inaugural Address had begun to have concrete, practical effect. In Baltimore, a middle-aged man who had been vacillating for weeks over the prospect of purchasing a new house listened attentively; before the speech was over he had rushed to the agent's office, checkbook in hand. "I liked what the President had to say," he explained simply.

Another listener even more moved by Roosevelt was Jesse Isidor Straus, president of R. H. Macy & Co., which in those days sold only for cash. Riding back to New York by train, he told friends that he was not merely changing horses in midstream. Roosevelt's speech, the crisis and the hopeful attitude of everyone Straus had met gave him much profound thought, and, as he sat in his Pullman, he began to compose the advertisement that would appear as a full page in every New York newspaper:

> I trust my government.
> I trust our banks.
> I do not expect the impossible.
> I shall do nothing hysterical.
> I know that if I try now to get all my cash I shall certainly make matters worse.
> I will not stampede. I will not lose my nerve. I will keep my head.

Even the most persistent pessimists had to admit that, at least for the moment, there was a general burgeoning of hope. Somehow the optimism crossed partisan lines that day and night. Amateur philosophers, speakeasy pundits, the gentlemen at the Racquet and Tennis Club, housewives, college students, agreed that something better was about to happen. No one could yet point to anything specific, but the promise of action—and action now—had an electrifying result.

In the White House, the man who had galvanized the nation stayed quietly in his study, yielding himself completely to a soothing lethargy. He removed the steel braces from his legs and discussed the events of the day with his friend and secretary, Louis McHenry Howe. At 10:30 P.M. the President went to bed. The first day of an era had ended.

Sieg Heil!

ONLY twenty-four hours separated the beginning of the twentieth-century American revolution and the death agony of German democracy. Roosevelt took office in response to a popular will whose sovereignty he meant to uphold. On March 5, Adolf Hitler, already Chancellor of Germany, staged a parliamentary election designed to destroy the rule of the people of his country and the Constitution under which the election had been called. The Roosevelt revolution, not wholly intended as such, was to strengthen the society in which it took place. The Hitler revolution, deliberate from its inception a decade earlier, was to doom the culture that had allowed it to grow.

Hitler and his original National Socialist Party came out of the miasma, the torment, the frustration of the Kaiser War. His calculated crusade against the Greco-Judeo-Christian culture of three thousand years burgeoned rapidly, first picking up the strays, the crackpots and the rejects, then attracting the fanatics, the frenzied seekers of a cause and finally the opportunists who saw in him a useful and expendable tool. From the time of his Munich beer-hall *Putsch* a decade earlier, he had been to the sophisticated a sort of

graveyard joke, but the week of March 1–7 saw him emerge
not as a joke but as a scourge, not as a tool but as the master.

As leader of the largest party in the Reichstag, Hitler had
approached President Paul von Hindenburg in August, 1932,
with a request that he be made Chancellor and given the same
powers held by Benito Mussolini in Italy. Hindenburg, a
national idol, was somewhat in his dotage at 85. Still the
traditional aristocrat and soldier, he regarded Hitler with
conflicting emotions. On the one side he approved of Hitler's
posture of uncompromising autocracy. But, as he confided
later to an aide, he could not shake the revulsion he felt at
the thought of the proud German people coming to heel before that upstart house painter. He therefore rejected Hitler's proposal. Other members of the old German nobility
did not share this feeling. Although Kaiser Wilhelm II, in
exile in the Netherlands, held Hitler in disdain and contempt, his two sons, August Wilhelm and Friederich, were
working eagerly with the Nazis, perhaps with some vain hope
that Hitler might restore the monarchy.

Hindenburg, however, did not take into consideration the
political agility of another aristocrat, Franz von Papen—a
gentleman with the fortunate facility of always being on the
winning side. Von Papen, the complete patriot and scoun-
drel, was aware of what Anne Morrow Lindbergh was to describe sympathetically several years later as "the wave of the
future." He negotiated privately with Alfred Hugenberg,
publisher and arch-reactionary agrarian leader, and on January 28, he presented a *fait accompli* to Hindenburg. Von
Papen argued that the government of General von
Schleicher, the last of five shaky administrations within 12
months, was totally ineffectual. It was true that there was a
slight economic improvement, but during Schleicher's 55
days in office the country had become restless and rudderless.
Von Papen peppered his conversation with such words as
communism and *anarchy*. What was needed, he urged, was

absolute leadership, and only one man in the Reich was able to give it. This man was Adolf Hitler. Hindenburg, the Junker, listened, but still hesitated. Two days later he surrendered. Hitler became Chancellor, appointing von Papen and Hugenberg to his cabinet.

This was at the end of January. Hitler did not yet have the powers he wanted. Moving cautiously, he instituted a purge within the government. At first it was conducted in the most civilized fashion. There was a genteel but steady weeding out of the Prussian bureaucrats. In one week, three provincial government presidents and ten police commissioners were placed on "permanent leave of absence." A Nazi police chief took over the lives of 15,000,000 citizens in the Rhineland and Westphalia. These industrial provinces were peopled mainly by Socialists and Communists.

Then came the first overt move against the intellectuals. Passports were denied to liberal and pacifist writers and speakers on the ground that their utterances in foreign countries would be harmful to the Reich. During all this time the Jew-baiting in the press and on the platform continued unabated. If the German people, still free to speak, resented any of these actions, they did not do so openly. After all, there were only about 600,000 Jews in a population of more than 66,000,000.

But soon the Catholics were startled and dismayed when their biggest publication, *Germania,* of Berlin, was suppressed. It had printed a manifesto saying: *We declare ourselves against all forms of bolshevism. Germany must not be abandoned to the extremes of either the right or the left.*

It must be said for the Nazis that they never kept their intentions secret from the German people. Hermann Goering, Minister of the Interior for Prussia, issued the following instructions to the police:

> You must refrain from even a mere semblance of an antagonistic attitude toward . . . the Nazi Storm Troops or the

Stahlhelm [reactionary veteran's group]. Every manifestation of a Nationalist purpose and Nationalist propaganda must be supported with full vigor. With respect to them, police restrictions or instructions must be resorted to only in the most urgent cases. On the other hand . . . the police must proceed against Communist acts of terrorism with the utmost severity and must use their arms ruthlessly when necessary. I will protect every policeman who makes use of firearms in the exercise of his duty. Every police officer must always bear in mind that failing to act is a greater fault than error made in action.

Goering also addressed himself to the population two days before the March 5 election. "I hereby summon the whole line to the onslaught on Communism," he announced. "My measures will not be hampered by legal considerations. It is not my business in this matter to practice justice, but only to annihilate and to extirpate."

If the people of Germany were listening and watching, they were treated to another "truth." Bernhard Rust, Nazi Minister of Education for Prussia, told them that freedom was "inconsistent with human nature." And to prove his point, he forced the resignation from the Prussian Academy of Art of Heinrich Mann, writer and elder brother of Thomas; Kaethe Kollwitz, the artist; and Dr. Martin Wagner, the architect. Mann and Frau Kollwitz had signed a manifesto urging Socialists and Communists to unite in preventing the "threatened destruction of all personal and political liberty."

But whatever doubt the Germans might have had about the fullest intentions of the Nazis was dispelled by Hitler himself when in a radio broadcast from Stuttgart he said: "I am firmly resolved . . . under no circumstances to let the German people return to a Marxist regime. I shall know how to preserve what we have attained."

As soon as these awesome utterances were made, the apologists leaped forward with their specious arguments. There were too many in Germany and other countries to be quoted, but *Time* magazine deftly summed them up:

> Today most Germans are agreed that Hitlerism, with its bombastic counsels of violence, treaty-breaking and Jew-baiting, would have swept the country years ago had not Germans been lulled by a false postwar prosperity induced in the Fatherland by a flood of U.S. loans. These loans enabled Germany to pay reparations with borrowed money, turned the shackles riveted on her by the Treaty of Versailles almost into gold bracelets. When Depression showed the bracelets to be iron, the Germany-in-chains was ready to break them by turning to the doctrine of Messiah Hitler, who had been preaching repudiation from the first.

Nevertheless, private creditors in the United States, Great Britain, France, Italy, The Netherlands, Sweden and Switzerland extended their short-term credits to German debtors for another year. Headed by Albert H. Wiggin, former president and chairman of the Chase National Bank of New York, the committee representing the creditors extended a revised "standstill" pact that had been created in August, 1931, as a result of the Hoover moratorium. The agreement had prevented the withdrawal by foreigners of balances in German banks and halted attempts by German banks and businesses to obtain foreign funds with which to pay maturing short-term credits. American creditors bore about 40 per cent of the burden. The committee was happy to report impressive results and praised the "steady co-operation of the government, the Reichsbanks and the community."

If George Orwell had done any research for his *1984*, where he created such words as *newspeak* and *doublethink,* he could not have missed the double talk in the definition of capital as put forward by Gottfried Feder, a building engineer who had been named by Hitler to the Finance Committee of the Reichstag. The way Feder postulated the dogma, there were two kinds of capital.

There was the grasping, greedy hoarding by banks that gave all the interest to the Jews. Then there was the creative capital that was the very sap of German business, which was good and kind even though it paid interest.

This was the kind of thinking that Hitler loved, because he could send speakers to meetings of workers where they would threaten expropriation of *bad* capital, while others, wearing swallowtails and silk hats, would assure boards of directors that their capital would be protected. Even the name of Hitler's party, the National Socialists, was a masterpiece of double talk. Until Hitler dinned confusion into the willing ears of most Germans, the two words were a contradiction in terms.

Having assumed the Chancellorship, Hitler faced with hidden misgivings the Reichstag elections of Sunday, March 5. There were actually two elections, one for the German Reichstag and the other for the Prussian Diet, which included almost two-thirds of the country. He had unleashed his propaganda machine, and some significant repressions had been accomplished with less than expected resistance, but the overwhelming victory that Hitler sought was by no means assured.

And then the guardian angel of dictators sent him a gift. It was the Reichstag fire. On February 27 the main chamber and the great dome of gilded copper were destroyed by a roaring blaze. Police immediately blamed the Communists. Goering stepped to the microphone of a national hook-up and charged that the "fire was to have been a signal for the outbreak of open civil war. The Communists had in readiness terror squads . . . to commit their dastardly acts disguised as units of our own Nazi Storm Troops and the Stahlhelm. The women and children of high government officials were to be kidnaped as hostages and used in the civil war as living shields. The Communists had organized to poison food . . . burn down granaries. . . . From all these horrors we have saved the Fatherland. We want to state clearly that the measures taken are not a mere defense against Communism. Ours is a fight to the finish until Communism has been absolutely uprooted in Germany."

Hitler pounced with an alacrity that belied his inner fears that he would be stopped. But he was not stopped. He ordered that pistols and rifles be issued to 60,000 auxiliary police in Prussia. Fifty per cent of these came from the Nazi Sturmabteiling; 30 per cent from the selected Schutzstaffel shock troops; 20 per cent from the Stahlhelm. This swift increase of men under arms was an open violation of the Treaty of Versailles, which limited Germany to a total army of 100,-000. Moreover, with astounding audacity Hitler decreed that these auxiliaries be paid full wages by their private employers regardless how little time their new duties left them for their regular jobs. The employers assumed this burden without audible demur.

Hitler then confronted Hindenburg with "the facts in the national emergency." This time Hindenburg did not hesitate. He signed a decree that finally gave Hitler the total tyrant powers he had sought. The decree suspended seven articles of the Constitution. These articles had provided that:

> . . . freedom of the person may not be impaired.
> The home of every German is his place of refuge and may not be violated. . . .
> Secrecy of letters and of postal, telegraph and telephone services may not be impaired. . . .
> Every German has the right within the limits of the general laws to express his opinion by word, in writing or printing, by picture or in any other way. . . .

All Germans have the right to gather in meetings peaceable and unarmed without announcement of particular permission. . . .

All Germans have the right to form societies or associations for purposes not contrary to the penal law.

Property is safeguarded by the Constitution.

Thus did Hitler stifle all the Germans under one monstrous blanket of repression. This was followed swiftly by a set of laws designed to thwart any action by those few areas of resistance remaining. The death penalty was fixed for anyone attempting to obtain or revealing military secrets. Prison for ten years was provided for those who transmitted news of any kind to foreign governments that was not in the good interests of Germany. Even foreign correspondents were not permitted to act freely within this new ring of iron. A penalty of not less than three months' imprisonment was provided for those reporters who might transmit "news that should be kept from foreign governments." The reporters were informed of this as they learned that the entire opposition press had been suppressed. Walter Funk, chief government press officer, was not arbitrary in his announcement. He offered an explanation: "You must realize, gentlemen, that what has happened in Germany is no ordinary change. A new era has begun! Parliamentary and democratic times are past."

Somehow the news did get out. American, British, French, and Scandinavian newspapers printed the story of Hitler's ascendancy in detail. Many included in their columns well-reasoned speculation that the Reichstag fire was caused by the Nazis themselves and not Communists.

The London Times wrote:

The threat of a general massacre of political opponents by the Nazis might have been dismissed two months ago as crude bravado but cannot be rated so lightly now.

The London Daily Herald reported:

> A quarter-million Nazi Storm Troops, including desperate characters over whom even Chancellor Hitler cannot exercise control, will, it is stated, invade the large towns of Prussia and slaughter all progressive leaders and Jews, of whom, both men and women, a long list has already been prepared.

Hitler was fuming when he heard of these published reports, and the entire Nazi thought-control apparatus was mortified when it discovered that a large number of these publications had found their way into Berlin. Verified reports of more arrests were received by the foreign press corps in Berlin. Several Reichstag deputies were among 350 Communists arrested. Funk bragged that "every Communist ballot will be thrown out" in the forthcoming election. A high Berlin police official boasted that if Professor Albert Einstein were to return from California, he would be arrested as a Jew and a sympathizer with the radicals.

Der Fuehrer, marching on to his spectacular campaign speech in Berlin's Sportspalast, was getting the personal adulation of the now captive press. Portrayed as a devotee of Wagnerian music, an ascetic, a lover of Aryan humanity, and dedicated completely to the salvation of Germany, he was expected to follow the glorious philosophies of Bismark and Frederick the Great, whose busts were the only adornments in his austere office. This evaluation omitted any mention of a definite program of what he intended to do for and with Germany. In his Sportspalast address to the inspired cheers of 20,000 followers, Hitler lumped Socialism, Communism, and Democracy under one massive curse. "Marxism," he shouted, "proceeds on the assumption of all being equal. As a corollary to this principle, democracy also postulated not only that nations must be appraised as equal in quality but that individuals also must not be differentiated. This obviously leads to the throttling of individual capacity. We will take up the struggle against this insanity. Not because we are in love with capitalism—I am myself a child of the lower classes—but because we want to spare the people. We will rebuild the Reich by tenacious work. The rise of the German people cannot be prevented."

If the speech was somewhat incomprehensible it did not matter. The stentorian delivery, the fury, the frenzy and the searing heat of unrestrained patriotism were enough for the mad multitude in the Sportspalast. At the conclusion, Hitler announced that after the election the Reichstag would meet in Potsdam, the symbolic citadel of Germany's aristocracy and imperialism. It would convene in the Garrison Church where Frederick the Great was interred.

On the eve of the election there were still some Germans capable of analytical thought, who must have realized that despite heroic campaign oratory Hitler had made no specific pledges, had proposed no specific political platform other than his tirades against Jews and radicals and his professed love for the *Vaterland*. There seemed still to be some hope in the sullen attitude of the organized workers at the mention of Hitler; there were still the loyal followers of the Socialists, the Communists, the Catholic Centrists, the Bavarian Populists and the many little, confused and disorganized splinter parties. But all these hopes vanished on election eve under the magic wand of Dr. Josef Goebbels, Hitler's publicity chief extraordinary, who understood the German mass mind better than anyone. He decreed that Hitler would make his final appeal to the German people in a national radio broadcast from Koenigsberg on the Polish border.

Hitler's party flew in three Junkers planes across the narrow Corridor that cut Germany in two, a dramatic demonstration of the denigration of the Reich by the Allies after the Kaiser war. He decreed, and the Nazi discipline responded fervently, that bonfires and patriotic conclaves be held all over the Reich from the tiniest hamlet to the largest cities. As the party flew over Danzig, that Free City responded with the screaming of sirens and the tolling of bells. And as Hitler stepped to the microphones the Nazis—and many others— were gathered in front of the "flames of Nordic destiny"— from the dreary sand dunes of the Baltic on the north to the Bavarian Alps in the south; from the hills of the Rhineland in the west to the swamps of the Masurian Lakes in the east. Everywhere there were torchlight parades illuminated by monster magnesium flares; the sounds of boots on cobblestones; the throaty notes of the *Horst Wessel Song,* and the binding oath of blood brotherhood standing strong and fast against all that was not pure German. And when the strident voice of the Fuehrer came over the loud-speakers, the excited multitudes stood as if mesmerized to accept their thralldom from the "divinely appointed savior of the Reich."

Hitler, Goebbels, Goering and the others had wrought well. After 88 per cent of the free electorate had cast ballots, an all-time record on this bright and balmy Sunday, this was the score: of 652 seats in the Reichstag, the National Socialists had captured 288 and the Nationalists 52. This was one bloc. The Socialists got 120 seats and the Communists 81. In the Catholic bloc, the Catholic Centrists got 73, the Bavarian Populists 20. All the splinter parties got 18. In the Prussian Diet the National Socialists got 44.6 per cent of the vote and the Nationalists 9 per cent, the Socialists 16.9, the Catholic Centrists 14.4, the Communists 13.4 and the splinter parties 1.7.

The Nazis knew the entire world was watching, but it did not matter now. Moving swiftly as the victorious vote was being counted, triumphant Storm Troops seized the muncipal government of the Free City of Hamburg, whose 1,000,-000 inhabitants had enjoyed until this brutal moment the status of a state in the German Republic. Dr. Karl Peterson, the Socialist mayor, confronted by the force of Storm Troopers, promptly resigned.

Historians maintain a continuing debate as to how much Hitler fooled the German people and how much they wanted to be fooled. They listened to his voice rather than his words and they saw only what he wanted them to see. For example, on election day the Nazis had forbidden the flying of the black, red and gold flag of Republican Germany. Instead, they displayed the old Imperial Hohenzollern colors of black and white. When the election was over, having won it under borrowed colors, the Nazis hoisted their own flag—red, with a white bull's-eye containing a black swastika.

At a command from Goebbels, all the Germans stood still once more and heard Hitler declaim: "The National Revolution is on its way and will continue."

The first day of an era had ended.

CHAPTER 8

Render Unto Caesar

   . . . ON SUNDAY NIGHT, March 5, as Hitler was sweeping to victory, Roosevelt decreed that the next four days were to be a bank holiday for all banks and financial institutions in the nation. He also declared an embargo on the export of gold. This thwarted the hoarders. The *Paris* sailed without her $9 million in bullion. All those who held gold were warned that they would have to surrender it to the government.

The action was not too late to prevent the depletion of the Government's gold holdings, but the run on the precious metal had forced the U.S. to expand its currency, causing a good deal of discomfort and loss to Americans abroad. One day the dollar was worth 28 piastres in Cairo, the next day it was 17. In Montreal, the dollar lost 35 cents within 24 hours. Americans in Havana had nothing to worry about. Cuba had declared a bank holiday of its own.

The order closing all the banks created some confusion, including the question whether owners of safety-deposit boxes could get to them. On Monday afternoon therefore Woodin, looking fresh and chipper in a blue shirt, checked suit and spats, called in the press to explain the rules he had issued that morning:

All banks were allowed to make change to relieve the shortage of small bills and coin.

All banks were empowered to make loans to expedite the movement of food for the people and feed for animals.

All banks were to permit free access to safety-deposit boxes so that holders could bring out their hoardings, and others could get to their belongings.

All Postal Savings Banks would remain open.

All banks were to cash checks drawn on the Treasurer of the United States.

All banks were to be allowed to receive payments due them.

All banks were cautioned against paying out in gold or gold certificates.

These rules cleared the atmosphere, removing some doubts and fears. By Tuesday many banks were paying out currency for payrolls and the necessities of life. The sturdier banks allowed withdrawals in large amounts for proved emergencies. But the hoarding of gold and gold certificates was obviously a condition that called for speedy executive measures. The Federal Reserve Board found the answer. On the Wednesday following the inauguration, it announced that its member banks would prepare lists of all persons who had withdrawn gold since the first of February and had failed to return it within five days.

Newspapers and radio broadcasts spread the news and within an hour banks began to receive telephone calls asking for details. The banks were co-operative. They said they would open for anyone who wanted to return gold. They promised that newspapermen would be kept out of lobbies and there would be no publicity. Where the law had been stumped, moral suasion, or pressure, succeeded in spectacular fashion.

Out of mattresses, cans, cookie jars, home safes, hidden cabinets and every other manner of cache came the gold. Long lines formed at banks throughout the nation. Paper bags, sacks, satchels, brief cases, clutched by anxious men and women, began to disgorge. A 56-mile-an-hour gale whipped through the queues in New York, where banks got back on the first day $30,000,000 in gold and gold certificates. One business firm brought $6,000,000 in bullion to the Federal Reserve Bank. One man accounted for $700,000. In line at a Sixth Avenue bank stood a woman trying feverishly to keep the gale from blowing through her skirts and petticoat. Suddenly a gust loosed the stitches of a hastily sewn seam, sending hundreds of gold certificates flying across the street. People broke the line and helped her recover her hoard. Whether she ever got back all of it will never be known.

Some were meek; some repentant; some shamefaced; some defiant; some even posed as patriots, but they came trooping back with the hoards, large and small. Boston collected $350,-000 in one day; Cleveland, $300,000; Minneapolis, $185,000; Philadelphia, $700,000; Richmond, $168,000. In Wilmington, Irénée du Pont turned in a gold-coin collection he had been saving for 20 years. By the time the queues had thinned out to a few obdurate hoarders, the country had recovered $300,000,000 in gold and gold certificates, enabling the Federal Reserve banks to put $750,000,000 worth of greenbacks into circulation.

Financial centers of the world were amazed at Roosevelt's unilateral proclamation of the gold embargo. Even in the United States most legal minds, caught up in the infectious fantasy of the times, did not question the legality of Roosevelt's action. It was not until the Thursday after the inauguration that a bewildered and willing Congress passed a conglomerate bill ratifying all acts "heretofore and hereinafter taken by the President." It also provided prison terms for hoarders and created another charming euphemism. In the conventional manner it provided receivers for tottering banks but it called them *conservators*. The age of official self-delusion by semantics had begun.

Now that the bank holiday was nationwide, newspapers were filled, on the one hand, with serious stories of the grave situation, and on the other hand, with the little absurdities created by a short-changed imaginative people.

Some ministers in New York, Boston, Philadelphia, St. Louis and San Francisco urged their congregations to keep their silver and place IOU's in the collection boxes. While they were doing that, merchants were begging churches to accept checks and large bills in exchange for their collection coins. Most clergymen were co-operative, encouraging and sympathetic in their sermons on this mock holiday, the first Sunday of Lent, which had begun March 1. They preached for the most part on secular themes, endorsing bank holidays and urging patience and good will, prayer and hope, humility and unselfishness, as good companions for the duration of the crisis. The more brash among them ventured to prescribe for the ills of the nation and the world.

The depression could be ended in 24 hours, Norman Vincent Peale told his congregation in the Marble Collegiate Reformed Church on Fifth Avenue, through the simple expedient of "a good prayer meeting in Wall Street" attended by all the bankers and brokers. "Let them," he counseled floridly, "look God in the eye and tell him how they felt the pressure of the social whirl. Let them tell him how, to keep up with the Joneses, they had to build finer homes, buy expensive cars and yachts, and more and more luxuries for their families. Let them admit to God, at least, that, to keep this dizzy pace, they had, as many suspect, to issue new stock and deflate old stock far above its value [sic] and sell it to the unsuspecting public to get the money to pay the piper."

For the rest of America's Christians, Lent had begun with somewhat less fanfare and much more sober thinking, for churches too were caught in the economic vise. Protestant ministers' salaries had declined from 10 per cent to 33 per cent; those in rural areas were suffering the most. Yet at the same time only one church in every 2,344 had been forced to close in 1932; and in that same year $30 million in church building contracts had been let. Nonetheless church income had been falling steadily; it was salaries that had to absorb the blows. On the third day of Lent, which was also the third day of March, Protestants marked a world day of prayer for foreign missions, for which they had just voted a reduction in budget. The Presbyterian General Council, meeting in Philadelphia, voted a 10 per cent salary reduction for all its officers and employees, and reduced the per capita tax on congregations for assembly purposes from 11 to 10 cents. Reluctantly, the Council voted also to discontinue its magazine in order to save $18,000 more per year. The Brooklyn Diocese of the Roman Catholic Church took similar action: Bishop Molloy, citing such things as a $20,000 loss in the income of a single parish in the preceding year, decreed a 10 per cent reduction in salary for all pastors, who had received $1,380 yearly, and all curates, who had been paid $840 yearly. Their maintenance by the Church was of course continued; nothing was said of cuts in the salaries of the higher ecclesiastics. The Orthodox and Conservative rabbinate had already suffered successive reductions in salary, but the more fashionable Reformed rabbis in big cities, like the modish Protestant pastors on Fifth and Madison and Park avenues, were still serving God for five-figure honoraria.

It was only the Orthodox rabbis who openly recognized the peril of their co-religionists in Germany (most of whom would have refused to associate with them) and, on the Sabbath Eve of March 3, offered special prayers for the welfare of the German Jews. Reform Judaism, itself a German-Jewish product, ignored the obvious—neither Protestants nor Catholics at this time appreciated either the strength or the implications of German anti-Semitism. Mexican anti-clericalism had long occupied the attention of American religious leaders, but by now it was taken for granted and when, over the weekend, the State of Chiapas joined the many others that had sealed the churches and sequestered their property, almost no notice was taken.

Two Protestant ministers stand out of the record of those days. Dr. George M. Stockdale, a New York Methodist, was unique in recommending the study and emulation of Jesus rather than presupposing His blessing for what He might very likely have damned. The Rev. Thomas F. R. Beale of St. Paul, a native of Britain, lost his plea for American citizenship when, taking his stand on essential Christianity, he refused to bear arms for the United States. But much more publicity and praise went to the Presbyterian congregation in Milwaukee that proved its religious worth by providing free gasoline and oil to everyone who drove to church on March 5. . . .

CHAPTER 9

And Caesar's Wife?

... THOUGH there were a number of minor financial scandals at this time—virtually every city of any size had at least one—there were two major ones that overshadowed all the rest. Five thousand miles from the scene of his depredations, Samuel Insull Sr. was sitting on suitcases containing $10 million in cash, secure in the knowledge that he could not be dragged back to Chicago from his refuge in Athens, because the United States had no treaty provisions with Greece to permit extradition on charges of mail fraud. A similar loophole in our extradition agreement with Canada allowed one of Insull's sons, Martin, to languish comfortably north of the border while Samuel Jr. remained active in the utilities industry in Chicago despite having been indicted, with his father and brother, on twenty-five counts of mail fraud. Each count carried a penalty of five years in prison and $10,000 in fines so that, if convicted on all counts, each of the defendants would face 125 years in a cell and $250,000 in fines.

The Insulls—indicted after a four-month investigation by the Department of Justice—had carried the relatively new device of the utility holding company to a breathless peak.

Their Corporation Securities Co. had been set up to deal in the issues of companies that operated public utilities, and had ultimately acquired control of a great number of these with the help of bankers and brokers. In this there was nothing illegal or even immoral. It was what had happened afterward that had brought into being the 120-page indictment that included not only the Insulls but such impeccably respectable financial leaders as Stanley Field, chairman of the board of the giant Continental-Illinois National Bank & Trust Co.; Edward J. Doyle, president of the Commonwealth Edison Co., one of the operating companies acquired by the Insulls; and Harold L. Stuart, president of the hitherto irreproachable investment-banking firm of Halsey, Stuart & Co.

The indictment was returned at the end of February. It accused the men of mail fraud in that they had offered shares in Corporation Securities to the public on the pretense that it had great physical properties when in truth it or its subsidiaries had lost many of these and in many cases its assets consisted of paper as worthless as that in any ignorant margin speculator's odd-lot portfolio. In addition, despite an existing agreement with the holders of debentures of Corporation Securities that the debentures would be fully secured before any of the company's assets were pledged, the firm's whole portfolio had been deposited as collateral for $15 million in bank loans. The investigation had not reached the climax of the handing up of the indictment when the elder Insull and Martin fled, the one to Greece and the other to Canada, while Samuel Jr. remained at the shaky helm of the foundering vessel called Corporation Securities Co.

Until they were actually indicted, of course, the Insulls could not legally have been denied their passports or stopped from leaving the country. But both were safely out when the Grand Jury acted, and the outgoing heads of the Departments of State and Justice must have been secretly relieved that the problem could plague them no longer than a few days. It was a prickly part of the inheritance assumed by Secretary of State Hull and Attorney General Cummings, and, like their predecessors, they could only voice polite hope that the respective foreign governments involved would be good enough to make the fugitives unofficially but no less sensibly unwelcome. No sign of such a tendency manifested itself during that bank-holiday week.

The other major scandal had a much more intimate relation to one or more of the underlying factors in the fragility of the whole banking structure. Even while Roosevelt was trying, in the first days of March, to persuade Hoover to close the banks, and then during the whole of the bank holiday that ensued, a proud man, liked and respected even by his bitterest opponents, was destroying the work of a lifetime as he testified before the Senate Committee on Banking and Currency.

Charles Edwin Mitchell had risen in the Horatio Alger tradition from the platitudinous humble beginning to become chairman of the board of New York's huge National City Bank and of its various affiliates, as well as a director of a dazzling array of financial and industrial corporations in both the United States and Latin America. The story that he had begun to trace before the Committee some weeks earlier and that reached one of its many climaxes even as the new President was closing the banks was an intricate one in which even the trained financial and legal mind had difficulty in assessing whether there had been any actual violation of the laws—aside from one point, which Mitchell admitted without hedging: a purely personal dereliction in connection with taxes on his private income. This became a heinous crime solely because of the curious dichotomy of the American mores, under which it is not only good sport but downright ethical for every workingman to reduce his taxable income by claiming charitable contributions that he never made, while it is debatable whether a rich man's tax fraud may not be worse than Benedict Arnold's treachery.

Mitchell's personal fortune when he became chairman of the board of National City in 1929 exceeded $20 million; by the end of the year it had vanished and he had gone $3 million into debt in a vain effort to halt the plunge in the price of the bank's stock. It was this attempt to protect all the holders of National City shares, whether their portfolios contained one share or thousands, that was the crux of the question whether, in his official capacity, Mitchell had caused the bank to violate the federal law that forbade national banks to deal in their own securities. But what Mitchell and National City did after the Wall Street disaster of October, 1929, was only a part of what every big bank in New York was engaged in; a coalition formed specifically to try to arrest the avalanche. This too was an unimpeachable purpose; it was the means that the Senate Committee was savagely attacking during the bank-holiday week.

Day by day Mitchell had stripped the complex operation until by now it was almost bare bones. As long ago as 1911 the National City Bank had formed a wholly owned subsidiary, the National City Company, for the purpose of underwriting and trading in security issues of public companies. These companies included, of course, the National City Bank itself, and the National City Co. had hardly been formed when the then Solicitor General of the United States gave it as his opinion that the establishment of the subsidiary was an illegal act. This view was never officially acted on, and other national banks followed National City's example. But the Senate Committee's counsel, Ferdinand Pecora, had steeped himself in the 1911 opinion and proceeded to make a strong case that, through its subsidiary, the National City Bank, under Mitchell's direction, had been violating the law by trading in its own securities and by lending its of-

ficers money—without interest or security—to enable them
to hold their imperiled shares of the bank's stock. In 1929 it
lent them $2.4 million; by March of 1933 only 5 per cent of
that amount had been repaid. Pecora also cited the view of
Hoover's Attorney General, Cornelius W. Wickersham, who
had declared at the start of the Committee's investigation
that he concurred with the 1911 view that the National City
Co. had been illegally established and that it was a tempta-
tion to the bank to speculate disastrously at the same time
that, in a booming economy, it had offered the bank the opportunity to monopolize economic power through control
of a vast complex of industries.

Mitchell's admission that he had sold $2.8 million in the
stock of his bank to his wife to establish a capital loss in 1929,
and that he had omitted to report $600,000 in income re-
ceived from the National City Company for the same year,
was for the moment overlooked in the maze he was unravel-
ing. (Later it formed the basis for a criminal prosecution
for tax fraud, of which he was acquitted, and for a civil
suit for tax payment, which he lost; stripped of everything
he owed, he refused to go into bankruptcy and ultimately
paid his creditors 100 cents on the dollar and made a new
fortune in Wall Street before he died in 1955.) Besides lending money without interest or security to its officers, the
National City Bank had advanced credit through stockbrok-
ers to enable investors to purchase its stock. In 1930 it had
lent its *alter ego,* the National City Co., enough money to
buy almost two million shares of the bank's stock, which
were then sold to the public for $650 million; but Gordon
Rentschler, president of the bank, indignantly denied that
this constituted a violation of the legal prohibition against
the bank's selling its own stock. The National City Co. was
also accused of selling the bank's stock short and, to meet its
commitments, borrowing 30,000 shares from Mitchell's
personal holdings and paying him $128,850 in interest.

Just before the inauguration, Mitchell resigned an impressive list of chairmanships and directorships: the National City Bank, the National City Co., the National City Realty Corp., the National City Safe Deposit Co., the International Banking Corp., the General Sugar Corp., the Banque nationale de la république d'Haïti, American & Foreign Power, American I. G. Chemical, Anaconda Copper Mining, Andes Copper, Chile Copper, Chile Exploration Co., the Discount Corp. of New York, International Telephone and Telegraph, New York Edison, Consolidated Gas Co., Postal Telegraph, U.S. Realty & Improvement, and the Teachers' Insurance and Annuity Association.

The following Monday, the first day of the bank holiday, President Roosevelt received a New York financier whose name was previously unknown to the general public. He was James H. Perkins; the next day he became chairman of the National City Bank, and it was generally believed—without confirmation or denial from any source—that he had gone to the White House that Monday to receive the Presidential blessing. One of his first acts, on the day he took office, was to announce the impending divorce of the bank from its subsidiary National City Co.; within hours New York's Chase National Bank announced that it was severing the umbilical cord that had bound it to the Chase Securities Corp. For National City, the divorce was a mixture of gain and loss. It would take some time, of course, to complete the severance, and during that interim the National City Co. would deal only in government and municipal issues and high-grade corporate bonds. Its municipal list was the largest in the country; it had also been the loan broker for many foreign countries, cities, and corporations, including the gigantic Kreuger Match swindle. In addition, the National City Co. had financed such outstanding public utilities as Consolidated Gas, New York Edison, the New York Steam Corp.,

Brooklyn Union Gas, Pacific Gas & Electric, Postal Telegraph and Chicago Rapid Transit.

Chase National and National City, in cutting off their underwriting connections on March 7, were in effect merely stealing a march on the executioner. Before the year was out the Banking Act of 1933, based in great measure on Mitchell's revelations to the Senate Committee, was to forbid all banks to underwrite any issue of securities. But these two major banks, as well as lesser institutions that followed their example as quickly as they learned of it, made it plain that, when they should be allowed to reopen, they were prepared to remain in the banking business and to eschew speculation. . . .

CHAPTER 10

Pedagogues and Politics

THE nation's educational system was having as much crisis in that first week of March as any other segment. Teachers' salaries had been reduced as deeply as 30 per cent —in some of the largest cities in the country a high school teacher, if he could find an appointment, received $1,800 a year to start and, after ten years, a maximum of $3,200 unless he had taken two graduate degrees; their aggregate value was $400 more annually. Assistant instructors in the finest universities began their academic careers at $750 per year (men without private means or working wives were urged not to seek the posts) and the full professor who, after decades, could command $9,000 annually was a plutocrat of his profession.

The Department of Superintendents of the National Education Association was holding its national convention in the beginning of March, and it was in a desperate fighting mood. The pupil population of the public schools had risen by a million since 1930; in the same period the teaching force had lost 15,000 members through sheer force of economics. Worst of all, the average per-child-per-day fund had declined from the already inadequate sum of 63 cents to 49. Speaker

after speaker exhorted the pedagogues to abandon the political neutrality that had been a tradition of their profession, to
initiate political action that would assure the elimination of
the clubhouse politician's domination of the nation's schools.
No one denied the shortage of money; but the issue, educators insisted, was real economy against bogus economy.

Professor John Dewey of Teachers' College of Columbia
University, the hero of the progressive educators of the day,
warned that public schools could never be secure as long as
they were dominated by the great financial interests. Scornfully he pointed to the occasion when Franklin Roosevelt,
still Governor of New York, had been petitioned by teachers'
groups to increase the state's appropriations for its schools.
Before he could reply, Roosevelt had said, he must consult
various bankers in New York City: in the end the increase
had been denied. Hence, Dewey concluded, the only course
left to teachers was to form a labor union and to affiliate with
the American Federation of Labor.

As great a menace to the public school as the financier, according to William McAndrew, former superintendent of
schools in Chicago, was the politician and the politically appointed Board of Education. But neither McAndrew nor
Dewey took strong issue with the basic practices of public
education that geared the curriculum to the progress rate of
the lowest common denominator. Their concern was wholly
with political and financial considerations. It remained for
Dr. Goodwin Watson, a Teachers' College colleague of
Dewey, to try to bring his fellow educators' attention back
to education. Watson urged that schools go beyond the
teaching of basic skills, personal or social, and consider the
future needs and desires of the individual. One of the duties
of the school, he contended, was education for the enriching
use of leisure; and this, he held, should be begun in the
earliest grades by making intellectual activities attractive

and interesting. Adult education as it was getting under way in big cities, he conceded, was helping to fill the gap left by lack of opportunity or exposure during the normal student years; but it was at least equally important to eliminate that gap in the future.

This was already being done by the private schools but only a fraction of the population could benefit from their superior staffs, curricula and methods. Heavily endowed schools could charge as little as $150 to $350 for a full school year; but many were being forced to retrench, if not to close, as the economic storms battered their assets. Intrinsically, the greatest defect of the good private school was its relative indifference to the sciences, in contrast to its strong emphasis on languages, history and the arts. A radical departure was announced in this week by Major Enoch Barton Garey, who had long headed St. John's College in Annapolis, Maryland. He planned to open a small boarding school on an old Eastern Shore estate and he proclaimed that it would be what he called ultraprogressive. By this he did not mean permissive, for he made it plain that his concept of progressive education was learning by doing. Unlike the usual private school, Major Garey's institution would start teaching science in the earliest grades. "The school will train boys," he said, "to do something today, not only tomorrow." Like other private educators, however, he did not speak in terms of the "units of learning" and the "units of teaching" that were the key phrases in the liturgy of Teachers' College and its apostles, who could define either only in terms of the other (units of learning were components of units of teaching, *e per contra*). Nor did private schools place the same trusting faith in the growing "batteries" of tests—for both mentality and personality—that were rapidly overwhelming the public schools.

Outside New York City, public higher education was

limited to the traditional state universities. In New York there were two free colleges—Hunter for girls, and the College of the City of New York, for men—that could then match academic standards with the finest of the private universities. Being publicly supported, they had of course to pay lip service to the dogmas of educational democracy; but it was extremely difficult to enter them and even more difficult to survive until graduation. A survey of the freshman class at Hunter made during this week showed that 88 per cent were under 18—three of the girls were 14—and that relatively few planned teaching careers. Young women in college had their eyes on what had always been the men's professions: architecture, politics, advertising, chemistry, diplomacy, psychiatry, journalism.

The whole question of fitness for college was under discussion, which was not always clearly rational and dispassionate. There were those who felt—and there was much more feeling than thinking—that anyone who could pass the entrance examinations and had the money should go to college; there were others who felt that only those of outstanding ability should benefit by the limited facilities and should be aided, if necessary, by scholarships; and there were also those who felt that everyone, by reason of having finished high school, was irrevocably entitled to go on to college at the expense of society.

Dr. George E. Vincent of New York was one of the few who dared to use the word *élite*. In a speech that week to the Wesleyan University chapter of Phi Beta Kappa, he warned the colleges against barring all mediocre students, implying that the selectivity he urged should eliminate only what might be called the most mediocre. Vincent contended that the intellectual élite, for whom the university can do most, need to study among their inferiors in order to avoid being seduced into ivory-tower concepts and thinking and, since it is the function of the élite to lead, they can best learn how to lead the mediocrities only by living and working among them.

In practice, of course, this was what universities had always done without any conscious thought about it. The facilities were there, the atmosphere was available to all; whether one attended Yale or Princeton or Harvard—at $400 per year tuition—to "make contacts" or to enrich one's inner life was entirely one's own option. Harvard was—as it has remained—the only university in the United States that refused to admit students in business administration until they had a thorough grounding in the humanities. Its Graduate School of Business Administration ranked with its Law School; but early in March, Harvard announced an experiment to be made with its traditional rival, Yale University. Students in Yale's School of Law who had completed their first year satisfactorily would be allowed to take the next year in Harvard's School of Business Administration, after which they would return to the New Haven Law School to complete their legal studies. This, it was hoped, would give the fledgling lawyer some knowledge of the field in which he would presumably be applying his professional skill and knowledge.

One problem Harvard had not been able to solve for itself, and in this it had the companionship of Princeton and the universities of Virginia, Illinois, Toledo and North Dakota. Each of these disparate institutions needed a new president to replace a man taken by death or retirement; and each, regardless of its prestige or its relative wealth, was having the same difficulty. Like a girl dreading the advent of spinsterhood, a university cannot appear overeager—nor can it accept every suitor. As usual in both instances, the most desirable choices were those who were least interested. Even the kind of able executive who was most needed and whose private means would enable him to afford the luxury of heading a university was reluctant to assume the task in a period so unusually charged with uncertainty. The events—and more, the implications—of the first week of March only aggravated the problem for the would-be bride, and the would-not-be bridegroom as well.

CHAPTER **11**

"Funny Money"

PREACHMENTS and problems notwithstanding, life had to go on, limited only by the lack of the smaller change. The Reno divorce mill reported that fewer than a dozen suits had been filed, these by women who were already in town. The hotels and rooming houses in that uninhibited city were empty because there were no new arrivals. They didn't have the price of a train or bus ticket. In New York's Roseland Dance Hall the dime-a-dance girls accepted iou's from men who could show bankbooks. All others didn't dance. They sat on the sidelines, griped and waited. One newspaper called them wailing wallflowers. Prostitutes had either to trust their customers or withhold their services. Police reported a significant reduction in this kind of activity. However, several enterprising madams in the French Quarter of New Orleans informed their steady customers by penny post card that the barter system was in force, suggesting that food, jewelry and women's apparel would be welcome. One madam in Providence, Rhode Island, who had just refurnished her establishment, informed regular patrons that she needed books with fine bindings for her décor and these would be accepted as legal tender. The contents of the books did not matter. A high-priced Chicago house gave all the girls a two-week holiday—without pay.

The male denizens of the nation's skid rows, who lived and drank by cadging pennies and nickels, were the hardest hit. Police noted fewer stupefied drunks on sidewalks and in doorways. The missions reported a brisk trade in quiet, sober men, some of whom even asked for work. Fewer pickpockets were arrested during the week than ever before. Penny-vending machines remained filled with their goodies. Chicago, Boston, Philadelphia and New York reported that more of them were broken into for the coins alone than ever before. Gambling houses accepted checks and large bills for chips—and paid off in chips only. Their attendance fell sharply for a while. The floating crap game—big and little—so beloved of the half-world in the big cities, virtually vanished during the shortage. Two race tracks folded in Florida and at others in the nation only the big-money windows got a good play—and these had difficulties making change for the winners.

Long before Roosevelt closed the banks, responsible business leaders, bankers and state and local officials moved to stave off the total paralysis of all commerce threatened by the lack of cash. Merchants were issuing credit certificates. They were encouraged and helped by their communities, which issued scrip. Before the week was over, Nashville had printed $1,000,000 in scrip; Philadelphia, $8,000,000. Knoxville, Atlanta, Richmond, Chicago, Boston, Providence, New Haven, Detroit and many others were having the scrip printed and ready for distribution.

Governor Herbert Lehman of New York, who had declared a bank holiday on Saturday, March 4, appointed Al Smith chairman of the Emergency Certificate Corporation to distribute rainbow-hued bills in denominations from one to 50 dollars.

Daniel Ellis Woodhull, president of the American Bank

Note Company, was called to the New York Federal Reserve Bank and given an order for $250 million worth of scrip to be used for New York's Clearing House. Woodhull's Bronx plant increased its labor force to 2,500 and proceeded to function on a 24-hour basis with experience and tradition that had begun when the firm was founded in 1795. (In its collection of old plates were some bearing the name of Paul Revere.) While the Bronx plant and other plants were running off the scrip with the greatest possible speed and enthusiasm because it made for more jobs, the U.S. Mint in Philadelphia continued calmly with its normal coinage of $20 gold pieces and copper pennies. An official explained that the Mint was not concerned with policy. "We have no orders with regard to the present situation," he said. "This is just a factory."

The roar of the presses in the Bronx, the excitement of eager men and women working again, had a curious effect on its neighbors. Hundreds congregated around the building, gaping, chatting, peering. Police were assigned to keep the crowds orderly, and their task was a lighthearted one. Good-natured shouts of "Let's have some samples" and "Don't tell Hoover" filled the air. There was an atmosphere of relaxed tension and hope. A sergeant in charge of the police detail later told a reporter that "these people seemed to feel that tomorrow they'd all get jobs." The press of the nation picked up the infectious enthusiasm about the "fake money that was not fake at all." Some called it substitute money, some said it was legal counterfeiting, but almost everyone felt that if it worked it was worth the attempt.

Scrip, as a financial stopgap, had an excellent record. During the panic of 1907, U.S. banks issued $238 million in scrip. In New York alone it was used as legal currency for six months. Elsewhere, communities admitted that they would have been unable to get along without it. But to Secretary Woodin it was an appalling, confusing and dangerous expedient. He reasoned correctly that scrip presented a ponderous procedural problem. Scrip was difficult to transfer from one clearinghouse district to another. One district's scrip might be at a discount in another district. The Federal Reserve's job was to facilitate interstate as well as interdistrict exchange, and when everyone was issuing some sort of scrip, the result could be only a financial tower of Babel.

While many were willing to accept scrip simply because it was there, others were confused as to its function. One banking house bulletin described the working of scrip as follows:

> John Citizen marches into a bank where he has $1,000 on deposit. He presents his personal check for $500. The teller gives him $500 in scrip. This carries no promise of redemption in legal money, but does present proof that John Citizen's bank is good for the $500. He purchases some furniture and pays for it with the scrip. The retailer passes the scrip certificate to a wholesaler, who deposits it in another bank associated with the local clearinghouse. That bank can either issue the certificate again or return it to the first bank for collection. In this way the scrip has been circulated like lawful money although all concerned know that it is not a promise to pay. However, it does represent the tangible assets of the bank and will be honored when real money is available again.

Because there was no law against issuing scrip, and those who accepted it did so at their own risk, private institutions such as factories, newspapers, stores and hotels issued credits of their own. For a while a good deal of the retail commerce of this country was conducted on these terms.

The exclusive and expensive Huntington Hotel in Pasadena issued scrip negotiable only within its confines for such conveniences as tips, cigars, cigarettes, newspapers, cosmetics, shoeshines and haircuts. Among the distinguished clientele, most of them millionaires, who lined up in front of the cashier's window for their portions of scrip were former Secretary of State Frank Kellogg; former Speaker of the House Frederick H. Gillet; Boston banker Henry G. Lapham; Edward Bausch of Bausch & Lomb; William G. Stuber of Eastman Kodak; Charles Doran, former president of Sperry Gyroscope; Edward A. Cudahy Jr., the meat packer; Princess Erika of Denmark; Louis B. Kuppenheimer, the clothing manufacturer; Dr. Arthur D. Bevan of Chicago's Rush Medical College; and Sir Montagu and Lady Allan of Montreal.

Many newspapers followed the policy of the Louisville *Courier-Journal,* paying their employees in private scrip, which was eagerly accepted by local merchants. Salt Lake City printed colorful paper money that could be used within the city. *The Princetonian* printed promissory notes in 25-cent denominations for students, who redeemed them as soon as the banks reopened. Many banks and business houses gave out tokens made of wood and worth from 5 to 25 cents.

Days and weeks later, when the time came for the redemption of the scrip, Americans proved themselves fundamentally honest. Everybody was paid off. There were no counterfeits, and there are no records of litigation as a result of the makeshift money. Many followed the example of one man in St. Paul who papered his basement with 25-cent certificates as others had done with worthless stock certificates after the 1929 crash. Scrip also became a collector's item, a brief exciting piece of Americana.

No matter how casually the public accepted the scrip system, Secretary Woodin didn't like it. He confided to Moley Monday morning that he had been up most of the night brooding over the peril of scrip. He insisted it was not needed. "The Government can issue currency against the sound assets of banks," he said. "It won't frighten the people. It won't look like stage money. It will be real money that looks like money."

Moley agreed, especially after Woodin took the attitude: "There is nothing to lose. We're on the bottom. We're not going any lower."

As a result of this decision, $2 billion in currency, based on bank assets, was authorized. The Bureau of Engraving and Printing put on 375 new workers. There was no time to make new plates. Dies from the series of 1929 were used. Within a few days planes took off from Washington carrying sacks of good green cash to all parts of the money-hungry nation. The Roosevelt administration was demonstrating its "action now" philosophy.

CHAPTER 12

Find the Piece that Fits

. . . THE vast American stage over which the bank holiday held sway gave the people a splendid opportunity to dramatize, and they did not disappoint the editors and the newsreels.

One housewife in Milwaukee placed a sign on her door offering to sell her delicious preserves (famous for years among her friends and neighbors) for 25 cents a jar. She had no takers. A dentist in Toledo announced he would pull teeth for as little as 25 cents in coins. He had two patients in four days. A taxi driver in Atlanta (he owned his cab) offered rides for postage stamps. He had many customers. When his story was carried by The Associated Press, the post office did a brisk business. Old coin collections were found in attics and used. Mexican pesos and other foreign coins suddenly appeared and were accepted. It was possible to go into Canada and get dollars for large bills at a discount. Most communities on the Canadian border were using Canadian money. Two prize fighters in Buffalo agreed to do battle for two sacks of potatoes and a case of canned tomatoes, winner take all. The winner, it was reported, graciously gave the loser half the tomatoes. A New York State legislator arrived in Albany with a side of bacon and several dozen eggs. He had bacon and eggs for the rest of the week and enough left over to invite friends of both parties for a snack.

Probably the most dramatic demonstration of barter took place at the semifinals of the Golden Gloves tournament sponsored by the New York *Daily News* in Madison Square Garden. The announced price of seats was 50 cents or any article of equal value. The only proviso was that the 5-cent amusement tax be paid in cash. As the crowds filed in past the stiles, appraisers inspected the merchandise offered. When the night's box office was counted, it included false teeth, spark plugs, canned goods, foot powder, tools of all sorts, golf knickerbockers, cameras, steaks, frankfurters, salami, baseballs, golf balls, bats, sweaters, mattresses, fishing tackle, one large box of egg noodles, nightgowns and infinite sundries.

When all the items were neatly stacked and classified, it was discovered that the largest pile consisted of jigsaw puzzles. This astonished no one. The country was enveloped in its latest fad, jigsaw puzzles, and whatever else one didn't have, one did have a jigsaw puzzle to fill the long and lonely hours while waiting for a job.

More than 6,000,000 puzzles had been sold during the winter of 1932-33 alone to feed the fad that had become the nation's most successful tranquilizer. Priced from 10 cents, for those made of crude pasteboard, to $5 and more for the gilt-edged plywood creations, these jigsaw puzzles were indeed a happy parallel to an unhappy reality. Groping for the elusive little pieces, finding them and achieving the completion of a picture was evidently more rewarding than trying to put together the puzzling pieces of politics and economics which never seemed to fit into an understandable pattern.

The puzzles had another advantage. Once they were solved, they could be taken apart and passed on to the next enthusiast. In addition, many storekeepers accepted them as legal tender during the emergency. The demand was so great during those dark winter days that it created a minor economic boom. One manufacturer of the puzzles in St. Paul, who regularly employed 400, announced that because of an 87 per cent increase he was adding 425 workers. The Einson-Freeman Company of Long Island City, suppliers of the less expensive puzzles to newstands, turned out about 2,500,000 a week and was increasing its output to the point where it had to employ 350 more artists, die cutters, machine operators and printers. Related industries, such as steel, engraving and paper, also benefited. Dies, for example, had to be changed after every 100,000 cuttings.

The American and Interborough News Companies issued weekly puzzles containing suggestions for jigsaw races, jigsaw parties and jigsaw relays. Psychologists set time limits for performance. The standard for most puzzles was three to four hours for 12-year-old children and two and a half hours for adults. One puzzle contained the challenge that adults who took more than two hours should have their IQ's examined.

The hucksters whipped the fury of the fad with *The Jig of the Week, The Jig Surprise, Every Week Jigsaw Puzzle, The Jig Quigg* and *Jig Your Troubles Away.* People who had never been inside a museum or an art gallery pieced together the works of the great masters and viewed them for the first time. Rubens, Rembrandt, El Greco, were among the favorites. Da Vinci's "Last Supper" was a big seller. The masters who covered their paintings with huge skies or expansive seas were especially in demand because they made the puzzles more difficult to solve. There were series covering American Presidents, great battles, stars of stage, screen and radio, sports figures, scenes of famous places, and maps. You could have a jigsaw puzzle made from photographs of your family, your home, your pets or your factory. And people did just that. It was discovered to be an evocative advertising medium because the audience was held captive until the message was completed.

In La Grange, Georgia, a woman received a marriage proposal in the mail in the form of a jigsaw puzzle. She said yes in the same way. An old man in Dallas wrote his will on a piece of plywood two feet square, sawed it into odd-shaped little pieces and sent it to his attorney to be solved after his death. A vindictive man in Lexington, Kentucky, sent his creditor a check on a jigsaw puzzle. After it was put together, the bank honored it. Several private mental institutions reported that disturbed patients became quiet while concentrating on finding form and reason in the demented little pieces. In Los Angeles, a woman suing for divorce said her husband bought her large, elaborate puzzles and then held out pieces. She charged mental cruelty. A psychiatric patient in Cleveland claimed he had been helped by solving blank jigsaw puzzles because he was able to substitute his own inner conflicts for the white space he was putting together.

It was inevitable that a craze of this magnitude would become the basis for clubs. They flourished in every hamlet and metropolis in the country. When too many people stayed home, moving picture houses gave puzzles as premiums. At New York's Hotel Algonquin, headquarters of America's more affluent intellectuals, several teams competed in a grand jigsaw puzzle contest. They pitted writers against publishers; extroverts versus introverts; Harvards versus Yales and Bimetallists against Buy American. Stan MacGovern, cartoonist and untiring observer of the passing scene, speculated that if all the mental energy expended throughout the nation in one evening on the solution of these puzzles had been directed toward the solution of the world's woes, Utopia would have arrived instantly.

The craze seeped into every area of American endeavor. Editorialists commented upon it; clergymen preached about it and scholars gave learned dissertations on it. It became a celebrated case in jurisprudence and tax policy. The U.S. Government sought to collect $50,000 in excise taxes from the Viking Manufacturing Company of Boston on the ground that jigsaw puzzles were a sport and therefore should be taxed as sporting goods. The Federal District Court upheld the Government, and the Viking firm appealed. The U.S. Circuit Court of Appeals, sitting in Boston, ruled unanimously that the jigsaw puzzle is a game and not sporting equipment. The decision, written by Judge George H. Bingham, quoted a dictionary definition that said a jigsaw puzzle is "something which perplexes or embarrasses, a difficult problem or question, hence a toy, contrivance, question or problem designed for testing ingenuity." (On Nov. 8, 1937, the U.S. Supreme Court ruled that it was not a game.)

But the craze gave only momentary surcease from the ever-present sorrows and frustrations of the Depression. The country was being stifled by lack of employment, lack of money and lack of hope. All the games, puzzles, sporting events, movies, theatres and radio could not obliterate the sensation that the people were on a treadmill that was moving more and more slowly every day. They looked to the White House to find the answer. But there were many who were aware of events in the rest of the world—Hitler, Japan and the League of Nations were filling at least half of the front pages. . . .

CHAPTER 13

The Sixth Sense

IT IS written on tablets of jade that God gave man a sense of humor because he alone of all the animals needed it. The ancients who made this observation would have found perfect proof of it during this week. The radio, the stage, vaudeville and the movies were supplying laughter in abundance. Newspapers, magazines and books were encouraging laughter. The parlor joke, the locker-room joke and the office joke were flourishing. People were telling jokes, they were repeating jokes and they were listening to jokes.

What were people laughing at? They were laughing at themselves. They were laughing at others in the same predicament. They were drawing humor from the reliable old sources and finding the grim or hilarious jest in current affairs.

The hardiest perennial of the moment was the definition of the Depression: when prices are reduced to where you could afford them if you were still enjoying prosperity. Or the definition of a dictatorship: where everything that is not compulsory is forbidden. Or the boastful industrial statistic that the United States uses more soap than any other country, which was interpreted to indicate that this made it either

the cleanest or the dirtiest nation in the world. Or the last
of the speakeasy jokes: "I like this place. Good food, good
liquor and bad girls." Or the office joke in which the boss
complained, "If there were more self-starters, the boss
wouldn't have to be a crank." (*Explanation for the young:
A crank was used to start the engine of an automobile before the self-starter was invented.*)

The people were eager to laugh. They sought out the
comedians, the clowns and the humorists and paid them the
largest salaries in the amusement industry. They roared at
slapstick and the broad joke, the subtle joke and political
humor. Will Rogers, a cowboy entertainer who had made
good on Broadway twirling a lariat and uttering a patter of
rustic wisdom, had become a nationally syndicated columnist
with a loyal following. He was the only regular columnist
in *The New York Times*. Farmers and factory workers, financiers and office workers got their daily chuckle from his
comments on the news.

"The bankers," he said when the *holiday* began, "are asking us to bear with them. We will bear with them. If the
bankers are handing us the baloney we will know what the
country needs—new bankers."

Of Al Smith he said: "He told us exactly what his ideas
were on every important question. No wonder he can't get
elected. Imagine a man in public office that everybody knew
where he stood. A man like that is not a statesman. He's a
curiosity."

Of Roosevelt he said: "America hasn't been as happy in
three years as they are today. No money, no banks, no work,
no nothing. But they know they got a man there who is wise
to Congress and the so-called big men. The whole country is
with him. Even if what he does is wrong. If he burned down
the Capitol we would cheer and say, well, at least we got a
fire started, anyhow."

When Henry Ford was forced to take over some banks in

Detroit, Rogers wrote: "He's going to have a bank where you can leave your money and come back and find it before the banker does." He was following the fashion of the day by blaming everything that went wrong on the bankers and Wall Street.

In an interview he reported that John Nance Garner had told him the story of two brothers. "One ran away to sea and the other became Vice-President. Nothing was heard from either of them again."

He voiced a majority opinion when he discussed scrip. "Everybody is all excited over scrip," he wrote. "We're all for it. The way it sounds, all you need is a fountain pen and a prescription blank. That's what we've been looking for all these years. A substitute for money. Come on with your scrip. The psychology of the stuff not being actual money is going to make everybody buy something."

Magazines such as *Life* (not the Luce publication), *Judge*, *Ballyhoo* and the college publications went in for the pun, the reliable old wheeze and the *He-She* joke.

Example: SHE: Did you vote for the honor system in your school? HE: Yes, four times.

HE: Have you heard the story of the nasty military officer? SHE: No, what about him? HE: He was rotten to the corps.

There were others of this genre too painful to repeat.

Life had a cartoon showing a rich young man getting out of bed and saying to his valet: "I think I'll shave myself this morning, Reeves. I need the exercise." Another showed junglelike rough on the golf course with a voice coming out of the thicket, pleading: "Never mind the ball, caddy, find me." And there was the rich host saying to the violinist in his drawing room: "You are just tuning up? Why, I hired you a week ago." Readers were allowed to draw their own social-significance conclusions from a cartoon showing a boy drawing words on a back fence, and a dignified gentleman saying to him: "Son, would you like a job as a gossip columnist on my paper?"

The sick joke and the small-car gag seem to have had their beginning during the week. A cartoon showed a young woman at a greeting card counter saying: "I want something really nasty in a Valentine card for a boy who smokes a pipe in an Austin sedan." Another drawing showed the teacher telling her eighth-grade pupils that one of their classmates had gone sleigh-riding on a very cold day and died of pneumonia. There is a moment of silence and then a voice from the rear says: "Can I have the sled?"

The Depression, of course, supplied most of the material. A drawing showed a choir loft in a fine old church where one singer was saying to another: "Well, we're all working, thank the Lord." At a wedding ceremony the bridegroom says: "And with all my worldly goods I thee endow." His father whispers: "There goes his dollar watch." One librarian says to another: "Business must be terrible. They're all returning books on time." One wag observed that when a man looks at his watch these days, he's not interested in the time. He's wondering how much it will bring in a pawnshop. Or: "Lend me a nickel to phone my pawnbroker. I want to find out what time it is. He has my watch." A cartoon shows a man sitting in an employment office saying: "Can you use anybody with ten years' experience on the Ways and Means Committee?" Another cartoon shows the magnificent stage of the Metropolitan Opera House, crowded with famous singers, and one of them is saying to the plush audience: "The artists will now pass among you. Anything you can give will be greatly appreciated." One jokester reported that the dictionary makers were describing *wages* and *dividend* as obsolete words.

A story that made the rounds during the week had a touch of the bitterness felt by many able people who had been thrown out of work. It concerned the relief client who reported to a charity clinic for treatment of a sore throat. The busy doctor was annoyed and asked rather testily: "Tell me, if you weren't on relief would you have come to me with a minor complaint like this?" "No, Doctor," the relief client replied. "I would have sent for you."

It must be mentioned with genuine reluctance that the week saw the birth of a snappy-remark type of saying that endured for many years. Two samples will more than suffice: "She was only a vegetable man's daughter, but she certainly knew her onions." "She was only a mason's daughter, but she certainly knew how to get plastered." These grew into an entire literature that mercifully disappeared from public places when they went into ribaldry and smut.

Comedians in night clubs, speakeasies and vaudeville found their audiences responding to topical humor. One said he had invented an alarm clock without a bell for people who were not working. Another explained inflation in this way: "Instead of not having the money we haven't got now, we wouldn't have twice as much and it would be worth only one-third of what we haven't got now." The barter system was explained as "giving somebody a pig and a duck they don't want for an overcoat that doesn't fit for the benefit of the newsreel cameras." The impending repeal of Prohibition brought about the prediction that the new legal saloons would not have sawdust on the floor because it might get into the hair of the customers.

The Women's Christian Temperance Union warned that "some men *battle* their way to the top and others *bottle* their way to the bottom." A clergyman in the West told his congregation: "If you drink enough while driving, your car will last you a lifetime." When his sermon was over the sharper members of his flock had to explain it to those with a slower sense of humor. A church paper wrote of the job applicant who presented three letters of reference from three clergymen. The employer asked: "Don't you have any testimonials from people who see you during the week?"

Married life and the Depression combined to make the following cartoon funny at the time. It showed a woman, holding a bill, saying to her husband: "You and your suicide attempts. Look at this gas bill." *Ballyhoo,* an absurdist magazine, reported an interview with a woman on her golden wedding anniversary. Asked whether she had ever considered divorce, she replied: "Never, only murder." The romantic proposal joke was given a realistic turn in the following:

HE: If you don't marry me, I'll die.

SHE: I won't marry you.—And sure enough he died—65 years later.

Prudery and censorship came in for some cutting commentary. A censor was described as a man who had never recovered from the initial embarrassment of having been born naked in bed with a woman. *Ballyhoo* asked: "If a girl is innocent and sheltered, how does she know when to blush?"

Radio did not escape the barbs of the humorists. *Judge* pointed out that at one time a man had to write a good deal for the wastebasket before he became a success. "But now he can write for radio first." And then there was the snappy repartee:

HE: May all your children be radio announcers.

SHE: And may all yours have to listen to them.

A skeptic in *Ballyhoo* referred to it as the *bunk* holiday and struck out at invitations to purchase goods on time:

> Let us burn the festive candles
> At the giddy feet of Pan;
> I've arrangements with the piper
> For an easy-payment plan.

The hoarders were told: "Take care of your pennies, and the dollars will take care of your heirs."

Fred Allen, the radio comic, told the politically cautious:

"Progress always involves risks. You can't steal second base and keep one foot on first."

Jack Benny, who had not yet assumed the role of penny-pincher, was telling jokes on the radio in those days. One concerned the tramp who knocked on the door and told the well-padded housewife that he hadn't eaten in two days. "You should force yourself," she replied. El Brendel, a comedian with a Swedish accent, regaled fishermen with the observation that, since three-fourths of the earth was covered with water, it was clear that the Good Lord had intended that a man should spend three times as much time fishing as he does mowing the lawn. Al Jolson, who frequently interrupted his singing to tell a story, recounted to a vaudeville audience the story of a woman tourist posing for a photograph amid the fallen pillars of a Greek ruin. "Don't get the car into the picture," she pleaded, "my husband will think I ran into the place."

Eddie Leonard, the minstrel man, found favor with a rustic philosophy patter that seemed to be the thinking fashion in rural areas. He would begin by pointing out that there were 50,000 laws trying to enforce the Ten Commandments. Then:

> If a man refuses to go up in a balloon, he's called a coward. If he goes up, he's called a show-off.
> If a man makes a lot of money, he's money-mad.
> If he keeps it, he's a miser.
> If he spends it, he's a playboy.
> If he doesn't make it, he's a ne'er-do-well.
> If he doesn't try to get it, he lacks ambition.
> If he gets it after a lot of work, he's a fool who got nothing from life.

The audiences loved it and repeated these "epigrams" over and over again until the intellectuals winced. But they, too, had their favorites which, while not bright sayings, helped pass the time at gatherings. One was a game called "Whodunit," which had a strong vogue at the time and is still popular. It consisted of a mystery story told by the moderator. The others, by asking questions that could be answered only with yes or no, tried to solve it. One went like this: A man shoots and kills a woman in full view of witnesses. He confesses to premeditated murder and is tried and found guilty of murder in the first degree. When he comes up for sentencing the judge says: "I regret that I must set you free. You are guilty as charged, but under the circumstances and conditions I cannot pass sentence. And what is even more tragic is that if you commit another crime like this, I still shall be unable to send you to the electric chair." Why? The game was a wonderful exercise in logic and gave the players a chance to play district attorney.

Another popular parlor pastime was started by Wilfred J. Funk, poet, publisher and lexicographer, who selected the "ten most beautiful words" in the English language—beautiful, he maintained, in meaning as well as sound. They were: *dawn, hush, lullaby, murmuring, tranquil, mist, luminous, chimes, golden* and *melody.* It became incumbent upon everyone at once to amend the list. Long evenings were spent arguing about words that should or should not be included. The *Literary Digest,* a news and commentary weekly of the time, devoted columns to the debate and the new words. Among the literate, in general, there was an intense revival of all mental games. The jigsaw puzzle was a solo effort, but Guggenheim, charades, anagrams and Twenty Questions provided calisthenics for the mind and companionship after politics, sex and religion had been exhausted conversationally.

It was a week in which people were looking backward and forward at the same time. *Judge,* which seemed more aware of the temper of the times, summed up the week with: "We are asked to worry about the future generations going soft.

But that can't be so when we think of the bond issues they're going to have to pay off."

Across the Atlantic there was laughter, too. Democracies like Great Britain and France laughed openly mostly at the same frailties that evoked humor in America. In Russia, Germany and Italy there was laughter, bitter, surreptitious and dangerous. Two that made the rounds in the dictatorships were: "When nobody disagrees with you, you are either exceptionally brilliant or a dictator." The other told of a man who was overheard saying to his friend: "The madman will ruin the country. He ought to be put away." He was promptly arrested (in Germany, Russia or Italy) and charged with insulting the leader. "But I didn't mean (Hitler, Stalin or Mussolini)," he pleaded. "Whom else could you have meant?" the angry judge demanded. While this was a revival of the joke told about the Kaiser, Louis Napoleon and Cromwell, it played to a vast and secret audience wherever repression reigned.

The British had their parochial jokes such as the visitor's remark to the vicar's wife: "What lovely buttons you are sewing on your dress," and her reply: "Yes, I get all my buttons out of the collection plate." Or the little boy who was saying his prayers in a low voice. "I can't hear you," his mother said. "I wasn't talking to you," the boy replied.

The British stage and its music halls were filled with laughter. *Punch*, the comic weekly, purveyed humor in a more dignified manner. Typical items were: "International diplomacy appears to be the ability to bury the hatchet with one hand and grind the axe with the other." Or: "Umbrella frames are to be marked with the name of the country of origin. Patriots will of course be particular to 'Borrow British.'" The currency problem was the subject of a humorous essay and there was a piece on birds. The birth of the summit conference was suggested in a cartoon that showed Prime Minister MacDonald dressed as a Pilgrim Father carrying a wallet labeled *Debt Remission* "to complete Mayflower style." This was part of the campaign to have MacDonald visit President Roosevelt on the matter of war debts. Sir A. P. Herbert wrote a savage and caustic article on traffic deaths, demanding the imposition of speed limits. The editor of *Punch* replied that the only way to stop speeding was to dig potholes in the roads. A comment in the *News of the World* on American radio advertisements suggested that what most people in the United States were looking for in a cigarette is a less irritating commercial.

In the dictatorships the published humor avoided topical subjects, resorting mostly to the banal, slapstick type of joke. *Simplicissimus* and *Fliegende Blätter* made fun of the upper classes who couldn't pay their bills; they ran such naïve items as:

OPTOMETRIST TO WOMAN PATIENT: I must look deep into your eyes.

PATIENT: You can do that only if we become engaged.

Women were likened to geography:

From 18 to 27 women are like Africa—part virgin and part explored.

From 28 to 40 women are like the United States—aggressive and high-toned.

From 40 to 50 they are like Asia—fascinating and mysterious.

From 50 to 57 they are like Europe—decadent but still interesting in places.

From 57 on they are like Australia—everybody knows where it is but few people go there.

On the subject of women, one German paragrapher declared: "A woman doesn't make a fool out of a man. She merely directs the performance."

Preoccupation with the English across the Channel made up two items—one of admiration and one of scorn.

The first concerned the arrival in heaven of Sherlock Holmes who was promptly presented with a mystery. He was told that Adam and Eve had disappeared. It was explained that they had become tired of being gawked at by all new arrivals and had lost themselves in the vast multitude. Holmes looked intently at the assemblage, walked up to two angels and brought them forward. They were Adam and Eve.

When asked how he had accomplished this remarkable feat, he replied: "Elementary—they were the only two who had no navels."

The other was a revival of a World War I story when the British Royal House changed its name from Saxe-Coburg-Gotha to Windsor. The Germans recalled with delight that immediately thereafter, a Berlin Shakespeare company put on a play entitled: *The Merry Wives of Saxe-Coburg-Gotha.*

Political humor on the Continent was violently partisan. Almost every publication pictured Uncle Sam as a bloated capitalist whose main interest was money, with no feeling for the real problems of the world. Prohibition, gangsterism and the loose morals of American womanhood were favorite subjects in cartoon and joke. John Bull, leading Uncle Sam by the nose in international diplomacy, was almost standard fare.

An Italian humorist reported that there was an American bar in Rome with a clock that had only two numbers on it— 5 and 3. "The bar," he said, "opens at 5 P.M. and closes at 3 A.M., and the drinkers feel that these are the only two numbers that are important."

In print and on the stage it seemed that Americans were singled out more than any other national group to be the butt of jokes. Special scorn was heaped upon the "noisy tourist, his fat wife and their bad-mannered children." The jokes were not good-natured. They were bitter, resentful and openly hostile.

As in America and France, the general tenor of political

humor was self-critical. The weekly commentary in *Punch* on Parliament was irreverently witty and pungent, sparing no one on either side of the House. Social changes that were constantly manifesting themselves in tradition-bound England were noted in such music hall quips as: "Remember when a wife asked her husband what he'd like to eat instead of where?" or "The lad who received a wrist watch when he was graduated from college now has a son who wears one to kindergarten."

French humor columns supplied their readers with the rapid-laugh type of joke such as these:

VISITOR TO AN INSANE ASYLUM: Do you have to keep the women inmates separated from the men?

ATTENDANT: Of course, sir. The people here aren't as crazy as you think.

Fashion people were told that "considering what has been seen of the latest in bathing suits, the designers are working themselves out of a job."

The Austrians threw a homily to their womenfolk by observing that a man who thinks he's smarter than his wife has a smart wife. Then they concerned themselves with the national *Schlamperei* with the following:

TRAIN PASSENGER: Is smoking permitted?

CONDUCTOR: No.

PASSENGER: Then where did all these cigarette butts come from?

CONDUCTOR: From people who don't ask questions.

The week was no different from any week in humor. There were the topical jokes understood and felt only for the historic moment. And there were all the old jokes, dressed up in contemporary raiment, to be forgotten for a while and then revived or discovered by the eager young. There is no new joke. There are only new listeners.

CHAPTER 14

Bias and Bigots

As IN every moment in history, the accepted pattern of prejudice, hatred and bigotry prevailed. In commerce there was fear and suspicion between capital and labor. The Socialists hated the Communists and the Communists hated everybody. The rich feared the poor, and the poor envied the rich. The educated scorned the illiterate and the unlettered scoffed at the intellectuals. People who held one viewpoint disliked their neighbors who held a different viewpoint. No one was visibly disturbed by this situation, which was regarded as normal in a competitive and restless society.

Even more *normal* were the prejudices and hatreds that continued among the religions and the races. The Protestants resisted the inroads made by the Roman Catholics. The Jews distrusted the Christians and fought to maintain or increase their status. The Negro in the North and the South was kept in his place by the Caucasian. The Mexican laborer in America's Southwest envied the position of the Negro. All these conflicts were beneath the surface. Except in Germany, there were no overt acts of violence.

Hate was divided into two parts. There was the traditional

passive or unspectacular kind, and there was the professional kind in which certain interests could gain by heaping abuse and invective on other interests. There were also those who fought hatred and prejudice, and they were scoring a signal advance in the reopening of the famous Scottsboro Case.

The case, which had aroused international interest and indignation, had its beginning on a quiet afternoon on March 25, 1931. A freight train, going through the northeastern corner of Alabama, carried a strange human cargo. Aboard were two girls, Ruby Bates and Victoria Price, mill workers, who were bound for their homes in Huntsville. They were wearing overalls, an unusual garb for ordinary women of that time. With them, on an open gondola car two-thirds full of gravel, were seven white boys. When they reached Stevenson, about 20 or 30 Negro boys and men got aboard and scattered themselves on different cars of the half-mile-long train.

It was inevitable that before long a quarrel developed between the Negroes and the whites. No one could tell who or what started it, but the Negroes got the better of the fight and the whites either were thrown off the train or got off voluntarily. Impelled by rage, wounded pride or possibly chivalry, the white boys told police about the affair, and when the train got to Paint Rock, a sheriff's posse arrested nine young Negroes. Word had spread that the two girls had been raped and a mob soon gathered around the jail. Sheriff M. L. White and a group of picked citizens spirited the nine boys to another town. It was never clearly determined how these particular nine were chosen from the larger group of Negroes.

They were indicted on March 31 and six days later Charlie Weems, 21, of Atlanta, and Clarence Norris, 19, of Chattanooga, were brought to trial in Scottsboro with all the panoply of a military guard and police keeping the crowds orderly. Then Heywood Patterson, 17, of Chattanooga, was brought to trial. After that, Eugene Williams, 15, and Andy

Wright, 17, both of Chattanooga; Ozie Powell, 16, of Atlanta; Olen Montgomery, 17, of Monroe, Georgia, and Willie Robertson, 17, of Columbia, Georgia, were placed on trial. All were found guilty, and on April 9 Judge A. E. Hawkins sentenced them to death. It was the first time in the history of Alabama that a judge had given the death penalty to eight men at once for a single offense. The ninth boy, Roy Wright, 14, was not convicted. There were no Negro citizens on the grand jury that indicted the boys or on the petit jury that found them guilty. There were three trials, each one taking only one day.

The press of the nation displayed the story in large headlines. It was pointed out that the defendants had in effect been railroaded. Questions were raised as to the character and vocation of the Misses Bates and Price, and it was noted that the court had refused to admit into evidence any reference as to their background or previous behavior.

While the National Association for the Advancement of Colored People sought to help the nine doomed, illiterate and destitute members of their race, the Communists leaped into the breach and used the Scottsboro Boys as a perfect springboard for their propaganda. The International Labor Defense, known for its strong Communist leanings, organized rallies in Harlem, the Bronx, Brooklyn, Chicago, and Philadelphia. There were Communist riots over the case in Dresden, Berlin, and Cologne, in Paris and Rome.

There were many sincere sympathizers. Many European notables, including church leaders and Albert Einstein, sent protests to Governor B. M. Miller of Alabama. Legal authorities pointed out that the young men had not been given the proper defense by their court-appointed attorneys.

With the help of the NAACP, the case was appealed to the Alabama Supreme Court, which on March 25, 1932, affirmed the death sentences of all except Eugene Williams. The exception was made on the ground that Williams was a juvenile.

The case was brought before the United States Supreme Court and, on the day when the Justices agreed to consider it, extra police had to be ordered to keep Communist rioters in line. It was tragic that the true issue was constantly being obscured by the Communists. Many prominent sympathizers who had agreed to address Scottsboro rallies found themselves giving aid and comfort to the entire Communist philosophy, which was invoked at every meeting.

In November, 1932, the Supreme Court ordered another trial. Therefore, on Monday March 6, 1933, in the little brick courthouse at Scottsboro, the new trial began. The attention of the world was centered on the courtroom. There was to be more bitterness and hate, but the rest of the nation was satisfied that law and justice were at least getting a better chance to function in Alabama.

The Scottsboro Boys' trial threw into eclipse the South that always insisted: "We love our Nigras and our Nigras love us"; it portrayed in sharp relief the South that was suspicious of foreigners, radicals, Catholics and Jewish Yankees; the South in which the Jewish merchants of such cities as Athens, Georgia, and Birmingham, Alabama, had pusillanimously joined the Ku Klux Klan and used their shop windows to advertise its meetings so that they might be considered *white Jews;* the South in which the "loved Nigra" was the stock figure out of an Uncle Tom show, loved because he knew better than to try to shed his inferiority or to make himself other than a laughingstock.

The "separate but equal" doctrine was unquestioned even by the majority of Negroes; they accepted the separateness but were still waiting for the equality. Their schools were inferior in quantity, physical plant and staff; their living quarters were slums, whether urban or rural, except for those of the small minority who had by unimaginable effort (and sometimes with the help of anonymous white benefactors) scraped out a precarious toe hold on a somewhat higher economic level. Even the unusual Negro—and there were some even in the South—who occupied a responsible position on a white man's plantation, owned a business, practiced medicine or law, or held a pulpit was never addressed as *Mister* by a white; the Negro and his wife alike were always greeted by their first names, and this applied as high as the occasional court in which a Negro lawyer found himself trying a case before a white judge, who almost invariably regarded him as a sport of nature.

Though the mass of Southern Negroes had only the rudiments of schooling and worked as laborers in city or country, they held education in the same esteem as did the European immigrants of a half-century earlier, and they strove to direct their children toward it in spite of the economic hardship entailed in sacrificing the income that the young might have brought into the family budget. At the same time they viewed their aspirations with a certain humor; those Negroes who strove too hard for a chimeric status they could never really achieve were known among their own people as "strainers." Within their own community there were certainly social stratifications; but what made a Negro middle-class would have been considered proletarian among his white neighbors.

In no case, whatever his background or achievement, could he use the same public sanitary facilities as the white man; he had his own sections in public transportation and in those theaters that admitted him; his contacts with the master race were limited to those instances in which the latter could not avoid them—employment and business. The Negro could buy in a white man's shop or serve at a white man's table, but he had to exercise the utmost circumspection. A glance or a word that might have been construed as insolent meant a beating for which there was no legal redress; and underlying the entire racial relation was the ill-repressed unconscious sexual jealousy and fear that erupted intermittently in charges of rape of white women by Negroes, followed almost inevitably by the savagery of lynching. While the dwindling white upper class had no toleration for Negro-baiting, the middle- and lower-middle-class whites accepted it, when they did not take part, as a matter of course. The most charitable prevalent view was that of the Negro as a perpetual child; and children, after all, were made to be teased and bullied.

Not only the Negro's human dignity was ignored; his basic economic rights fared no better. Negro sharecroppers were regularly lured to jobs by cash advances to cover the expense of moving with their families and to provide for Christmas gifts; but when, at the end of the year, the Negro came for the reckoning of what was due for his labor after compensation to his employer for cash advances and food and other commodities supplied on credit, he was regularly cheated. Those who cheated him argued in their own defense that he liked to be cheated, and besides, he was inherently dishonest and had undoubtedly cheated them all year long in one way and another. If, in resentment at this treatment or in response to sweeter bait, he changed jobs at the end of his contract year, it was because he was of bad character, shiftless, improvident; it was never even hinted that the bad habits imputed to him were the inevitable result of the treatment regularly meted out to him by the ruling group, which, consciously or otherwise, did all it could to discourage the Negro from any attempt at thrift, initiative, or self-betterment. The South was still as fundamentalist as it had been ten years earlier, at the time of the great Scopes trial, and found it easy to believe that the Negro's universal subhumanity had been divinely ordained and could not—and therefore should not—be altered.

The Negro in the North was kept in his place quietly. He was not subject to obvious discrimination. He was not called *nigger* or *nigra*. He was called *Negro* or *colored*. He could ride in any public conveyance and select any seat he wanted. He could take a civil-service examination. He could bring a lawsuit against a white man and get fair treatment. He could use the same rest rooms as whites. He went to the same schools as whites. He could sit in any seat he wanted at a ball park. He could make a speech in any properly designated place. He did not have to get off the sidewalk to let a white man pass. If he showed the proper deference, he could shop in any store.

On the surface the Negro in the North was enjoying the same rights and privileges as the white citizen. In many states his rights were protected by law. New York had passed a civil-rights law as far back as 1909.

Beneath the surface, the Negro was merely tolerated as a second-class citizen. He was the last one hired on a job and the first one fired. He had to be better than good to get a civil-service job even after he had passed the test for it. He could picket, but many unions wouldn't let him join. He could not get a seat in the orchestra of any theater or motion-picture house. He was refused service in any restaurant except one catering to Negroes. He lived in a ghetto, and in many cities was not permitted to leave it after certain hours. He had freedom of religion, but could join only Negro churches. He could shop in any store, but was generally shunted to the bargain basement. Many of the better shops just "didn't have what he wanted," even if he saw it on the counter.

If the Negro in the North resented these restrictions, he did not show it openly. Perhaps it was because he was becoming aware of the power he was finding in organization, unity and education. More northern Negroes were attending sec-

ondary schools and colleges. Negro political clubs were showing white leaders that under the proper conditions they
could vote in a bloc. In cities such as New York and Chicago
they were beginning to wield a balance of power in local elections. In Negro ghettos slogans began to appear saying, BUY
FROM YOUR LOCAL NEGRO MERCHANT or, JOIN THE CLUB.
The Scottsboro case was a heartening experience because it
showed the Negroes that there were millions of whites who
felt strongly that justice should show no color line. Remarkably enough, the Negroes were able to resist the frantic woo-
ing of the Communists. They were told by their leaders that
if the Negro was to win equality in the United States, it
would have to be under the American system.

The master-race theory, as propagated by Hitler, was quietly making itself felt in the United States. While the Ku
Klux Klan was generally discredited, small crackpot organizations, such as the Silver Shirts under the leadership of William Dudley Pelley, were beginning their inspired hate attacks against Negroes, Catholics and Jews. They were openly
pro-Hitler and they filled the mails with their attacks against
all but "100 per cent white Protestant Americans." They
found ready converts among a small group that was to be referred to years later as the "lunatic fringe."

The insidious propaganda machine of Dr. Josef Goebbels,
which had done so much harm to the Jews in Germany, was
also beginning to make gains in the United States. In a tiny
room in New York's Yorkville section, Joseph Schuster, a
former beer-hall entertainer, and a group of German-Amer-
icans formed the *Freunde des Neuen Deutschlands* on the
basis of blueprints supplied by the office of Dr. Goebbels.
The *Friends* eventually became the German-American
Bund, which had a complete master plan for taking over the
United States when *Der Tag* should arrive. Similar organizations were being established in South Africa and Great Brit-

ain, despite the relatively recent fiasco of Sir Oswald Mosley's British Union of Fascists, shreds of which now preached Nazi-ism.

But in England generally, as in Western Europe, the Jew enjoyed full civil rights and a fairly large measure of accept-ance, tempered in more conservative circles and blunted in the lowest classes. Though Jews served with honor in the government and the armed forces and held hereditary peer-ages, socially they were often still on probation. In contrast, France, despite the lingering scars of *l'affaire Dreyfus*, really accepted the Jew without question or hesitation; and the same thing was true of the Low Countries. In Italy, the "Jew-ish question" had not yet been suggested by Hitler to Mus-solini, who numbered many Jews among his higher lieu-tenants. What was ironic was the ardent support some Jews in Germany continued to give to Hitler, whether in secret or with flagrant bids to be made "honorary Aryans." It was a self-deluding snobbery that made it easy for these Jews to believe that the Nazi hate campaign was directed solely against the Jews of Russia and the rest of eastern Europe, whom they themselves despised and feared, and that Hit-ler's mouthings against the Jew in Germany were only a tem-porary expedient.

A large number of American Jews preferred to believe that, if official anti-Semitism were not a policy of expedience, it was temporary if only because the conscience of Germany and the world would destroy it. The Jew in America had, for the most part, learned to live with a quiet casual kind of bias that kept him out of certain companies and industries, barred him from many clubs, hotels and resorts and, in most areas outside New York, made it almost impossible for him to form partnerships or close social contacts with Christians. Catholics and Jews alike were barred from owning or even renting property in some of the country's most exclusive areas; the presence of Al Smith in the inaugural parade re-

called to many the apocryphal story of the one-word cable
that he was supposed to have dispatched to the Pope after
his rousing defeat, solely because of his religion, in the 1928
Presidential election. But none of these manifestations of
religious bigotry in the United States was based on more
than "gentlemen's agreements" that were already showing
signs of wear, and the injured parties did not fight too hard
against them. They had, in this week, far more immediate
problems.

The inauguration of Roosevelt generated so much and so
wide a hope and expectancy that people for the moment sub-
merged their prejudices in a sea of optimism. Jobs and
money were preoccupations that kept hate far below the surface, though there was an awareness of the Scottsboro trial
and of the Nazis' triumph. In addition, there were vague stir-
rings of a new national hatred in the United States.

For years the American market had been glutted by cheap
goods from Japan. Workers felt that they were being cheated
out of jobs, as their employers felt that they were being un-
justly deprived of profits, because American industry could
not compete with the low wages being paid in Japan. *Buying
American* was gaining in popularity and there was the beginning of the beloved oversimplification; America was the
good guy and Japan was the bad guy. As in every moment in
history, it was gratifying to know there was always something or someone to hate.

CHAPTER **15**

Bankruptcy of Heart and Head

THE world, which had been pointed toward nobler achievements at the end of the war that had been fought to make it safe for democracy, was behaving in this first week of March, 1933, in its usual schizoid pattern, pressing hysterically toward extremes of right and left, flouting the urgencies for peace and creating the foundation of greater tragedies to come. "The paradox of the world of today," according to *The Economist* of London, was "a combination of technical virtuosity with a bankruptcy of heart and head in everything that appertains to human relations."

While the postwar whimpering of the have-not nations was surging into a roar, the three great democracies were, on the whole, too busy with their own affairs to give proper heed to the approaching peril or to those brave solitaries within their boundaries who pointed to Germany and Italy as tomorrow's bully-boys. In America, twelve years of Republican isolationism that spanned a fabulous, if irresponsible, prosperity ending in an economic debacle had turned the nation's interests even further inward. France, preoccupied with constant internal financial and political crises, momentarily relaxed her wary watch over discontented neighbors. Great Britain, heartened by an increase in trade and striving to maintain her empire, also missed in the larger sense the portent of events in Europe and Asia.

Even Soviet Russia seemed to be concentrating mainly on affairs at home. Having signed nonagression treaties with France and Italy and resumed diplomatic relations with Spain, Stalin was making overtures for similar ties with the United States in continuing moves calculated to give the Soviet the security it needed to enlarge its own economy with a second five-year plan and to combat the "deviationists, wreckers and saboteurs" typified by the 66 functionaries of the Agriculture Ministry and the collective farms on trial and about to be convicted of counterrevolution (35, including Commissar F. Konar, were executed). Aside from the diplomatic maneuvers, the only international *démarche* from Russia was the Comintern's plea to Socialists everywhere to join Communists in a united or popular front and its pledge never again to call them "social-democratic lackeys." The Parliamentary Labour Party in Britain replied that, even if it came from the left, dictatorship was still dictatorship; but the Independent Labour Party eloped with the British Communist Party.

Only the League of Nations, the greatest idle gesture ever made for international harmony, seemed actively aware of dangers and responsibilities. At the League-supported Disarmament Conference in Geneva someone quoted these lines from Tennyson's *Locksley Hall:*

> *Heard the heavens filled with shouting, and there rained a ghastly dew*
> *From the nations' airy navies grappling in the central blue*

The quotation entered into the discussion of means of abolishing the prime terror of the next war—aerial bombing. All the delegates agreed in sanctimonious rhetoric that they were unalterably opposed to this kind of death for "helpless men, women and children." However, the proposal dealt also with some form of sovereignty for the League because it entailed persuading the nations of the world to submit their civil as well as military aviation to international control. It was suggested that a League of Nations Air Force administer an international law of the air. France endorsed the idea and was joined by Britain. Germany refrained on the ground that the Treaty of Versailles had forbidden her to have an air force, but she wanted her civil aviation to remain untouched. So did the great land empires, Canada and the United States. Hugh S. Gibson, the American Ambassador to Belgium and delegate to the conference, declared:

"So far as our part of the world is concerned, we would not accept any international control of aviation. Our commercial aviation is more extensive than any other nation [sic], having more planes than all Europe combined, meeting unparalleled geographic and weather conditions. Ours is the only civil aviation in the world without government subsidies [postal contracts were delicately ignored]. Our machines have been designed not for military but civil use, a recent examination of them showing only 74 fit for military service."

Salvador de Madariaga, the scholarly Spanish delegate, asked Gibson: "Does your objection mean that your happy country accepts, nevertheless, the abolition of military aviation?" The happy country's uncomfortable representative replied with an amendment proclaiming that "international control of aviation is not feasible, desirable or necessary for the United States." It was not voted on and, by the March 1 deadline for debate, the impasse had not been resolved.

But by then the League itself was facing a far greater problem. Imperial Japan, the youngest of the great powers, was to become an outcast among the nations by a vote of 42 to 1. In her headlong expansion Japan had marched into Man-

churia in September, 1931. The League's Committee of
Nineteen, after protracted study, had certified China's innocence. On the day of the voting, the League Assembly's president, Paul Hymans of Belgium, outlined the question to be
decided. The Committee's recommendations included the
withdrawal of Japanese troops from all seized areas and the
League's refusal to recognize Japan's new puppet state, Manchukuo. There was a momentary hush after verdict and sentence had been pronounced. China's chief delegate, Dr. W.
W. Yeh, nodded approval. The diplomats, at their polished
pine desks, looked to Japan's delegation head, Yosuke Matsuoka. "Manchukuo belongs to us by right!" he shouted in
vibrant fury. "Read your history. We recovered it from Russia. We made it what it is today." He sat down amid an excited murmur.

It was reasonably clear what the Assembly would do, but
all doubt was removed when the foreign minister of Lithu-
ania rose to parade a ghost. Dr. Zaunius, in very certain
terms, reminded the delegates that, after Vilna was seized
from his country by Poland in 1920, the League had let the
problem drop. It did not matter much, he insisted, that the
League had tried bravely at first to prevent this injustice.
Poland still held Vilna. And, Dr. Zaunius asked, will Japanese troops still hold Manchukuo in 1945? As the alphabetical
voting began, "Oui" was heard from delegation after delegation until the finite "Non" of Japan. Thirteen countries
either abstained or were absent. Hymans ruled that the committee's recommendations had been adopted unanimously,
since the votes of the parties to the dispute did not count. In
a brief summary of the day, Hymans described Japan as "a
land that seems desirous of retiring into isolation and carrying on its policy without taking into account the opinion of
other nations."

Matsuoka was about to reply; the delegates had a moment
to look beyond the railing to the seats of the nonmember ob-

servers, including Gibson and Boris Stein, Soviet Minister to Finland. It was universally regretted that America and Russia could not participate in the debate or the decision. Matsuoka's reply was diplomatic but firm. He implied his country's withdrawal from the League: "The Japanese Government is obliged to feel that it has now reached the limit of its endeavors to co-operate with the League regarding the Chino-Japanese difference." Then he stepped down and walked out, beckoning a few reluctant retainers to follow him. They were those who had made it plain to him that they opposed any sort of histrionics.

Hymans still had several chores. The first was to thwart an attempt by Dr. V. K. Wellington Koo, a Chinese former premier, to make a gloating speech. The next was to stress the need for support from the two great nonmember nations, the United States and the Soviet Union. The Assembly enlarged its committee to 21 by appointing Canada and The Netherlands, and it instructed the group to invite America and Russia. Hymans voiced the universal belief that unless these two great powers co-operated with the League in word and act, Manchuria was certain to become another Vilna.

A cable went off to Washington with the question; Russian Foreign Minister Maxim Litvinov was in Geneva and was broached directly. He said he must consult his government and implied that it would make no decision before the American inauguration. Litvinov noted that Tokyo had invited his country to resume negotiations for a nonaggression pact after Japan herself had broken off the talks only three weeks earlier.

The American reply was a dual effort by outgoing Secretary of State Henry L. Stimson and his successor, Cordell Hull. It expressed "substantial accord" with the League's report on the Manchurian affair, "general accord" with the League's action and "general indorsement of the principles thus recommended." These fine phrases fooled none of the diplomats: America had omitted any assurance that she would act with the League. Just before Hoover left office, Stimson issued a statement saying that the Administration would co-operate with the Committee of 21, which, he stressed, was an advisory group. The best picture of the American attitude came from Matsuoka a few days later in Paris: "The League is now making an attempt to elevate itself to the status of a super-state," he told American reporters. "Is the world at this stage of progress prepared to accept it? Are the Americans prepared to accept it? Why, you are not prepared even to join it."

Historians may wonder whether the actors were aware of the mockery of the drama. For, while the League was acting in assembly and virtually every statesman was composing righteous denunciations, Japanese troops were rushing relentlessly toward the conquest of the Chinese province of Jehol. While journalistic pundits were pondering the possibility of a world arms embargo, violent opposition flared simultaneously from munitions makers, shipping interests and professional pacifists. Meanwhile Sir John Simon, Britain's Foreign Secretary, astonished the House of Commons by announcing that a British arms embargo against China and Japan was in mild effect: it was only temporary, pending international consultation, and it did not embrace existing contracts and commitments. Even had it been what it purported to be, critics noted the overwhelming superiority of Japan's arms factories over China's and recalled Sir John's long record of favoring the Japanese.

Having safely occupied Manchuria, Japan had begun the absorption of Jehol into its imperial bosom. In a series of swift and dramatic military moves begun on January 1, 1933, troops were thrusting toward an effective conclusion by March 4. Jehol was described by the conquerors as a renegade province of Manchukuo. One-third the size of Japan, with a climate like New England's and a population of more

than 6 million, Jehol was rich in farm land, forests and tremendous opium crops. During the first three weeks the Japanese troops had battled subzero weather as well as the badly
equipped regiments of Governor Tang Yu-Lin, and during
the first week of March they hurtled toward their objective
in a kind of relay race that amazed even their own general
staff. Brigades were picking off cities one at a time in the
headlong push toward the capital. As soon as a battle-worn
brigade had captured a city, it withdrew and was replaced
by another, fresh and spirited. While the invaders' dash over
the snow-swept mountains was of unquestioned military
credit, due consideration must be given to the treachery and
bungling of the Chinese war lords who called themselves
generals.

As the Japanese advanced, the Chinese generals deserted
their troops and fled, or if time did not permit, broke out the
flags of Japan and Manchukuo and cheered the conquerors.
The comic-opera aspect of some of them was exemplified by
Tang himself. A week before Jehol fell, according to *Time*
Magazine's correspondent, he "put on a one-man Chinese
rodeo in his *yamen* at Changteh, delighted correspondents
with his Chinese cowboy feats. Spurring full speed on a
shaggy Mongolian pony, War Lord Tang flourished his repeating rifle, drew bead on a stationary target, riddled the
bull's eye with lead. Two-Gun Tang alighted from his pony,
served tea and faced questions. 'I will resist the Japanese
with all the troops and resources at my command,' said he.
Six days later he was found in an opium stupor. 'I don't even
know where my troops are,' he admitted." That night he
vanished from his throne room and from history with 242
truckloads of treasure, to the distress of the chief of his government, Chiang Kai-shek. The former war lord, now running the nationalist state in Nanking, was busy keeping his
own post and left the defense of Jehol mainly to Marshal
Chang Hsiao-liang, the Manchurian war lord who ruled

North China from Peiping. Chang resigned a few days after Jehol fell. Though he shared Tang's acute sense of self-preservation, he was considerate enough to leave a forwarding address, in Italy. Meanwhile a shipment of 102 Fords consigned to him, at first halted by the Japanese, was again on its way, Tokyo having found it was not formally at war with Chang despite labor unions' protests.

The Orient was by no means the League's sole problem. A European mutual-security pact was voted, 14 to 5, with 30 abstentions. It was vigorously opposed by Austria, Hungary, Germany, Italy and The Netherlands. The Dutch explained their uncomfortable position by citing Britain's lagging on the pact and her refusal to regard herself as a part of Europe —"Words," Anthony Eden had just said, "will not dry up the Channel." *The Economist* reminded him tartly that "words will not turn the air over England into a vacuum." But to many experts in Geneva in that week, a European war, despite Italian denunciation of the "threatening" new Little Entente of Czechoslovakia, Yugoslavia and Romania, was far less likely than a Japanese-American conflict arising out of commercial rivalry in the Orient. Japan, the experts believed, would be the loser, if only because she had only 800 war planes against America's 1,800 and only 234 warships against America's 523. (The disinterested appraisal of American military aviation was in some conflict with Ambassador Gibson's statement.) It was generally felt that Britain would add her 387 naval vessels to America's in any war, despite the extremely vocal adherence of the youth of both countries to the so-called Oxford Oath—a pledge never to fight for one's country under any conditions.

Latin-Americans were untroubled by such problems: they were fighting with gusto while the League was debating their rivalries as well as greater ones. A League Committee of Three, having investigated the patrol skirmishes, gunboat bombardments and aerial sorties along the upper Amazon

near the malarial jungle town of Leticia, decided that the
League would have to intervene between the combatants,
Peru and Colombia. Peru had ceded the area to Colombia
in 1922, but in the past six months it had been overrun by
Peruvian irregulars. The Committee recommended that
both nations evacuate the region and that the League assume
its protection; Peru's terse reply served for Colombia as
well. The Colossus of the North agreed that it would send a
delegate to serve on a consultative committee that would observe the continuing conflict.

Paraguay and Bolivia were engaged in a more whole-
hearted war, raging for the past eight months for possession
of the Gran Chaco, a fertile agricultural area claimed by both
countries. The major sufferers in this conflict were 5,000
peaceful Mennonites who lived in the Chaco. This common-
law scuffle, which Argentina, Brazil and Chile had tried to
mediate, only to be accused of threatening to establish peace
by force, was about to be made an honest woman of by a Par-
aguayan declaration of war sought by President Ayala. The
League was studying the Argentine-Brazilian-Chilean proposal while at the same time its attention was brought back
to Europe by the Free City of Danzig.

This war-born city-state had brought charges against Pol-
and because the Poles had made an unauthorized landing
on Danzig's Westerplatte peninsula. The purpose of the
landing was to thwart Germany's planned seizure of Polish
arms stored there; but the latter project stirred no official
protest from the Danzigers. It was almost a relief for the
League to observe the preparations for the World Feminist
Congress, about to renew its war of words for equal rights
for women in Marseilles, second only to Buenos Aires as a
world brothel center.

International relations outside the League were more har-
monious than the grandiose efforts undertaken under its
aegis. The Little Entente had been hammered out peace-

fully by the participants and enjoyed the blessing of the French. Whatever her internal troubles—and they were numerous—France was further reassured when Roosevelt, on the eve of his inauguration, summoned her poet-ambassador, Paul Claudel, and his British colleague, Sir Ronald Lindsay, to hear enunciated a relaxed policy toward both countries' war debts to the United States. Two days later both envoys sat down with Secretary Hull to evolve a plan for world economic recovery that their three countries would lead.

France was trying to pick up the pieces after the budget crisis that had ushered in the month, Edouard Daladier had somehow managed to survive as premier despite his program for salary reductions for the vast army of French civil servants and income-tax rises for everyone; he had ridden roughshod over counterproposals for a national 4 per cent sales tax. Former Premier André Tardieu insisted that the crisis resulted solely from government by a leftist coalition—the Radical Socialists and Socialists—and cited Britain and Germany as evidence that Socialist rule always stagnates industry and aggravates unemployment. His concern was the restoration of Parliament's independence by breaking its thralldom to "the twin oligarchies of electors and spenders," and the means he envisaged was the creation of a unicameral legislature that could be dissolved by the executive when the question was one of confidence in individuals; basic issues would be submitted to referendum.

But more Frenchmen were interested in the reactions of the distinguished Italian anti-Fascist exiled in Paris, Count Carlo Sforza, to the historic changes in the United States. While Sforza—speaking for much of the European intellectual stratum—believed that the American hero-cult of the businessman had been mortally wounded, he viewed Roosevelt's election as a rejection of Hoover and his policies rather than an endorsement of new men and ideas. Hoover's greatest service to his country, in Sforza's view, was the destruction of the myth of the expert; and Roosevelt, the Italian said, had many qualities Hoover lacked: understanding and love of Jeffersonian ideals, human sympathy and—perhaps to excess—political sagacity. Sforza wondered openly whether Roosevelt would have the courage to tell his country frankly that isolationism was an anachronism; the Italian had noted the new President's tendency to talk largely on such sore issues as Prohibition and the war debts without really letting anyone know where he stood. In Italy itself, as in Germany, Roosevelt was hopefully hailed as a "strong man" who must become a dictator.

More immediate matters concerned other countries. On March 1 the Dail Eireann of the Irish Free State voted to abolish the oath of allegiance to the King of England, and the Irish Government notified London that it was taking over the moneys deposited with it in 1932 for a sinking fund. The British army was pointed toward the goal of motorization—a goal set by a little-known French colonel called Charles de Gaulle as the essential in any future war, though he did not share the British view that such a war—if indeed all wars were not soon abolished—would be short, confined and economical of life and money. The French colonel, whose first book was already a text for the revitalized Reichswehr, was continuing to evolve his revolutionary military ideas with constant relation to the changing international scene and to present them in an austerely elegant prose that was the envy of professional writers. But to the British public in this week the most important news was the approaching trial of "the prisoner in the Tower."

Lieutenant Norman Baillie-Stewart was a young career officer of impeccable background whose arrest under the Official Secrets Act caused bitter divergences of opinion. The formal charges specified that he had stolen army secrets and sold them to German agents for the wretched price of £90. Like the typical novel of espionage, this real spy story had a mysterious woman—Baillie-Stewart's mistress, known only as Marie-Louise. Under Britain's admirable libel laws, the papers could print only the bare facts of his arrest and the charges, as well as his denial of guilt; and speculation as to what he might have done and how he might have done it sparked the conversation in every Corner House and licensed premises.

In other parts of Europe, politics held the public interest because it was so closely tied in with day-to-day life. Greece voted on March 5, as did Germany, with substantially the same outcome. Premier Eleutherios Venizelos' coalition of Liberals, Progressives, Labor and Conservatives was defeated by the Populist opposition under Panayoti Tsaldaris and John Metaxas, and Venizelos resigned, to return to Crete. General Nicholas Plastiras, a tough professional soldier from Macedonia, seized power at once to balk the Royalist elements under Tsaldaris in the Populist group, though, like all the other dictators west of Russia, he told the country and the world that his "action was taken to annihilate Communism and secure public order." The best means he knew toward this end was a military dictatorship, but it had barely taken shape when the dictator backed down at the threat of a Royalist march on Athens and opened the door to a successor.

Only a day before the Greek and German elections, Austrian Fascists—knowing that their former compatriot, now the German Chancellor, was holding an election of his own —brought on a Cabinet crisis over the suppression of the railway strike that had begun March 1. The strike and the crisis were aggravated by the so-called Hirtenberg arms incident, in which Austrian railway functionaries and workers had connived at the illegal shipment of Italian arms to Hungary from the Austrian factory at Hirtenberg to which they had been sent ostensibly for repair. The Austrian Government's action in suppressing the strike was so vigorous that it provided a pretext for the Greater Germany Party—the Austrian branch of Hitler's Nazis—to make vociferous demands for leniency. Renner, the Speaker of the Austrian Chamber, and two vice-speakers resigned; on the weekend of March 4–5 Chancellor Dollfuss declared Parliament incapable of functioning and imposed virtual martial rule through a series of decree-laws.

Democracy was having equally hard going in Europe's youngest republic, Spain. Only two years old, the republic had already lost the collaboration of its outstanding sponsor, José Ortega y Gasset, disillusioned by the factionalism and petty personal rivalry that set in almost as soon as Alfonso XIII abdicated. The Government of Premier Azaña, dependent on the adherence of the Socialist Trade Union Party, had been badly shaken in January when the Civil Guard killed 14 peasants in cold blood during a Syndicalist riot.

As March arrived, Azaña fearfully faced a motion of no-confidence in the Cortes; it was based solely on the January massacre. He renewed his pledges to the Socialist Trade Union Party on the two points that meant most to its leaders: new laws setting up state rather than church schools and establishing tribunals to enforce constitutional guarantees. In return, the party assured him of its support at least until these laws should take effect, and as a result, Azaña retained power by a vote of 173 to 130 as the week ended.

Spain's former Western Hemisphere outpost, Cuba, was in much greater turmoil though technically far from a government crisis. President Gerardo Machado, a typical Latin-American dictator, had long since suspended the constitutional rights with which every such regime has always decked itself, and the whole island was in effect the fief of a tightly knit oligarchy. Throughout the country, however, resentment had been gathering for months and now, as March began and a new administration came into power in the United States that in fact, if not in law, viewed Cuba as a kind of protectorate, hopeful rebels were striking at the heart of the Machado Government's power: the sugar plantations and the railways that served them. No one leader had appeared among the rebels; but from one end of the island to the other, plantations were burning and railway tracks thrust toward the sky. Bombs flew in the cities, strikes were called suddenly and sometimes carried out, and repression, as it has always been in the Caribbean regardless of the public credo of the party in power, was ruthless but useless.

CHAPTER 16

The Show Went On

THE living theater was active and vibrant during the week. It was shielded from world events by its traditional impregnable preoccupation with itself, and its footlights glowed brightly and bravely in every civilized country.

Despite the money shortage, playgoers were keeping the lights burning in 40 theaters on Broadway; London, Paris, Berlin and Vienna were having strong seasons.

Circuses in the Northern Hemisphere were coming out of their hibernation, preparing their "greatest shows on earth and colossal spectacles for children of all ages" despite financial distress. Vaudeville, lingering obdurately in its death throes, was drawing renewed vigor from the movie palaces that combined films with live variety shows. People wanted to be entertained and somehow they found the money for it.

How well they found the money is best illustrated by the salaries drawn by the stars of the moment. Jack Pearl, the comic Baron Munchausen of radio, was getting $8,500 a week at the Capitol in New York. A week earlier in the same theater, Ed Wynn, "The Perfect Fool", had drawn $20,000. His rate for one radio appearance was $5,000. George Burns and Gracie Allen, a husband-and-wife comedy team, were get-

ting $1,200 for a radio show and $2,000 for a single stage appearance. Singer Kate Smith was touring the vaudeville-
movie circuit at a minimum of $7,000 a week. Milton Berle
was doing night clubs at $1,500 a week; Ruth Etting, a
singer, $6,000 a week; Jimmy Durante, $2,000 a week. Walter
Winchell was earning $3,000 a week for his radio show and
syndicated column; Rudy Vallee was averaging $4,000 a
week for crooning and, according to friends, was salting away
every bit of it. Jack Benny was making $4,000 a week, and
Clyde Beatty, the lion tamer, $5,000 a week. Circus rousta-
bouts were getting food, lodging and two dollars a week. Ordinary actors and actresses were working for Equity minimum and happy to get the jobs.

The theaters were almost untouched by the bank holiday
in New York. Governor Herbert Lehman declared the moratorium on Saturday, March 4. All places of entertainment
lost about 10 per cent of their business over the weekend.
The legitimate theaters, normally closed on Sundays, felt the
money shortage for the next four days only lightly.

The offerings on Broadway during the week were neither
brilliant nor weighted with importance. The critics were
kind, sympathetic and amiably hopeful. Broadway seemed
content to hold the line with reliable revivals and varied new
fare.

Eva Le Gallienne was charming audiences with her repertory version of *Alice in Wonderland* at reduced prices. Another revival was *As Husbands Go,* by Rachel Crothers, a
pleasant evening with two ladies from Iowa who find romance in Paris and try to bring it home with them. The humorous consequences seemed to bring satisfied chuckles
from the audience. Miss Crothers also had a new play on the
boards, *When Ladies Meet,* apparently directed toward the
same type of audience. It was an urbane tragicomedy in
which a wife and her prospective successor talk it over before
discovering each other's identity.

The critics agreed that Katharine Cornell was giving a glorious performance in *Alien Corn,* the Sidney Howard play produced by Guthrie McClintic, the star's husband. The press agent described it as a "pulsating study of a unique temperament in the grip of ordinary circumstances." The play dealt with the question whether Elsa Brandt (Miss Cornell), a talented piano teacher at an American woman's college, should go to Vienna to continue her studies in the face of her own dread of material insecurity and various other complications relating to campus life. *News-Week* declared the play was not up to the mark previously set by Mr. Howard, but that if a newcomer had written it, "*Alien Corn* might well be hailed by not too exacting critics as a minor masterpiece."

New York's drama critics were in violent disagreement over *American Dream,* a first play by George O'Neil, poet and novelist. Written with passion and sarcastic humor, it spoke out boldly on American culture, contrasting the outlook of a rebellious son of an established American family in 1933 with the outlook of two rebellious ancestors in 1640 and 1849. This Theater Guild production had a stinging third act that left some of the audience exhausted or shocked. Richard Lockridge in *The New York Sun* called it "eloquent, violent . . . and strongly dramatic." Percy Hammond in the *Herald Tribune* called it "inert, incoherent, somewhat sluggish."

Those who were not seeking an important play found easy amusement in *Autumn Crocus,* starring Dorothy Gish and "that newly imported and justly popular matinee idol, Francis Lederer," in a sentimental romance about a wistful English teacher on holiday in the Austrian Tyrol. Mr. Lederer charmed the ladies consistently every evening and Wednesday and Saturday afternoons. The big production number was a "spontaneous" moment when the innkeeper and his guests made music in the old-country fashion. It was whipped-cream cake served with delight and good taste.

S. N. Behrman was represented with *Biography,* in which Ina Claire gave a charming and spirited performance as the tolerant lady portrait painter in a study of the modern temper. "A *laissez-faire* attitude," the critics said, "is the lady's refuge in an uncouth world as she contends gracefully against a blundering senatorial candidate and a snarling magazine editor."

The Hamlet theme, in modern dress, was presented in *Conquest,* written and produced by Arthur Hopkins with Judith Anderson and a highly competent cast. Hopkins, telling the story of a contemporary family of manufacturers, upheld the triumph of old-fashioned standards over certain influences of the boom and Depression on commercial and private life.

Crime was represented in two plays. Edgar Wallace, the inexhaustible Briton, who turned out detective stories by the gross, had written an old-fashioned melodrama called *Criminal at Large* that starred Florence Reed and was described as the "mystery thriller of the year." J. B. Priestley, on a more lofty level, was the author of *Dangerous Corner,* a quietly intense play containing a provocative climax in which the truth was extracted from a group of characters, and a past of crime and passion was exposed. Colin Keith-Johnson headed a commendable cast.

The prevailing conversation piece in drawing rooms and speak-easies was Noel Coward's *Design for Living,* which the critics called "daring, witty, swift, decorous, wanton and immaculately clever." It put forward the hitherto unmentionable theme of a triangle in which the two men are more interested in each other than the woman in the case. It was never quite clear who was pursuing whom. Coward and the Lunts (Lynn Fontanne and Alfred Lunt) were the protagonists.

If the theatergoer wanted fatalism in full dress, there was *Dinner at Eight,* an ironical comedy by George S. Kaufman

and Edna Ferber. Millicent Jordan, a catalyst in the plot,
plans an elaborate dinner party at her Park Avenue mansion.
Deeply distressing things happen to her guests between the
day the invitations are sent out and the hour of the dinner.
It was excellent theater, well done. (Years later it became a
motion picture with the "greatest all-star cast ever assem-
bled," including John and Lionel Barrymore, Wallace Beery,
Marie Dressler, Jean Harlow, Edmund Lowe and Billie
Burke.)

Goodbye Again was called one of the brighter and funnier
plays of the season, having to do with an author who meets
an old love while barnstorming on a literary lecture tour in
Cleveland. Critics said the play was made doubly entertaining by the fine performances of Osgood Perkins and Sally
Bates.

For those who loved nostalgia replete with a barrel organ
playing "In the Good Old Summer Time" and the characters dressed in old-fashioned clothes, James Hagan wrote and
Leo Bulgakov produced and directed *One Sunday Afternoon.* Lloyd Nolan played Biff Grimes, a small-town dentist
with a heart of gold, who finds in his chair the prosperous
banker who twenty years before had won away his girl. Biff
has married her less colorful friend. The play draws to a pre-
dictable end when Biff finds that Providence was really favoring him through all these mellow years. There wasn't a
dry eye in the entire theater as the curtain fell.

George M. Cohan was the author and star of *Pigeons and
People,* which contained no perceptible plot but was, according to Cohan, a "comic state of mind in continuous action."
There was an abundance of profound and entertaining discourse in the familiar Cohan manner that left the audience
with the feeling that it had witnessed something deep while
enjoying a chuckle. Mr. Cohan was on-stage most of the time.
The other characters came on as foils for what was mostly a
monologue.

Pauline Lord was appearing in *The Late Christopher Bean*, an engaging and novel comedy adapted from the French about the sudden posthumous fame of a painter and the furore that takes place when some of his masterpieces are discovered in a sleepy New England village.

Ben Hecht and Charles MacArthur brought the power of the lampoon to its hilarious best with *Twentieth Century*, taking Broadway for a rough and uproarious ride from Chicago to New York. Eugenie Leontovich and Moffat Johnston headed a good cast that revealed the backstage madness of a producer and a star. It was Hecht and MacArthur at their zaniest and audience as well as critics loved every moment of it.

Elmer Rice was on Broadway, too, with his *We, the People*, a drama dealing directly with the tragedy of the times. In frank, humanitarian propaganda, Rice rose in towering wrath and indignation over the political and economic slovenliness that had forced the country into depths. It was a mighty polemic about and against the Depression, showing mass victimization of wage earners, teachers, farmers and intellectuals. The critics praised the "bitter and violent protest," the "long-smoldering outburst," the "undeniably powerful and interesting theme," but damned the play as "too pessimistic and disturbing for the public fancy." The audiences evidently agreed. During the week the theater was half empty. The play closed after 50 performances.

The Pulitzer Prize winner for the year was Maxwell Anderson's *Both Your Houses*, which concerned itself with the two legislative branches of our national government. Under Hoover there had been deep dissension in the Senate and the House of Representatives, arousing nationwide criticism. The promise of a united legislature under Roosevelt seemed to make Mr. Anderson's play almost prophetic. It had none of the heaviness of Elmer Rice's argument, and attracted good audiences.

Peggy Wood returned to Broadway after four years in London to star in *A Saturday Night,* a folksy story about a woman's birthday party, her husband's desire to give her at long last a big evening and all the things that happened to prevent it. Owen Davis wrote the play, which lasted only five weeks despite the fact that it got better notices than *One Sunday Afternoon.*

Another American repatriate, Tallulah Bankhead, who had been appearing in London plays, returned in *Forsaking All Others,* by Edward Roberts and Frank Cavett. It also marked the stage debut of Fred Keating, a handsome personable night-club and vaudeville magician. Miss Bankhead portrayed a young woman who is about to be married to her childhood sweetheart. While waiting at the church, the bride-to-be declares she would "really rather live in sin" than go through with the ceremony. She is half obliged by her bridegroom, who jilts her for a lovely lady he has met abroad. Miss Bankhead had another good line at this: "Well, anyhow, Jesus loves me." Then comes Mr. Keating and a fine ending.

The Negro theater as such was represented with two highly effective offerings, *Run, Little Chillun, Run,* and *Louisiana.* Hall Johnson, the choir leader, who wrote the former, presented it more as music and libretto than as a play. Critics acclaimed it as "the finest all-Negro musical spectacle the town has seen in years." It was the story of a preacher caught in the toils of flesh and the Devil, lightning and thunder, half-naked dancers "writhing in ecstasy," and a delirious evening for the playgoers. *Louisiana* was described as "a genuine Negro drama of the conflict between voodoo and the Baptist church," and acted to the hilt.

The playgoer this week had an abundance of choice. Nazimova was starring in *The Cherry Orchard;* Maurice Schwartz was in *Yoshe Kolb,* the Yiddish classic; a Shakespeare repertory theater was popular at a dollar top; and *I*

Piccoli, Italian marionettes, were called brilliant and charming by happy critics.

And then, of course, there were the musicals.

Mary Boland was bright and funny in *Face the Music,* a revival from the previous season. It was a satire about the lavish tendencies in musical show business, with politics and "tin boxes" thrown in to make it timely.

Fred Astaire proved that he could dance without his sister, Adele, who had broken up the team to marry a British nobleman. The vehicle was *The Gay Divorcée,* which, according to the advertisements, was a "smartly costumed, intimate musical comedy about professional corespondents at a Mediterranean seaside resort. Claire Luce is decorative and graceful and Louella Gear is the droll chaperone." It was apparently all that, playing to full houses.

Drenched in romantic song, *Melody* gave everyone an opportunity to sway in three-quarter time to the *schmaltz* of Sigmund Romberg with book by Edward Childs Carpenter and lyrics by Irving Caesar. The tender story covered several generations of one family, Evelyn Herbert appearing as both the heroine and the heroine's granddaughter. Its impressive cast included Everett Marshall, Hal Skelly, Victor Morley, Harrison Brockbank, Walter Woolf and Jean Aubert, with a typical George White chorus. Bobby Connolly was the director.

Reinald Werrenrath headed a group of excellent voices to make another Jerome Kern score part of the Broadway scene with *Music in the Air.* Tullio Carminati, Natalie Hall and Walter Slezak kept the operetta moving with fine performances. *Take A Chance,* a Schwab and De Sylva concoction, was extremely funny and melodious, with enough blue material to keep a sophisticated audience happy without bringing in the censor. Ethel Merman belted out "Eadie Was a Lady" with verve and enough decibels to make it the hit of the season. Jack Haley, Jack Whiting and Sid Silvers handled the rest of the chores commendably. *Walk a Little Faster,* a revue, was not received with great plaudits, but the critics reminded everyone that Beatrice Lillie and Clark and Mc-Cullough could make any pedestrian presentation move just a little faster.

Strike Me Pink, a new musical, opened during the week, with Jimmy Durante, Lupe Velez and Hope Williams. Lew Brown and Ray Henderson did the words, music and production. Hal Le Roy of the spidery legs did some fine dancing. Gracie Barrie won a storm of applause with "It's Great to Be Alive"; Durante, wearing white tie and tails for the first time, gave impetus to "Am I mortified," a phrase that was to become a snappy remark for the younger generation for years to come. "Let's Call It a Day" and "Memories" were two songs that lingered on radio and records.

The London season was flourishing at cut prices, offering a satisfying variety of theater fare to please any palate. *A Bit of a Test,* a fine farce by Ben Travers, was attracting a large audience, as was *The Streets of London,* a comedy-melodrama with song and dance that, the critics said, evoked "more continuous laughter than heard in years." *Ballyhoo* was called the best revue in town. Edward Poor Montgomery had a lush and showy piece called *Double Harness.*

Ivor Novello, the actor-playwright, was scoring a triple success in two light comedies. He was the author of *Fresh Fields* and the author and co-star, with Gladys Cooper, of *Flies in the Sun.* Both pieces were enjoying a good box office after generous critical praise.

Jessica Tandy and Cathleen Nesbit were co-starred in *Children in Uniform*; Raymond Massey, Francis L. Sullivan and Yvonne Arnaud appeared in *Doctor's Orders; While Parents Sleep* was in its second year; and *Mother of Pearl* and *The Glass Wall* were continuing to draw responsive audiences. *It's You I Want,* with Seymour Hicks, and *Ten-Minute Alibi* were having successful runs.

Two importations from America were enjoying large audiences. *Once in a Lifetime,* by Kaufman and Hart, and *Dinner at Eight,* by Kaufman and Ferber, were to encourage other imports later in the season, among them *The Gay Divorcée* and Eugene O'Neill's *All God's Chillun Got Wings,* which starred Paul Robeson.

The outstanding hit of the year, *Richard Bordeaux,* a historical drama by a Gordon Daviot (a pseudonym), firmly established John Gielgud as one of the important men in the British theater. Another that evoked predictions of perennial success was *The Green Bay Tree,* by Mordaunt Shairp. The Old Vic had *Mary Stuart,* a good play by John Drinkwater. *Road House* starred Godfrey Tearle (he played the part of Franklin Roosevelt in a film about the atomic bomb sixteen years later) and Marion Lorne. *The Princess in the Cage,* by C. B. Fernald, was holding its audience, and *Cock Robin,* a collaboration of Elmer Rice and Philip Barry, was getting well-deserved plaudits. Anny Ahlers starred in *The DuBarry,* and at the Sadler's Wells Opera Puccini and Verdi were being featured.

Whatever doubts were held about the financial success of the season were dispelled by the enthusiastic audiences that crowded into the variety theaters. The Palladium starred Cedric Hardwicke and Company and Lew Stone; the Windmill Theater joyfully advertised its *Non-Stop Revue;* the Victoria Palace had the Joyful Jovers and the London Pavilion had a ten-hour uninterrupted show, unhesitatingly featuring "the world's greatest stars." Balieff's *Chauve-Souris* offered an evening of "unconfined fun and laughter." *Jolly Roger,* a new musical burlesque of melodramas, opened during the week, and got fine notices with special praise for its star, George Robey. *Night of the Garter,* another laugh-pro-

voking offering, was described by happy critics as "the fun-
niest show London has had for years." Another favorite was
The One Girl, a Ziegfeld musical comedy. *Sleeping Beauty,*
a pantomime, and *Tout-le-Temps,* a "stupendous French
revue from the Folies Bergère," rounded out the formal entertainment for the week.

London producers were beginning to sense a change in an
old theatrical pattern. It had been the tradition to send met-
tropolitan stage successes on tour through the towns and
provinces. However, this was being supplanted by a perceptible increase in the number of local professional repertory
companies and "little theater" groups. As the trend progressed it was noted that frequently these "little theater"
organizations were responsible for first showings of considerably greater significance than those originating in London.

The theater on the Continent was vigorous and entertaining. There, too, the variety acts, singers, dancers, magicians,
acrobats, animal acts, were drawing large crowds in the
provinces as well as in the large cities. These performers
operated on an international scale, many of them having been
seen in England and the United States.

Paris was having a bright season. Among the outstanding
offerings were Jean Giraudoux's *Intermezzo* and St. Georges
de Bouhelier's *Napoléon. Intermezzo* was a poetic-ironic play
about a young woman teacher who experiences mysterious
lakeside ecstasies with a specter, which created scandal and
set up complications. The critics described it as rich in
imagery and ideas, an allegory of prosaic, rigid routine versus
romanticism and lyricism. The play, produced by the
Comédie-Francaise, had incidental music by Poulenc.
Napoléon was a heroic type of pageant of the Emperor's last
years, from Vilna in 1812 to his death in St. Helena. *Prin-
temps mortel,* translated from Lajos Zilahy, was a mildly
received mystery drama. *Maman, marie-toi,* by Maurice

Dekobra, was a pleasant comedy, bordering in its presentation on vaudeville, in which a young playboy tries to arrange for his mother, a Russian princess, to marry a rich industrialist. The young man then falls in love with the tycoon's daughter, developing an exciting cliché that the audience enjoyed thoroughly. The American influence was making itself felt with plans for an operetta entitled *Bootlegger,* as well as translations of *Dinner at Eight* and *Abie's Irish Rose,* which appeared under the title *Bloch de Chicago.* A notable absence was Marcel Pagnol.

The German stage was about to undergo the transformation from freedom to Nazism. The persistent anti-Semitic campaign had already taken some toll among the directors of the leading producing theaters in Berlin, most of them Jews or liberals. By the time Hitler came to power Berlin had lost much of its prestige as a theatrical center. Better and more important productions were found in the smaller cities. Those plays that remained were riding on momentum and the prestige of their stars and authors. Werner Krauss was appearing in the title role of *Faust, Part II;* Heinrich von Kleist's *Prince Frederic of Hamburg* was drawing large audiences; and Goethe's *Iphigenia* was being well received. Max Reinhardt's final activity in Berlin was Hugo von Hoffmannsthal's *Grosses Welttheater,* an elaborately staged translation from the Spanish of Calderón. *Ball at the Savoy,* by Paul Abraham, starring Gitta Alpar, was one of the best musicals Berlin had seen in many years. Richard Tauber, sustaining the Viennese tradition, starred with his discovery, Mary Losseff, in *Frühlingsstimme,* by the Czech composer, Jaromir Weinberger. Lucie Mannheim starred in Erich Korngold's adaptation of Leo Fall's *Divorced Woman.*

Four theaters in Vienna were doing pieces bearing on or about Franz-Josef. These included Robert Stolz's indefatigable *White Horse Inn.* The Scandinavian countries turned to O'Neill for their important fare, offering translations or adaptations of *Mourning Becomes Electra* and *Desire Under the Elms*. Later came *Dinner at Eight*.

The theater in Rome offered solid and satisfying story material that pleased audiences and critics generally. *A Man to Be Remade,* by Luigi Chiarelli, told the story of an innocent man convicted of murder. After serving 23 years at hard labor, he tries to get back to his old life and finds his wife married to his best friend, who turns out to be the real killer. Vincenzo Tieri's play, *Taïde (Thaïs)*, unfolded the story of a woman lawyer, a sort of female Don Juan. Critics said it was a psychological study of nymphomania, but charged that it missed the basic point. The problem is summed up by a prostitute who postulates to the heroine: "What is necessary is not to study all men—they are all alike—but to study one man and make him happy." This drama played to full houses, the refinements of the critics notwithstanding. The play that got the most attention, in the press and in conversation, was Gino Rocca's *World Without Crawfish,* a science-fiction preachment that caught the fancy of the moralists and the pacifists. A scientist announced to the world that he had achieved a method by which anyone could kill anyone anywhere, without contact and with impunity. The world is at first startled, shocked and dismayed, but instead of the general slaughter, a great peace descends upon all and an exemplary morality becomes the rule. This is explained on the theory that man fears being killed even more than he longs to kill. Virtue becomes universal: hence it ceases to be good or pleasurable. Before there is a danger of all the people becoming passive and bovine, the scientist confesses that the entire theory is a pious fraud. The world returns to its normal vicious pattern and life becomes bearable once more.

Fantasy of a much less fertile kind, applied with a far heavier hand, dominated the stage in Moscow and Leningrad

too; but there it was called *Soviet realism,* in which the right
is always wrong and only the left is right. Such dramas as
N. Pogodin's *The Poem of an Axe* and *My Friend,* A. Afi-
nogenov's *Fear,* L. Leonov's *Skutarevsky,* A. Korneichuk's
Platon Krechet and *The Wreck of the Squadron* and V.
Vishnevsky's *Optimistic Tragedy* dealt only with one or the
other—sometimes with both—of two basic themes: the inception of the workers' and peasants' Utopia and its development under Stalin. Only in such Gorky plays as *Yegor Buly-
chev and Others, In the World* and *Enemies* did the famous
Moscow Art Theatre and its colleagues allow Soviet realism
to be upstaged now and then by human realism and even
by human idealism.

The movies were the world's biggest form of entertainment. They were escape, opiate, ready-to-wear dreams, all
things to all men. In their darkened palaces could be found
release from reality, sublimation and safety. A man could see
himself as a brave cowboy or a dashing war correspondent;
a youth could see himself as the college football hero; a
young girl could see herself as the pure and pursued
heroine; her middle-aged mother could change places with
the *femme fatale* or the wisecracking best friend of the
heroine. The children, little or big, were offered delightful
slapstick and cartoons. Hollywood gave its all to satisfy all.
Not until television mesmerized millions with mediocrity
and commercials was there such a mass medium. And, try as
they might, the hucksters could not break in with "a message
from our sponsor."

Financially the movies were doing poorly during the week,
although they were still earning more than other forms of
entertainment. Before the crash in 1929 the weekly gross
throughout the United States was more than $42 million.
Just before the bank holiday this had been cut to about
$3,000,000 a day, taking into account price reductions. Dur-

ing the bank holiday the gross was $2,000,000 a day. When the money was back in circulation again, the gross went back to $3,000,000 a day.

A listing of the top popular movies of the week, playing in first- and second-run houses of America, can be of special interest to those sleepless viewers of television's late and late, late shows. When science-fiction writers invented time travel they did not realize how soon their predictions would come true in the form of old movies. But these movies were new then—new and thrilling and exciting:

Rasputin and the Empress, with John, Ethel and Lionel Barrymore; *Ladies They Talk About,* with Barbara Stanwyck; *Dangerously Yours,* with Warner Baxter; *Sailor Be Good,* with Jack Oakie; *King of the Jungle,* with Buster Crabbe, boosted as the Lion Man, and Frances Dee; *Our Betters,* with Constance Bennett; *Rome Express,* with Conrad Veidt and Esther Ralston; *Perfect Understanding,* with Gloria Swanson; *Blondie Johnson,* with Joan Blondell and Chester Morris; *Grand Slam,* with Paul Lukas, Loretta Young and Frank McHugh; *Secrets,* with Leslie Howard and Mary Pickford; and *Clear All Wires,* with Lee Tracy and James Gleason.

These were the films that drew millions to the giant movie palaces in the big cities with live stars as added attractions. The neighborhood movies and the houses in the smaller towns lured their customers by adding bank night, free dishes or door prizes. For the average citizen the movie was the big night out. A four-hour show would include two full-length features, a cartoon, a two-reel comedy or travelogue and a newsreel. While popcorn had not yet made its starchy and buttery debut, its popular predecessors were peanut brittle, hard candy and tacky Tootsie Rolls. As the great drama unfolded in the darkened theaters, children watched with enviable absorption; young couples made love quietly; mothers sat dreamy-eyed and fathers snored contentedly. Here was true togetherness even before the word was coined. Assailed by intellectuals, buffeted by censors, confounded by economic instability, the movies went blithely on their way, secure in the knowledge that they were indestructible as long as the ordinary people continued to dream and to dramatize themselves.

Two movies made special news during the week. A new one, *King Kong,* dealt with the adventures of a 550-foot-tall ape-creature, captured in a remote island and brought to Broadway by an enterprising producer (Robert Armstrong), his leading lady (Fay Wray) and his first mate (Bruce Cabot). It was sensational and full of action. For further details see your current television screen. The other was *She Done Him Wrong,* starring Mae West and Cary Grant. This was a film that had sex as its main feature and was being thoroughly enjoyed by audiences of all ages. Suddenly the censors descended upon it in several states. It seemed that Miss West and others were speaking too frankly for some state authorities. Suggestive remarks such as the oft-repeated "You must come up to see me sometime," and "I'm tired, I just laid a cornerstone," spoken in a manner that no print can adequately convey, were stricken from the sound track. *Variety* reported that week that wherever the film had been censored, box office was poor, but as a result of the publicity, where the film had not been cut box office was "sensational."

Paradoxically, *She Done Him Wrong* shared popularity honors at the end of the year with *Little Women,* starring Katharine Hepburn as Jo, Jean Parker as Beth, Joan Bennett as Amy, Frances Dee as Meg and Spring Byington as Mrs. March. At first Hollywood was puzzled by this reaction to extremes in film stories. *Little Women* had a gentle, sentimental, wistful and nostalgic air that left audiences happily misty-eyed. Mae West's film was filled with vigorous humor and ribald gaiety and was an unashamed spoof of sex. It laughed rowdily at sex instead of taking it seriously. Miss

West's speech and mannerisms became part of the American scene; mothers encouraged their precious little girls to give imitations of her; she became a great fad among the French and Italians, and even sober and dignified men enjoyed repeating her libidinous gems. Hollywood was not long in finding the answer. Both films had nostalgia in common. The audiences were able to escape from the torment of the moment in these two films that showed bygone days when life was apparently sweeter and simpler.

In spite of the groans of producers, financiers and congenital crepe hangers, Hollywood was thriving. It was the biggest exporter of American culture. More American films were being shown abroad than those of any other country, Germany running a poor second. Of a total of 639 films shown in Great Britain during the year, 449 were American; in France there were 208 U.S. films in a total of 496; in Spain, 202 of 302; in Italy, 152 of 270; in Hungary, 322 of 717. To this very day, a demigod in chaps and ten-gallon hat rides heroically in the forbidding mountain fastness of Serbia, Albania and Bulgaria—on film, that is. He is Tom Mix on that gallant steed, Tony. The cowboy picture had a special appeal to peasants who could understand the simple formula, clearly presented, of the good guy and the bad guy. Amateur cowboy clubs were formed in France, Holland and Italy with regular meetings that were called rodeos, and the members dressed in the accepted manner. It did not matter whether one had a horse.

While the *western* was the steady fare or the second feature, the more expensive American films found solid popularity. Among the better exports being shown in London during the week were *Horse Feathers,* with the Marx Brothers; *Tiger Shark,* with Edward G. Robinson; *Mr. Robinson Crusoe*, with Douglas Fairbanks; *Madame Butterfly,* with Sylvia Sidney, Cary Grant and Charles Ruggles; *You Said a Mouthful,* with Joe E. Brown; *Tess of the Storm Country,* with Janet Gaynor and Charles Farrell; *The Son-Daughter,* with Helen Hayes and Ramon Navarro; *Night After Night,* with George Raft and Constance Cummings; *Hot Saturday,* with Cary Grant and Nancy Carroll.

Cecil B. DeMille was represented with his colossal, stupendous and gigantic *Sign of the Cross,* which had a cast of 7,500, including Fredric March, Claudette Colbert and Charles Laughton. England was represented by J. B. Priestley's *The Good Companions,* with Edmund Gwenn and John Gielgud.

Prominent in almost every movie program in the United States and abroad was the newest and best effort made in the animated cartoon field, *Mickey Mouse.* Walt Disney, who had succeeded with *Silly Symphony* in capturing public appeal, was overwhelmed with the reception given to Mickey Mouse. He followed this with the classic *Three Little Pigs* and for the next year the country was singing *Who's Afraid of the Big Bad Wolf?* It was an inspirational song directly linked to the Depression's wolf at the door.

Mickey Mouse pointed up the star system. Good pictures sold well, but good or even slightly indifferent pictures with a star sold best. Surveys and popularity contests in America and in Europe, Australia, and South America showed these to be the leading box-office attractions: Janet Gaynor, Marie Dressler, Greta Garbo, Joan Crawford, Norma Shearer, Marlene Dietrich, Helen Hayes, Irene Dunne, Jean Harlow, Diana Wynyard, May Robson, Margaret Sullavan and Claudette Colbert.

Among the men were Maurice Chevalier, Clark Gable, George Arliss, Ronald Coleman, Lionel and John Barrymore, Charles Farrell, Gary Cooper, Cary Grant, Joe E. Brown, Clive Brook, Herbert Marshall, Lee Tracy, Spencer Tracy, Leslie Howard, Charles Laughton, Paul Robeson and Otto Kruger. Of writers and directors, little was said or noted. One Hollywood writer, watching the popularity returns, remarked that the people knew that all the world's a stage, but they should be informed that not all the men and women are actors: some are writers, directors, cameramen and scene designers. Louis B. Mayer answered that others not getting screen credits or public recognition were the bankers who gambled their money on the movies. The public wanted stars and Hollywood obliged.

While Hitler was beginning to use motion pictures for purely propaganda purposes, the Russians were showing a slight relaxation in their emphasis on the building of socialism. For the first time they began to delineate individual rather than collective themes in their movie stories. Three films, shown during the week only in Russia, were *Shame, Men and Jobs* and *The Patriots.* There were reports during the week that a musical comedy on film was about to start production with a truly light theme omitting such sturdy Muscovite film clichés as tractors, blast furnaces and power plants. If this movie was not produced it might have been because Stalin read the announcement.

Two films were in production in Hollywood that showed the beginning of a trend. One was *Gabriel Over the White House,* starring Walter Huston, which was based on an astonishingly prophetic book that foretold many of the actions taken by Roosevelt in his New Deal Program. The other was *This Is America,* a compilation of newsreels picturing the history of this country from 1917 through the inauguration of Roosevelt. It showed the foibles and fancies, the tragedies and triumphs of America and Americans, and ended with a frank editorial plea for co-operation with the Roosevelt administration.

Hollywood loved the movies. That's why it made so many of them to be seen everywhere in the world by all kinds of people. These people paid to see the movies and part of their payment found its way back to Hollywood and to the Wall

Street bankers who risked their money on a sure thing. This made them all happy, but for one item. There was another mass medium that held its audience enthralled—Radio. And there was no charge for listening. The spoken word had been refined to its commercial best. Great drama, music, news, commentary and comedy rode on invisible waves from the tall broadcasting towers into homes and automobiles. There was one tiny bit of payment that had to be made—listening to the commercial. But as of this week "the message from the sponsor" had not yet been distilled into the exquisite torture that was to come later.

Radio was growing up. There were 22 million sets in the United States. Only a few were leftovers from the static-ridden, battery-powered sets of the twenties. All others were good examples of the technical advances that had been achieved toward good listening. By the time the entire nation was ready to hear Roosevelt's inaugural address, radio receivers had been improved by the use of multifunction tubes, higher efficiency coils and dry electrolytic condensers that gave voice and music a hitherto unobtainable fidelity. The technical thingumbobs enabled manufacturers to create smaller sets, some weighing as little as six pounds. Prices were brought down to Depression levels. Americans were finding convenience in the ownership of the big living room set and several table models.

The family was no longer chained to the large console set. Many homes had small radios in bedrooms, kitchens and basements. The housewife could listen to her favorite soap opera as she went about her duties from room to room. It was no longer necessary for one member of the family to force his taste upon the others. Generally there were enough radios to go around. A generation of high school and college students was doing its homework while listening to the radio. This mystified and even disturbed the older people, but did

no evident harm to the students. The practice continued unabated until television made simultaneous reading and
watching an impossibility.

Radio was handy. One did not have to seek it out. Many
private automobiles had it; the taxis had it; the better
hotels supplied amplifiers in each room that could select five
stations from master sets. Stores and restaurants had radios.
Even some theater lounges had radios.

The people listened to a rich variety of offerings from
opera and concerts to jazz; Shakespeare, Shaw, soap opera;
high comedy and low. Religious sermons, prize fights, political diatribes, advice to the lovelorn, inspirational talks;
kindergarten class and general school work—there was a
program for every taste.

Anyone in the United States arising between six and
eight in the morning could get his setting-up exercise instructions on his local station, followed by gentle organ music
while he breakfasted.

Wednesday, March 1, was a good day on the networks.
WEAF in New York (WRCA), fountainhead of the NBC
Blue Network, followed its calisthenics and organ music with
an *Inspirational Talk* and more bright music on a program
called *Cheerio*. At 10:30 A.M. there was some dance music
(yes, dance music), followed by *Cooking Talk* and the
Household Institute. While the lady of the house was setting
the table for lunch, Johnny Marvin, tenor, sang to her, or,
if she switched over to NBC's Red Network, she could hear
John Fogarty, a sweet Irish tenor, over WJZ, followed by the
Farm and Home Hour. On the Mutual Network she could
hear *Mrs. J. B. Reilly's Common Sense Talk*, which was inspirational as well as practical, perhaps a little more preten-
tious than profound, but satisfying to the body and soul of the
busy housewife. On the same network Alfred W. McCann,
the food authority who had a large and loyal following,
was followed by a chat on *Sculpture in Modern Life* by Sonia

Brown. At 2:30 P.M. Adolf Hitler's address to the German people was carried on the CBS Network, cutting into the regularly scheduled program for that hour, *The American School of the Air,* which this week was covering literature, music, elementary science, current events, history and geography for intermediary and upper grades. The program was beamed to shut-ins, students temporarily at home because of illness, and adults who wished to learn. It was one of many scattered through the networks, on local stations and on regional hookups for those who wanted knowledge. Tony Wons ("Are You Listening?") and Little Jack Little were followed by Ash Wednesday services from the National Cathedral in Washington, with a sermon by Bishop James E. Freeman. Later there was a talk by Charles Ingersoll, "Technocracy Challenges Capitalism."

On any day you could hear *Sisters of the Skillet* or Howard Chandler Christy discussing great paintings. Bide Dudley talked of Broadway and an anonymous expert gave advice on filling out your income-tax return. Almost all the talking was sandwiched among musical programs. Nellie Revel interviewed Walter Winchell, and Dean Gleason L. Archer of Boston's Suffolk Law School gave an enlightening, noncommittal discourse, "If a Woman Has Independent Means, Is She Entitled to Alimony?" Walter Damrosch conducted a music-appreciation hour. On Friday over NBC from 1:30 to 4:30 P.M. you could hear the Metropolitan Opera Company's *Tristan und Isolde* with Lauritz Melchior. Programing had not yet reached its later thoroughness and precision and, since almost all programs were live, many studios kept on hand an organist who filled in 15-minute voids that arose quite frequently. Any radio listing in any section of the country contained several such spots marked *Organ Music.* The women in their homes and the men in their cars, lonely people in strange hotel rooms and shoppers in stores found these interludes relaxing. Some of the larger stations had stand-by ensembles, tenors, baritones or sopranos with a ready repertoire. Programs like *Jolly Bill and Jane, King Kill Kare Songs, Battle's Ensemble, The Phantom Organist, Crazy Capers* and *Clara, Lu and Em* were popular steadies that kept the radio waves filled with music and chatter. Market reports, health talks, weather reports and an occasional news flash rounded out the morning and afternoon programs. A regular news program was given over the Red Network by Lowell Thomas. Elsewhere in the nation, stations were beginning to experiment with local gossip chatter at fixed times, including announcements of civic, fraternal and social activities.

The magic hour of twilight was devoted to the children. *The Lone Ranger, Buck Rogers, Little Orphan Annie* were the favorites, with *Bobby Benson, Skippy* (another comic-strip character), *Paul Wing, The Story Man, Tarzan of the Apes, Uncle Don,* Booth Tarkington's *Maud and Cousin Bill, Seckatary Hawkins, Children's Club* and *Kaltenmeyer's Kindergarten.* The little darlings sat glued to their radio sets while mother spooned dinner into their mouths. The older ones played while they listened, and the school-age crowd was at last able to concentrate on homework.

But there was conflict in this paradise. A great disagreement developed between parents and children. Mother wanted news and historical broadcasts for her children of 8 to 13. These children wanted thrills, bloodcurdlers and action. It all came out in a study made by Teachers' College at Columbia University and the United Parents' Association. The mothers marked as "excellent" the following programs; *Roses and Drums, Current Events, Today's News, Great Moments in History* and *The March of Time.* The children failed to whip up any enthusiasm about them. The children loved Eddie Cantor, who was rated *good* by the mothers. *Little Orphan Annie* was rated *high* by the children and *poor* by their mothers because she was always having emotional problems that were not good for her fans, the mothers contended.

Ford Frick, the sports commentator, got a *very good* rating with *Don Lang—True Animal Stories.* Rated *good* were *The Singing Lady, The Lone Wolf Tribe* and *Buck Rogers in 2433.* The real favorites of the children got *poor* and *very poor* ratings. *Uncle Don* was described as an "old-time Pollyannic announcer who tells about his fans' birthdays, tells stories and sings nonsense songs while urging children to eat their spinach." *Chandu* was regarded as too much blood and thunder; *Skippy* was called vapid; *Myrt and Marge,* a story of two show girls, good for adults but followed by children for whom it carried too much sophistication; *Howard Thurston, Magician,* too mystifying; and *The Shadow* too frightening.

The conflict, of course, was never resolved. *The Lone Ranger,* having started a long career in January, was rising rapidly to the top among the favorites. The children did not read the surveys. They listened to the programs that gave them the most thrills, chills, and excitement, leaving the studies and surveys to helpless educators and parents. It was ever thus.

When the evening rolled around, the family gathered to hear Boake Carter and the news. Then came a choice of fine music, popular music, plays or just plain entertainment. Kate Smith, Easy Aces, Tommy Lyman, Jane Froman, André Kostelanetz and his orchestra; John Charles Thomas, baritone; Howard Barlow and his orchestra; Vincent Lopez; Major Bowes' Original Amateur Hour. You could enjoy the problems of *The Goldbergs* or tour America with Carveth Wells. Ken Murray was on the air to make you laugh right after Amos 'n' Andy and Harry Hershfield. Eddie Cantor, Jack Benny and Ed Wynn purveyed more laughter; or there was a "glorious musical mélange" called *Captain Henry's Showboat* with Charles Winninger and Lanny Ross. Sigmund Spaeth, the tune detective, was a steady favorite.

If serious matters were more to one's liking, Hans von Kaltenborn and Edwin C. Hill explained the day's news events while reporting them. Or one could switch on Phil Regan, tenor; Eddie Duchin, pianist; Ruth Etting, or Cab Calloway, song-shouting band-leader; Frank Crummit sang wonderful songs, Ethel Shutta and Olsen's Orchestra made merry and a program called *Waltz Dream* drenched the radio in three-quarter time. Bruno Walter and the New York Philharmonic had Ossip Gabrilowitsch at the piano; Leopold Stokowski and the Philadelphia Symphony Orchestra had Abram Chasins at the piano. Hans Kindler conducted the NBC Symphony Orchestra, featuring Rosa Ponselle, soprano; Efrem Zimbalist, violinist; and Lawrence Tibbett, baritone. On Saturday night CBS and the two NBC networks broadcast the festivities at the Inaugural Ball.

Like the movies, American radio catered to a variety of tastes and made available every form of program, allowing the listener to choose for himself. European radio, being for the most part noncommercial, was more restricted. The United States had more radios, numerically and per capita. Its 22,000,000 sets represented 177 people of every thousand; Great Britain, with 7,000,000 sets, had 160 per thousand; Germany, with 7,000,000, 107 per thousand; France, with 2,000,000, 62 per thousand; Russia, with 2,000,000, 16 per thousand; Italy, with 500,000, 12 per thousand; Spain, with 300,000, 12 per thousand. Unofficial count showed that in the whole world there were some 55 million radios.

A glance at British and European radio logs showed the glaring absence of soap operas, chitchat programs, variety hours and other pap to the housewife, her children or her husband.

The BBC on March 2 began the day with an elaborate weather forecast for farmers and shipping, followed by a talk, *The Week in Westminster;* Reginald Foort was at the organ from 12 to 12:45. The BBC then offered fifteen gracious minutes of silence and went back on the air with a program called *Tracing History Backwards,* which was followed by another *interval* of fifteen silent minutes. At 3:15 there was *Evensong* from Westminster Abbey and then fifteen minutes of silence. Then came a German Reading, music by the Hotel Metropole Orchestra and *The Children's Hour,* which was a learned discourse on the Influence of the Roman Road on the Roads of England.

At 6 P.M. the Londoner got his *First News,* followed by fifteen minutes of *Interlude* to digest it. Then, from St. Margaret's, Westminster, he got a musical dissertation on *Bach's Organ Works* played by Herbert Dawson. This was followed by a Spanish Talk, a talk on the Making of a Play and a radio drama entitled *A Joy Ride* by A. J. Alan. At 9 o'clock came the *Second News.* After some musical programs, including a recital by Peter Dawson, baritone, came *A Short Midweek* Service from St. Michael's, Chester Square. The day closed at midnight with dance music by the BBC Dance Orchestra.

If this was not particularly exciting by American standards, it seemed to satisfy the Britons. The BBC seemed utterly devoted to service. Detailed road information for motorists, announcements of civic importance and instruction of all sorts were the essence of the programing. Perhaps, dealing with a higher national intelligence level than that in the United States, the BBC ruled out the vapid, syrupy offerings that commercial sponsors foisted upon the Americans.

The European countries followed the general pattern found in British broadcasting. There was much music, classi-

cal and national. Talks on cultural subjects, the arts, literature, history, current news and the sciences held the attention of listeners. Frequent weather reports were listed.

On Thursday, all Germany was listening to a Sportspalast
speech by Adolf Hitler, while in the provinces lesser Nazis
were haranguing the people over the air. But Berlin Radio
put on Beethoven's *Eroica;* Leipzig Radio gave its Spanish
Lessons and a wind-instrument concert; and Munich Radio
presented three one-act plays entitled *The Seven Deadly
Sins.* Oslo broadcast German lessons; Madrid gave French
lessons; Prague taught English; Rome gave French lessons.
All stations listed American music, a euphemism for jazz,
which was gaining in popularity throughout the Continent.
Paris interspersed its reports on the stock market, the
weather and sports with religious talks by Protestants and
Catholics. The Vienna radio was heavy with music, the high
light of the Thursday broadcast being the Vienna Philharmonic Orchestra under Dr. (later Sir) Adrian Boult per-
forming Mozart's *Symphony in G Minor.* The program concluded with a "snow report" and American jazz.

While each side of the Atlantic was proceeding with radio
in its own fashion, each also displayed enough curiosity about
the other to undertake surveys and studies. British and European communications experts were studying the commercial American radio system, while Americans were surveying
the generally noncommercial operation on the other side of
the ocean. News reports and commentary were increasing in
both areas. Newspapers, at first frightened—especially in
the United States—by the possible competition of radio,
were generally relieved when they discovered that the
initial announcement of a news event on the air whipped up
enough interest among listeners to spur them to buy newspapers for more details. As the week ended, it was apparent
that the Americans had no intention of switching to the

European system and the Europeans were resolved to continue their methods of broadcasting.

There were two exceptions to the almost universal European rule of state monopoly of broadcasting. (The monopoly was achieved variously through outright ownership of transmission facilities, majority ownership, and private ownership combined with governmental operation.) The exceptions were not altogether parallel: in Luxembourg, the single transmitter was a purely commercial venture, while in France privately owned and operated stations and chains of stations shared the air waves with the government network. Though Luxembourg was one of the tiniest states on the Continent, Radio Luxembourg had one of the most powerful transmitters in Europe, able to reach every country, including the United Kingdom, and utilizing short, medium and long waves. The good British or Continental set of the period was built to receive all three.

The Luxembourg station was brand-new; its corporate owner had been granted a 25-year monopoly subject to minimal government control of management and programing. It was as purely commercial as any station in the United States and from its transmitter on the 1,000-foot-high Jünglinster plateau, programs went out in every language of the Eastern Hemisphere, sponsored by manufacturers and distributors of merchandise in more than a dozen countries. The program content, however, maintained a general level considerably higher than that of American radio, ranging from music-hall turns to concerts by the station's own symphony orchestra, often conducted by eminent foreign musicians and embellished with leading instrumental and vocal soloists of international reputation. From the first, this money-making radio company reserved a regular program for hitherto unperformed works of new composers.

Both private and public broadcasting had begun simul-

taneously in France and, though a 10-year-old law had proclaimed broadcasting a public service and hence a state
monopoly, privately owned stations had continued to appear. During this first week of March, 1933, however, the
commercial French stations were preparing for the extinc-
tion that they knew was ultimately inevitable—new laws
envisaged the imposition of an annual registration tax on
receivers and their components and the establishment of
advisory councils that would include representatives of
national and local governments and of the listening public.

In Paris itself the competition was still keen: the government ran the Eiffel Tower station and private industry controlled Radio-Paris, operating it on American principles
but programing only for domestic consumption. In contrast, the privately owned Radio-Normandie was more Eng-
lish- than French-speaking, for it could easily be tuned in
by English listeners and, like Radio Luxembourg, offered
English advertisers an excellent means of promoting their
wares by air to their fellow countrymen. Unlike Radio Luxembourg, which as a matter of policy sought to create audiences throughout the Continent, Radio-Normandie limited
its export programing to the United Kingdom, whose advertisers flocked to its microphones to such an extent that
French programs and French advertising were more the exception than the rule in its operations.

While millions were listening to radio, secure in their confidence that this was the ultimate in mass communications,
the infant ogre, Television, was struggling onward and upward. A report published March 5 declared happily that the
pictures were clearer than they had been in 1930, but
added sadly that many broadcasters were withdrawing from
the field because there was no profit in scientific philanthropy.
The boom years of the twenties had encouraged many to
join the promised gold rush, only to find that technology and
the public were not yet ready. There were few receivers,

mostly experimental; therefore no income from advertising. Scientifically, television was still in the experimental stage, making equipment obsolete almost as rapidly as it was manufactured. Regular, if extremely limited, programing was in effect nightly in France and England and technical experimentation was far advanced in Germany.

When New York's Station W2XAB withdrew from broadcasting, its technical director, E. K. Cohan, declared that "further operation with the present facilities offers little possibility of contributions to the art of television. It is our intention to resume our experimental transmissions as soon as we are sufficiently satisfied that advanced equipment can be installed." This was the position of all the broadcasters who withdrew from the field disheartened by letters from pioneer enthusiasts who meant to encourage but didn't. One Montreal observer wrote that the New York pictures were overlapping a broadcast from Station W9XG at Purdue University. From Indiana came a letter saying: "One-half the time the New York images are quite clear; the other half they are marred by fading and multiple images." An observer in Connecticut complained of being bothered by "ghosts." He said he received the pictures "one above the other and I would like to know if that is the way they are broadcast." A Long Island enthusiast wrote: "Was it a cat or a Scottie in the background? The man wiping his face with a handkerchief was excellent."

There were also many letters that indicated that television was on the way. From Maine came a letter saying: "It gives me great pleasure to inform you that I have been successful in receiving the image of a woman from neck to head over a distance of 600 miles. The lips showed white. The face was a shade between light and medium. The hair was light. I held the picture on the screen for a few minutes until power noise interrupted reception." A Jerseyite wrote: "Had good luck with the last half hour of your program tonight. I believe there was a young lady demonstrating cosmetics. We could see her rub cream on her face and then pat her face with a powder puff. We saw the pianist take the music from the rack, cross her arms while playing and move her fingers up and down the keys. Enjoyed the tap dancing and ballet immensely. Television is a lot more interesting when there is a lot of motion. I saw the young lady with the new hat styles." One Bristol, Tennessee, fight fan "received quite a bit of entertainment from your boxing bouts." A Pennsylvanian wrote: "I just finished looking in on your television program and enjoyed it very much, especially the fashion show. Also the man called George who plays the mouth organ. He wore dark glasses."

More illumination and larger pictures—the average screen was two by three inches—were urged in the letters received by all broadcasters. They in turn presented these problems to the manufacturers of equipment, who labored at their drawing boards and prayed for a single genius to give them the solution. But all they got that week was a report of a new development by Vladimir K. Zworykin, RCA-Victor television expert. He had created an electromagnetic lens to supplement glass lenses in the image receivers. He reported to the American Physical Society at Columbia University that cathode rays, used to "pencil" the pictures on a fluorescent screen, are feeble. Zworykin's plan was to focus the rays to a point nearly as fine as can be produced with an optical lens by circling them with a thin coil of wire containing a tiny flow of current. When properly adjusted, he explained, the coil causes the rays to converge to a point of intense brilliancy. The intense rays "fluctuate over the screen and paint the picture."

Zworykin's development was the latest step in a long history toward the perfection of television. It had begun in 1817 when the Swedish chemist, Baron Jons Jacob Berzelius, laboring over atomic secrets, unwittingly started television on its way when he isolated an element that he called *selenium* (after the Greek word for moon). In 1873 a telegrapher named May temporarily pried open Pandora's box when he noted that the flow of electricity through selenium varied with the intensity of light shining on it. This led to the discovery that the energy of light could be turned into the energy of electricity. Seven years later Maurice Le Blanc suggested the idea of scanning the image and four years after that Paul Nipkow, a German, created a disk of revolving mirrors. Then, in 1923, Zworykin and Philo Farnsworth, discarding moving parts, invented the inconoscope, which was based on the knowledge of electronics. On Thursday, April 7, 1927, Secretary of Commerce Herbert Hoover and others broadcast from Washington to New York and were seen on a screen two inches by three inches. On September 11, 1928, WGY in Schenectady went on the air with a full dramatic program—a one-act melodrama entitled "The Queen's Messenger." By the end of 1931 five experimental stations were on the air.

As the week waned, enthusiasts were heartened by the reports that laboratories were laboring with furious intensity to improve the wireless image. And even though the commercial entrepreneurs were pulling out, there was the feeling among scientists that soon, quite soon, a new mass-communication medium would appear on the scene. The general public was not aware of this great work at hand, and nowhere in the records can be found any prophecy by sociologists.

CHAPTER 17

"Health Makes Wealth"

LONG before the first bank closing, the American doctor had learned a major lesson of the Depression for the professions: a full appointment book did not mean a full pocketbook. Doctors, like lawyers, were as busy in March, 1933, as they had been four years before, if not busier; the difference was that they did not often collect their fees. Victims of the tough-fibered popular myth that all professional men are rich, they were the first creditors to be put off when belts had to be tightened.

The American doctor's situation was unique. "Socialized" medical and health insurance was a commonplace in Europe, where it had begun in Germany during the Kaiser's reign; Mussolini had incorporated it into his Fascist program, and the democracies of western Europe, from middle-of-the-road France to diluted-Socialist Scandinavia, had done the same. Even in England, which still retained some of the innovations of its first Labour Government, there was a rudimentary National Health Service, though it did not extend beyond the general-practitioner level; and, as the crisis deepened, there was strong agitation to expand it to the services of specialists and dentists. In Russia, of course, complete medical care for everyone was taken for granted. Unprotected by any of these devices, the American doctor continued to make his house calls, receive patients in his office, make his hospital rounds, send out his bills and hope that one day some of them might be paid.

He also continued to enlarge his knowledge through research, sometimes paralleling the studies of colleagues in other countries, sometimes charting new courses. Tuberculosis, cancer and mental health were the primary subjects of study almost everywhere; but in no country was there any evidence to indicate that the three years of depression had produced any new phenomena for either physical medicine or psychiatry and psychoanalysis to examine. In fact, despite all the economic hardships, infant mortality, typhoid deaths, diphtheria fatalities and tuberculosis deaths were at new low points in many areas.

More tightly organized than doctors in other countries, the American physician relied on the American Medical Association to protect his interests, to investigate and report technical developments and to keep him informed of everything affecting his profession. In its weekly *Journal* the Association warned him against recommending a new electrical air filter that did not produce what was claimed for it, as well as a home diathermy machine that was a menace to every user; it also passed on the claims of various prepared foods and demanded precision in the labeling of drugs.

The doctor was also concerned with legislation, such as bills in some states that would establish a mileage rate for house calls (similar legislation already applied to British panel doctors), or others that would give him a legal right to collect fees from those who had injured the patients he was treating. Even more controversial medical legislation was pending in some inland states: proposals to impose examinations for venereal disease, tuberculosis and insanity on all applicants for marriage licenses, to protect the treatment of illness and injury by prayer, to require doctors to report the names of all cancer patients to the public-health authorities, to order sterilization for the insane and for all felons with three or more convictions.

Injection—intracutaneous, subcutaneous and intravenous —occupied more and more of the American doctor's attention. In the treatment of pernicious anemia, for example, Drs. Raphael Isaacs, Cyrus C. Sturgis, S. Milton Goldhamer and Frank H. Bethell found that intravenous injections of the extract from 100 to 125 grams of liver were more effective than 40 times that amount given orally, because loss was minimized. A much more spectacular success for injection was claimed by Drs. August A. Werner and W. D. Collier, working with castrated women—that is, those who had undergone ovariectomy or hysterectomy.

Universally their patients, regardless of age, had suffered from atrophy of the breasts, drying up of the vaginal canal and loss of sexual appetite after the operations, to say nothing of more profound and complicated emotional effects. Using hormone injections with theelin in graduated doses over three periods of 28 days each, the physicians found that the castrated woman could be restored to normal life and happiness: the breasts and the vaginal canal returned to what they had been, desire was revived (and sometimes even increased beyond what it had been) and a normal emotional life was restored, going so far even as to revive periodic emotional changes like those of menstruation.

With one major exception, physicians abroad were turning with equal enthusiasm to hypodermic treatment for an almost unlimited variety of problems. The exception was tuberculosis prevention, for which oral dosage was claimed to have been as effective as inoculation. Two physicians, Vaucel and Boisseau, in the Pasteur Institute of Brazzaville in French Equatorial Africa, had orally administered a drug called BCG to several thousand children and had just reported virtually complete success. Professor Calmette of Paris was so impressed that he urged that similar immunization be made mandatory for all applicants for medical schools.

Some of the uses and materials of injection reported at this time were exotic enough to drive the economic crisis out of anyone's mind. Cobra venom was the choice of Lignel-Lavast and Koression to ease the anguish of cancer patients; they contended it was a far more effective painkiller than morphine, and much less habit-forming. Besides, a single dose was effective for from eight to ten days; and they hinted, though they dared not state, that in some cases the venom appeared to have been fatal to the lesions. One Gabriel, studying the treatment of psychotics, inoculated horses with radium and thorium X. He then made a serum of their blood and injected this into his psychotic patients, claiming 21 complete cures among 34 patients. Perhaps a more valuable report that appeared in the same week was that of A. Besvedka and M. Bardach, who found that intracutaneous injection of an immunizing vaccine could also act as a cure, whereas subcutaneous injection was useless once the infection had taken root. An equally valuable study, again relating to mental disease, was concluded by J. H. Quastel and R. Strom-Olsen, whose attention had been arrested by the growing use of narcotics in psychotherapy and the harmful side effects that kept pace with it. They found that injections of insulin given with the narcotic injection warded off the side effects and hence expedited the narcotherapy. Hemorrhoids, too, were now being treated by injection—alcohol or alcohol with quinine being used for the internal growths and sugar-glycerin combinations for the external.

What might be called the sociological aspect of health and medicine received particular attention in Great Britain. Tuberculosis was on the rise there, especially among young

women in Scotland, and Dr. Charles Cameron, who headed
a large sanitarium, ascribed the increase to overexpenditure
of both time and money on amusement and luxuries to the
detriment of rest and proper food. In England, where
slum betterment and housing had long been endorsed as
near-panaceas, Dr. G.C.M. McGonigle delivered the alarm-
ing report that in a group of 152 families moved from a slum
to modern housing, the death rate had risen 40 per cent
while the national rate had increased only minimally and
that of a comparable slum area had actually declined. Mc-
Gonigle noted that virtually all the families in the modern
housing were on the dole and that they were now paying 50
per cent more in rent than they had paid in their slum: inevitably, this money came out of their food budgets and they
were virtually forced to subsist on sugar and starches.
In this connection it was generally felt that Western Europe
was depopulating itself and at some unspecified date would
be overrun by Slavs. *The Lancet* quoted the noted American
expert, Dr. Louis I. Dublin, as estimating that the United
States would have reached a maximum population of 148
million by 1970 and that this figure would be halved in the
next 60 years. The experts hedged, however, by warning that
a better contraceptive, a new epidemic disease or new
methods of making mass synthetic foods might make a mockery of any and all prophecies.

The relatively new science of pediatrics was much stressed
by British doctors, who called on their medical schools to
give more of the curriculum to the prevention and treatment
of children's diseases.

On March 5, the day after this appeal was published in
London, President Albert Lebrun of France opened an institute in Paris devoted solely to pediatrics. Started with a
gift of a million francs from the American Red Cross, the
school was a part of the Faculty of Medicine of the University of Paris. Believing that the health of the children today

was the welfare of the nation tomorrow, the French were resolved above all to reduce the toll of tuberculosis, which
was killing 80,000 to 90,000 Frenchmen a year and accounted
for 13 per cent of all deaths in the country.

Just two days earlier, the fourth Australian Cancer Conference had been concluded. In both Australia and New Zea-
land, the death rate for this disease among patients under
79 had been falling, though it rose rapidly at greater ages.
The conference devoted most of its attention to radium
therapy, which was gaining in stature everywhere. The Aus-
tralians considered deep X-ray treatment both more effective
and more economical than the radium bomb, and the conference voted to concentrate its studies on the deep therapy.

Medical education was under the microscope in a number
of countries. Many American students, kept out of their
own schools by racial and religious quotas or by finances, had
been studying abroad, and the A.M.A. pointed out that they
would be wise to check the curricular requirements of their
respective state examining boards before choosing a foreign
school, since some did not adequately prepare them for
American examinations. The Russians, on the other hand,
fighting a chronic shortage of doctors, compressed the course
to two and a half to three years, devoting 77 per cent of the
class hours to the medical sciences and coupling practical
hospital work with all courses. In Romania—the only Eastern European country whose medical diploma was recognized in France—the curriculum had just been lengthened to
six years, during the last half of which the student had to
participate in hospital practice; nor was passing his examinations sufficient to win him a license to practice: he had also
to write a thesis on an approved subject.

Technical problems claimed much medical attention. One
of the most interesting was an electrical transfusion machine
that worked like the human heart to expedite the transfer
of blood from one person to another. Cunningly designed

to avoid coagulative influence, regurgitation or air embolism, it was powered by a tiny motor and controlled by a flow regulator and a quantity meter, all the work of Drs. V. Pauchet and A. Becart of Paris. In Lyon, Dr. A. Ceccaldi brought out at the same time a new infra-diathermy machine whose ultrashort waves and much higher frequency made it possible to treat the patient through his clothes without burning him.

Lyon was also the home of a folk myth about cancer, because in the preceding 20 years there had been 6,703 cancer deaths in 5,000 of the city's 23,258 houses. These 5,000 were firmly regarded as "cancer houses," and it required a learned paper presented to the French Academy of Medicine on March 7 by Drs. A. Lumière and P. Vigne to breach the gullibility of the myth's followers.

Cancer was prominent, too, in the thinking of some psychiatrists, notably in the United States, where many practitioners, strongly influenced by Alfred Adler, were stressing the somatic, or physiological, side of mental and emotional illness. It was noted that epileptics with cancer had a much lower convulsion rate than other epileptics (not much credence was given to V.V. Patrascono's attempt to prove that appendectomy eliminated epilepsy). Hereditary factors in epilepsy were examined by Dr. Calvert Stein, who concluded that neither epilepsy nor neuropsychiatric illness was hereditary; he conceded that there was a higher rate of neuropsychiatric disorders in the families of epileptics and explained this on the basis of an existing potential or a latent defect in germ plasm; this in turn, he suggested, might offer epilepsy a more than usually fertile soil when there was the contribution of such factors as trauma, birth injuries or alcoholism. Much study was also given to the effect of drugs in both bringing on and alleviating physiological and pyschological symptoms; even psychotics proved amenable to sodium amytal, especially when it was given intra-

Benito Mussolini

Italy's Man on a White Horse

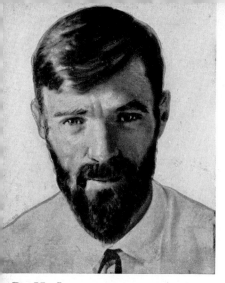

D. H. Lawrence
THE LOVELY LADY, *a posthu-*
mous volume of stories, was
published this week

Walter Winchell
Mr. Broadway

Douglas Fairbanks and Mary Pickford
America's Sweethearts

Cary Grant and Mae West in *She Done Him Wrong*

The Royal Family of the Theater. John, Lionel and Ethel Barrymore with "Crown Prince" John Blythe Barrymore

The New York Times.

First masthead (March 1, 1933)

"All the News That's Fit to Print."

LATE CITY EDITION

WEATHER—Fair today; tomorrow little change in temperature.

Copyright, 1933, by The New York Times Company

NEW YORK, WEDNESDAY, MARCH 1, 1933

VOL. LXXXII....No. 27,430

TWO CENTS In New York City

JAPANESE DRIVE SLACKENS BUT 2 ARMIES MAKE GAINS; ALL NORTH CHINA IS TENSE

CHINESE FIRM AT PASS

Hurl Back Repeated Flanking Attempts in South of Jehol.

Soviet Is Said to Be Sending Big Arms Supplies to China

HITLER SUSPENDS REICH GUARANTEES; LEFT PRESS BANNED

Emergency Decree to Combat 'Communist Terror' Voids Constitutional Safeguards.

CURB ON STATES PROVIDED

Berlin to Seize the Executive Power in Any Failing to 'Restore Law and Order.'

House Held Sure to Pass Bankruptcy Bill; Roosevelt Influence Wins Railway Aid

STATE SALARY CUTS IN LOWER LEVELS REPUBLICAN PLAN

Assembly Majority Proposes $4,100,000 Saving in Wages Under Lehman Budget.

$200,000 LESS TO SCHOOLS

Reduction of $700,000 for Reforestation Is Held to Be Counter to Constitution.

SMITH OPPOSES INFLATION, ASKS BOND ISSUE FOR JOBS; WOULD RECOGNIZE RUSSIA

British Royalty Go to Talkie For First Time to Aid Poor

HE STIRS SENATE INQUIRY

Currency Inflation Only a 'Shot in the Arm.'

Second masthead (March 2, 1933)

"All the News That's Fit to Print."

LATE CITY EDITION

NEW YORK, THURSDAY, MARCH 2, 1933

VOL. LXXXII....No. 27,431

TWO CENTS In New York City

CHINA'S MAIN LINE BROKEN IN HARD JAPANESE DRIVE; CHIHFENG TROOPS DESERT

LINGYUAN QUICKLY TAKEN

Two Armies Converge on the Stronghold After

HITLER INTENSIFIES DRIVE ON THE LEFT; HUNDREDS ARRESTED

Red Leaders Jailed, Socialists' Papers Banned and Homes Searched All Over Prussia.

NATION TOLD OF 'REVOLT'

60,000 Chinese Reds Defeat National Force in Szechwan

Boettcher Freed by Kidnappers; Payment of Ransom Indicated

Wealthy Broker Let Out of Auto Unharmed at East Denver, Cal.—Tells of Threats in Captivity—$60,000 Reported Tossed to Abductors.

ROOSEVELT WILL GO TO CAPITAL TODAY FOR INAUGURATION

Confers With Woodin on Banks and May Alter That Phase of His Message.

GREETED BY CITY CROWDS

HOUSE VOTES WIDE POWERS TO ROOSEVELT FOR CUTS; CONGRESS IN FINAL RUSH

Smith to March of Inaugural In Tammany Sachem Regalia

PRESS RELIEF MEASURES

House Body Reports Bill

Third masthead (March 3, 1933)

"All the News That's Fit to Print."

LATE CITY EDITION

NEW YORK, FRIDAY, MARCH 3, 1933

VOL. LXXXII....No. 27,432

TWO CENTS In New York City

ROOSEVELT IN CAPITAL, WILL CONFER WITH HOOVER TODAY; CUMMINGS MADE ATTORNEY GENERAL, RAINEY SPEAKER

CAPITAL HAILS NEW CHIEF

Crowd, Scorning Rain, Cheers as He Reaches City Heavily Guarded.

TALKS PROBLEMS ON TRAIN

THE START FOR WASHINGTON.

GARNER FORCES BEATEN

McDuffie Loses to Illinoisan by 166 to 112 in Democratic Caucus.

WALSH FOUND DEAD BY BRIDE OF 5 DAYS ON WAY TO CAPITAL

Senator Chosen for Attorney General Is Victim of Heart Attack on Train.

RETURNING FROM HAVANA

JAPANESE ADVANCE ON CHENGTEH ROAD; CHINESE IN FLIGHT

Invading Column Sweeps On, Taking Pingchuan, Only 50 Miles From Jehol City.

Poles Hear That Hitler Plans Talk in Plane Over Corridor

Fourth masthead (March 4, 1933)

"All the News That's Fit to Print."

5 A.M. EDITION

WEATHER—Cloudy today; fair tomorrow; temperature unchanged.

Copyright, 1933, by The New York Times Company

NEW YORK, SATURDAY, MARCH 4, 1933

VOL. LXXXII....No. 27,433

TWO CENTS In New York City

TWO-DAY HOLIDAY FOR BANKS HERE, LEHMAN'S ORDER

EFFECTIVE THIS MORNING

Governor Acts After an All-Night Conference With Banking Heads.

PERIOD INCLUDES MONDAY

All Banks and the Securities Markets Are Affected by Emergency Decree.

ILLINOIS TAKES STEP, TOO

Period of Closing There Is Put at Three Days—Federal Officials in Conferences.

McDONALD TO REJOIN ARMS CONFERENCE

JAPANESE CAPTURE CAPITAL OF JEHOL; NORTH CHINA UNEASY

Defenders Make Strong Fight, but Many Soldiers Are Forced to Flee.

SOME LEADERS QUIT FRONT

Losses of Chinese Are Put at 1,500 in Chy—Chengteh Is Said to Be in Chaos.

NEW JAPANESE DEMANDS

BANKERS SUPPORT ROOSEVELT'S PLAN

ROOSEVELT TAKES UP TASK AS PRESIDENT TODAY; GREAT CROWDS IN CAPITAL FOR INAUGURATION; EXTRA SESSION WILL ENACT A NEW BANK POLICY

Hoover Gets Last Pay Check; He Works Today for Nothing

CALL EXPECTED AT ONCE

Roosevelt May Even Set It for the Last of Next Week, Leaders Say.

TIME LIMIT IS PROPOSED

Aim Is to Restrict Work to Banking, Leaving Other Problems to Second Meeting.

PROGRAM IS NEARLY READY

President-Elect Is Warned to Have a Definite Course for Unorganized Congress.

BECOMES PRESIDENT TODAY.

ROOSEVELT PLANS SECRECY

He Rejects His Advisers' Plea to Reveal Aims Before Oath.

AGAIN CONSULTS HOOVER

But Declines a White House Offer to Spur Earlier Action by Congress.

CAPITAL AWAITS SPEECH

By ARTHUR KROCK

The headlines of the New York Times reflect the momentous events of the first seven days of March, 1933

The banks are closed and Wall Street is quiet. Only the flags stir in the gentle breeze to celebrate the Roosevelt inauguration.

venously, whereas sodium rhodanate had no effect even on the neurotic.

As if attempting to bridge the gap between psychosomatic medicine and pure psychoanalysis, Dr. Thomas M. French attempted to develop a complicated theory likening repressions to the conditioned reflex discovered by Pavlov. According to French, inhibitions were of two kinds—external, induced by fear, and internal, induced by frustration; he maintained that repressions could be similarly divided according to whether they arose from fear of an external event or from the repeated failure of a desire—the illustration he chose was the female Oedipus complex—to be gratified.

But the pure analysts ignored French's theory, just as they paid little attention to the use of drugs in psychotherapy. Freud, who was then director of the *International Journal of Psychoanalysis,* which was edited by his student and biographer, Ernest Jones, was still the supreme authority among psychoanalysts, and his preaching and practicing followers included A. A. Brill, Sandor Ferenczi, who was a dying man; Hanns Sachs, Franz Alexander, Melanie Klein, Princess Marie Bonaparte, Otto Fenichel and such later deviants as Karen Horney, Karl A. Menninger, Theodor A. Reik and William Alanson White, who was to become the *doyen* of the "interpersonal" school of psychiatry. Almost prophetically, psychoanalysis was giving particular study to the addictions, notably those of alcohol and narcotics. The origin of these was held to be purely psychic, arising from the needs of a narcissistic ego colored by masochistic and homosexual drives. That there was a physical aspect to alcoholism or drug addiction was not denied, of course, but the psychoanalytic view held that the physical factors in addiction were result rather than cause.

A violent rejection of the whole of psychoanalytic thinking came from Dr. Trigant Burrow, whose claim to the paternity of "phyloanalysis" no one disputed. The term derived from the Greek root, *phylon* (race), and the theory grew out of Burrow's long study of both normal and neurotic patients. Burrow contended that not only what is legally called insanity but all mental and emotional disorders were really physiological—reflections of tensions, alterations and disturbances affecting definite bodily processes. Mental disorders, he held, are discrepancies between those feelings that belong to the organism as a whole and the sensations that belong to the brain, "with its secondarily acquired ideas and images." Hence it was obvious to Burrow that conflict was not emotional but purely physical: "a disparity between two clearly defined body zones." From this premise he concluded that the only possible treatment of so-called mental and emotional illnesses must be physiological.

But to the American physician at large there was a much more immediate and pressing conflict: between what he had to spend and what he could collect. The issue of his Association's *Journal* that appeared on Inauguration Day reminded him that if he could not pay his already overdue subscription, his promise to do so would suffice to keep the magazine coming to him.

CHAPTER 18

The Undebasable Currency

I

CRISIS and climax tumbled one upon another so copiously in that week that the perception of them was all but numbed. Yet those seven days recorded also a wealth of artistic achievement that few similar periods before or since could equal. Music, dance, the visual arts, literature, lavished quality in quantity on capitals and county seats; the infinite varieties of the aesthetic experience took precedence even over the emptying purse, the ranting demagogue and—for the thoughtful—the subtly threatening future.

Even in economics there was an artistic influence, a barometric display that proved as accurate as any forecast by the Dow-Jones averages: auction prices of rare books had risen, on the average, 30 per cent from the lows of mid-1932, and the traditionally rapacious art dealers stood united with art editors in urging the owners of paintings not to sell them but to hold them if only as investments for capital growth. One French gallery owner who had just arrived in the United States hoping to amass a shipload of paintings at distress prices from suddenly former millionaires was virtually hounded back to Paris by collectors and editors.

The week's music offered the greatest contrast to the week's economic stringency and the political upheavals. Though the world's financial pages marveled at the day-by-day flight of great masses of capital from New York to Berne and London, enough remained to fill Carnegie Hall, the Metropolitan Opera House, Town Hall and scores of lesser auditoriums, as well as the major concert houses of cities across the country. Barely recovered from the gala of February 26, celebrating the 25th anniversary of Giulio Gatti-Casazza's reign over the Metropolitan—which had brought back from retirement such living legends as Marcella Sembrich, Olive Fremstad, Amelita Galli-Curci, Alma Glück, Frieda Hempel and Antonio Scotti—the company presented Debussy's exquisite *Pelléas et Mélisande* the next night with Lucrezia Bori, Edward Johnson (who was to abandon singing for the general managership) and Ezio Pinza; then it greeted March with *Rigoletto,* starring Lily Pons, Gladys Swarthout, Giuseppe de Luca and Lauri-Volpi. As the first week of March wore on, the bonanza increased to embrace *Tannhäuser, Tristan und Isolde, Lucia di Lammermoor, Il Trovatore,* embellished by such golden names as Elisabeth Rethberg, Maria Olszewska, Goeta Ljungberg, Lauritz Melchior, Friedrich Schorr and Giovanni Martinelli.

The standard works of the New York repertoire were equally standard in most other musical centers, regardless of nationality; but in Paris, Mozart was still represented on the opera stage (*The Marriage of Figaro*), and in both Paris and Berlin special attention was being paid to the 50th anniversary of Wagner's death. Paris commemorated it with an uncut *Tristan* conducted by Paul Paray and sung in a new French translation authorized by the composer's aged widow, Cosima, the daughter of Franz Liszt; she had been particularly pleased by the French version's fidelity not only to the substance but also to the intricate rhyme-scheme and complex meters of Wagner's original poem. In Berlin, Otto Klemperer, not yet barred by his non-Aryan blood from the podium, paid tribute with *The Flying Dutchman* and *Tannhäuser,* while the equally "impure" Erich Kleiber conducted the very early *Forbidden Love,* in which Wagner attempted to resolve the problem of free love against a score suffused with Auber and Rossini. It was in the same week that the music lovers of Dresden, hearing a *Rigoletto* conducted by Fritz Busch, broke up the performance when they realized that the conductor was partly Jewish.

Even as Deems Taylor in New York was berating the Metropolitan for paying its top singers as little as $1,000 or $2,000 a performance—he complained that South American companies were paying two to four times as much—both Paris and Berlin, as well as London, Milan and Rome, noted bitterly that they had to be content with second- and third-rate voices because the stars were all in New York. But almost in the same paragraph the Berlin critics were bowled over by Anny Helm's first major role as Brünnhilde in *Götterdämmerung* after a Bayreuth apprenticeship as Kundry and Brangäne. British enthusiasm was concentrated on Mozart and Bach cantatas.

The concert repertoire was much the same as it is today; yet at the same time new music was being introduced everywhere. Arturo Toscanini, who was bringing a number of new Soviet composers to the attention of American audiences, was singled out in a March 4 critique in the New York *Sun,* which charged that he had thus proved false his claim to political independence. In general, the taste of American concertgoers was not inaccurately reflected in a poll of Philadelphia Orchestra audiences, whose favorites were Franck's one symphony, Brahms' First, Tschaikowsky's *Pathétique,* Beethoven's Fifth, Rimsky-Korsakov's *Scheherazade* suite and their own Leopold Stokowski's excellent symphonic synthesis of the score of *Tristan*. But, even when a conductor dared to defy his audience with a symphony by Louis Gruenberg or Howard Hanson or a tone-poem by Arnold Schoenberg, even the standing room had been sold out by the time the house lights darkened, in Lincoln, Nebraska (whose orchestra was in its seventh deficit-free season), or in New York itself.

Toscanini's program for the weekend of the inauguration consisted of Wagner's *Faust Overture,* Hanson's *Romantic Symphony No. 2* and Richard Strauss' *Ein Heldenleben;* undeterred by the closing of the banks, the orchestra left New York on March 6 for a swing through Philadelphia, Baltimore (distinguished for its City Council's refusal to cut a penny from the budget of the Municipal Department of Music), and Washington. This program was more conventional: Beethoven's Third Symphony, the *Overture* and *Venusberg Music* from the Paris version of *Tannhäuser,* and the *Vorspiel* and *Liebestod* from *Tristan.* Toscanini's co-conductor was Bruno Walter; the season's guest was Issay Dobrowen, who served Philadelphia in a similar rôle. Ernest Schelling, the composer, conducted the Saturday-morning children's concerts, an innovation that won the praise of the Swiss journal, *Dissonances.*

New Yorkers may have had little or no money in the first seven days of March, but they turned out by the theaterful for a crowded calendar that comprised three concerts by the Boston Symphony under Serge Koussevitzky, a program of music by ancient sovereigns and modern Americans given by the Sinfonietta of New York under Quinto Magnani, a League of Composers evening of compositions by recent graduates of the Juilliard School, a Columbia University student production of *La Forza del Destino,* a National Orchestral Association concert in Carnegie Hall that featured the Seventh Violin Concerto of Mozart, only recently played in London for the first time by Yehudi Menuhin, chamber programs by the London String Quartet, the Budapest and Juilliard quartets, a recital by Fritz Kreisler and song recitals by Maria Olszewska and Roland Hayes, a singer who was brave enough to be his own and his competitors' manager. All these events of the week were in addition to the full Metropolitan Opera and New York Philharmonic programs. As if this were too little, Westchester County had its own full-sized Philharmonic Orchestra playing in White Plains. This group was organized specifically to give employment to musicians. There may have been few jobs, but there was a plenitude of good music.

In Philadelphia, the first big city to offer a conducting opportunity to Eugene Ormandy, who now shared with Artur Rodzinsky the post of assistant conductor, Stokowski and the Philadelphia Orchestra opened the month with a mixture of traditional and new music—Schumann's Fourth Symphony and Stokowski's synthesis of *Das Rheingold,* and the Piano Concerto No. 2 by a native Philadelphian, Abram Chasins, who played it as if he had never seen the envious caricature of himself on a wall of the gallery of that acoustic marvel, the Academy of Music. Philadelphia was also enjoying a prolonged season of Brahms' chamber music, sponsored by the Art Alliance and the Musical Fund Society.

Throughout the United States, music flourished as if the crisis had never existed. The great names of many nations were "playing the road"—the one street in America that was still paved with unembargoed gold. The famous Polish patriot-artist, Ignace Jan Paderewski, at that very moment seeking election to the presidency of Poland, was playing the piano night after night in American towns that no one in Europe except a concert manager had ever heard of. Walter Gieseking, the German who was supreme as an interpreter of Claude Debussy's piano music, was in Ohio; his colleague,

Vladimir Horowitz, was due back in New York; Sir Eugene Goossens was in Rochester, New York, a podium he shared with Sir Hamilton Harty and Walter Damrosch.

American music and musicians attracted capacity audiences in foreign countries during that frightening week. Werner Janssen, the son of a New York restaurateur, stunned Berlin when, leading its famous Philharmonic, he dared to play a Sibelius symphony—the Finnish master was virtually unknown in Germany, and orchestra, critics and public alike could not understand why Janssen admired him. The American was not unprepared for this: he had spent weeks with Sibelius in anticipation of this concert, and the composer had warned him that the Fourth Symphony would be a fiasco in Berlin, whose papers described the music as "childish . . . pallid . . . a kind of northern Bruckner." Janssen finished his concert with his own *New Year's Eve in New York,* and won high praise for his musicianship.

Though Hitler, the off-white German, was busily Teutonizing the music of the country he had commandeered by deposing such conductors as Fritz Busch and Carl Ebert because of their Jewish ancestry, other Germans were making the "inferior" Latin, Toscanini, an honorary citizen of Bayreuth, and applauding a new South American pianist, Claudio Arrau, when they were not filling the halls where such non-Aryans as Moritz Rosenthal, the pianist, and Emanuel Feuermann, the cellist, were playing Liszt and Haydn. A German conductor, Ernst Hoffmann, devoted a whole concert to the works of two Americans, Charles Griffis and the new Secretary of the Treasury, William Woodin. Howard Hanson of Rochester conducted his own *Romantic Symphony,* as well as the works of two compatriots, Professor Daniel Gregory Mason's *Chantecler Overture* and Richard Russell Bennett's *Concerto Grosso.* A French critic in the audience found them all pseudoromantic, but the Germans seem to have liked them. A tragic note sounded with the imminent bankruptcy of the world-famous piano maker, Bechstein.

France itself was the most receptive to new music, as Italy seemed the most wedded to the traditional in the concert hall as well as the opera house. Paris had four well-supported symphony orchestras, two opera houses and dozens of smaller musical events almost daily; from Bordeaux on the Bay of Biscay to Belfort on the German border there was serious music every day. In the capital, Alban Berg, whose Czech opera, *Wozzeck,* had scandalized America and, surprisingly, captured a good portion of Britain, presented a *Lyric Suite* and Francis Poulenc offered *Improvisations,* but the critics found both composers "victims of their own facility." It was only a few days since Felix Weingartner, a guest in Paris, had given the *première* of the Symphony No. 1 in C Major that Georges Bizet composed in 1848; on March 4, Dimitri Mitropoulos, conducting the Paris Philharmonic, introduced a hitherto unknown *Prelude and Fugue in B Minor* written 200 years earlier by Johann Sebastian Bach.

On the same day Maurice Ravel conducted the *première* of his new piano concerto, having chosen Marguerite Long as the soloist. A day later Mitropoulos offered Schoenberg's *Verklärte Nacht,* which, while not news, was still controversial wherever it was played (New York found it cacophonous, Paris found it hyper-romantically somniferous). Paul Hindemith, a German then living in Paris, whose music was known in the United States only to the self-conscious *cognoscenti,* won acclaim in France with his music for Rainer Maria Rilke's poetic cycle, *Das Marienleben*; the critics hailed Hindemith's work as reminiscent of the religious paintings of the Italian Primitives. The city's chamber-music groups filled the week with the sonatas and quartets of Franck, Debussy, Gabriel Faure, Florent Schmitt and Ravel.

Contemporary music's strongest advocate in Britain was Sir

Thomas Beecham. Independent of spirit as well as means, he was a conductor who went his own way or none; his great enthusiasm was Edward Delius, for whose music he formed the Delius Society. On March 5 he devoted an entire Royal Philharmonic concert to this composer, interrupting his campaign of popularizing the first three symphonies of Tschaikowsky. As in Berlin, Max Reger was getting a hearing. On the first of the month, the Bournemouth Symphony played Ralph Vaughan Williams' *London Symphony;* on the second, the Guildford Symphony, in quiet Surrey, devoted its entire program to British composers; the Birmingham City Orchestra played Ravel's new concerto on the sixth. Sir Edward Elgar interrupted his composition of a symphony dedicated to the British Broadcasting Corporation in order to conduct his chorale, *Gerontius,* with the Hallé Orchestra in Manchester, where Beecham, Pierre Monteux and John Barbirolli also filled in for the touring Harty. In a country whose critics admired Ravel's Concerto for using the piano lyrically, like Liszt or Chopin, instead of treating it as a percussion instrument in the manner of Hindemith, Stravinsky and Ernst Toch, Wilhelm Furtwängler's London visit with the Berlin Philharmonic, just after Janssen had conducted it in Berlin, was ill received and likened to an exercise in drill-master discipline.

Two of Europe's finest quartets were in England during this week—the Lener and the Busch, both victims of the Second World War. Both emphasized Brahms, in honor of the centenary of his birth. That ancient instrument, the clavichord, was rendered justice by Arnold Dolmetsch, one of the few men in the world who could still fashion a lute.

The Continent's first school of the lute opened that week —in Communist Russia. The Soviet Union's musical scholarship was second to none, and its artists and ensembles, acknowledged to be of the first rank, devoted most of their programs to the classic Russian composers. Parallel with the rather extreme nationalism characteristic of the arts in Russia under czar and commissar alike, a Marxist—or, to be precise, a Stalinist—musicology was being hastened to ripeness. It was in the atmosphere of the leading editorial in the new periodical, *Sovietskaya Musica,* that Lev Knipper's Fourth Symphony had its *première* in Moscow on March 2: a slashing attack on "rightists" who "smuggle in the ideological baggage of the rotting bourgeois world, all these 'atonalities,' jazz harmonies, etc.," coupled with an equally savage thrust at "all kinds of 'leftist' distortions of Marxism-Leninism, vulgarization and pseudosimplification." The new symphony was subtitled only *Four Études for Orchestra—Improvisation, March, Aria* and *Finale*—and apparently was neither rightist-rotting nor leftist-distorted.

In a sense, it was the dance that was undergoing the most drastic changes. The United States devotee, accustomed to classic ballet and to the romantic interpretations of Isadora Duncan, had just been seduced by the elaborate, exotic symbolism and stylization of the graceful Hindu, Uday Shan-Kar, and now his whole concept of the art of the dance was being shaken by the dynamic German, Mary Wigman. Discarding convention and artificial programing, Wigman believed that dance was an art only when every movement sprang from an emotion. Dance, to her, was a primary art, not the servant of some other; hence many of her creations were performed without music, while the music of the others was written to complement a previously conceived choreography (frequently abrupt and angular) rather than inspiring movements to interpret or accompany an earlier musical concept. The Dresden school, as her followers were known, was anathema to the classicists; but to those who wanted dance to be an art, not merely décor in motion, Wigman was a prophet. Her final American program, after a dramatic tour of the country that, if it did nothing else, made thousands of people think seriously about what made the dance an art-form, was given March 5 in New York and included the whole of her new cycle called *Sacrifice—Song of the Sword, Dance for the Sun, Death Call, Dance for the Earth, Lament* and *Dance into Death*—one of the most vigorous and believable dance performances of our time and one of the few to evoke true audience empathy. Wigman represented the quintessence of German expressionism made mobile.

Purely American dance, to Lincoln Kirstein, one of its most dedicated patrons and partisans, was appalling. He found it "part Dresden and part Duncan" and altogether "revoltingly self-expressive." The great Michel Fokine, who had created *Petrouchka, Prince Igor, Scheherazade* and *Les Sylphides* in Europe, was giving private lessons in New York, where professional ballet was nonexistent; though this week an amateur group was doing *Petrouchka* in a private theatre, and Fokine's pupils had to turn to musical comedy for a livelihood. The taste that Kirstein hoped was "more ignorant than corrupt" was being satisfied in Chicago by Harald Kreutzberg; New York could only wait for Martha Graham, and for the new choreographies being worked out, separately, by Agnes de Mille and Charles Weidmann. In Philadelphia Stokowski was preparing the *première* of Carlos Chavez' revolutionary ballet, *H.P.,* which was basically faithful to the traditional ballet technique.

The Ballets Russes de Monte Carlo were immensely popular in Europe, touring the Continent, as they had done for so many seasons, with an unvarying repertoire—*Les Sylphides, Coppélia, Swan Lake, The Firebird*—to which occasionally were added new compositions rigidly faithful to the classic tradition. In England, a former dancer called Ninette de Valois was breathing new vigor into the equally classic productions of the Vic-Wells Ballet. Beside the established stars like Serge Lifar and David Lichine such names as George Balanchine, Alicia Markova, Anton Dolin, were rising; Ruth

St. Denis and Ted Shawn were attempting, in America and Europe, to harmonize the old and the new.

Paris braced itself that week for the riots of the year before: the Ballets Jooss were returning for an engagement heralded by triumphs in Switzerland and the Low Countries. Kurt Jooss had much more in common with Wigman than with the classic ballet; he had also, as Wigman had not, a strong feeling about social problems. As antitraditionalist and expressionist as Wigman, Jooss was concerned with much more than the emotion or the experience of the individual, and *The Green Table*—for which, as for so many of his works, the music was especially composed by Alexandre Tansman—epitomized his art. It was this mordant dance-satire on war and its peace conferences that had brought on the Paris riots of 1932; but by March of 1933 Paris was more ready than it knew to appreciate Jooss.

Social consciousness in the dance, of course, was carried farthest in Russia, which was not then exporting its culture. Soviet audiences benefited by all the technical perfection handed down from the old Russian ballet. But in Moscow and Leningrad the aesthetic skill of generations was no longer employed for aesthetic delight alone: every ballet had a message. Some, like *The Red Poppy*, used new music by Reinhold Glière, or, like *The Golden Age*, by Dmitri Shostakovitch; others, like *Katerina*, were built around compositions of Anton Rubinstein and Adolphe Adam; but all preached the unallayed corruption of the ruling class and the monotonous virtue of the oppressed. However poor in dramaturgy, they were rich in technique and even in experiment, and there was even such novelty—*Katerina* was an example —as a ballet within a ballet. This was an invention of L. M. Lavrovsky, the choreographer, who built his ballet on the Serfs' Theater of the nineteenth century. An equally inventive creator of dance was V. I. Vainonen, who based *The Red*

Poppy in China and built *The Golden Age* on a milieu compounded of boxing and football where the most heroic and the most hounded athletes were Negroes.

II

The average share of common stock, the *Art Digest* pointed out on March 1, was selling for perhaps 10 per cent of its 1929 value, while great works of art were nowhere below 25 per cent of their prices four years earlier. And, in the face of bank failures and near panic, the Carnegie Institute of Pittsburgh announced that it would resume its annual international painting exhibit, suspended in 1931, with a $1,500 first prize, a $1,000 second prize and a $500 third prize. Against this background, the aging sculptor Paul Manship, who had designed the medal commemorating Roosevelt's inauguration, declared that "art is dying" because "this is a machine age. Work done with the hands in a machine age is no expression of the age, is personal art, and personal art can hardly be great . . . the only arts really of our age are the mechanical, the cheap trash of the movies, and so on. Besides, an art needs religion, belief in something, production for a purpose." Art may have been dying, but in that bitter week from Helena, Arkansas, to New York and Chicago and San Francisco, 216 separate art exhibitions were open every day.

Some of them were selling pictures as well as showing them. Business was brisk at the Chicago Art Institute's show of work by local painters, and the prices ranged from $100 to $750 a picture. More money was committed to art by the directors of the forthcoming Century of Progress Exhibition in Chicago, who had commissioned Thomas Hart Benton to paint a series of murals. Art magazines and the art sections of the Sunday newspapers were crowded with advertisements for summer art schools, winter art schools, art tours of Europe.

Much more than literature, painting was strongly influenced by the events of the moment. In the Prussian Academy of Art this influence was involuntary: the new German government forced the ouster of Heinrich Mann, Thomas Mann's elder brother; Kaethe Kollwitz, the outstanding woman artist of the Continent, and Martin Wagner, an architect—because they had signed a public appeal for a Communist–Social-Democratic coalition to block Hitler's barbarism. In the western world the artist's awareness of the social scene and his response to it varied from the out-and-out propaganda of the self-styled proletarian painters through the racial themes of the Harmon Foundation exhibit of work by 57 Negro painters and sculptors to the proclamation of the abstractionists against all racial, ideological or other limitations on art and against any form of oppression.

The outstanding American exemplar of propaganda in art flourished all this week in an exhibit at the pro-Communist John Reed Club in New York. Titled *The Social Viewpoint in Art*—*social* was the accepted euphenism for *leftist*—it embraced the work of such proletarians as George Biddle of the proud Philadelphia Biddles, Peggy Bacon, Benton, John Steuart Curry, Georg Grosz (who had just opened a school of painting in New York), Pop Hart, Louis Lozowick, Reginald Marsh, José Orozco, Boardman Robinson, Raphael Soyer, Benton Spruance (another product of the toiling masses of the Main Line) and the sculptors, Mary and William Zorach. While the exhibit was on, the club was seeking new works of art created specifically to mobilize sentiment for the liberation of Tom Mooney, an old I.W.W. agitator whose imprisonment for a fatal bombing was based on evidence of a nature that could hardly stand examination. Art's role in freeing Mooney (and thus depriving the Communist Party of a decade's beloved platitude) was to be fulfilled by a post-card campaign: the cards would carry reproductions of the winning creations. Artists themselves, including some of those represented in the John Reed Club's show, were violently divided on the ability of art to retain its artistic integrity if it were used as propaganda; the most vocal, of course, were the ultras on either side. In Great Britain it was the religious aspect of art that was under fire: the Bishop of Liverpool, the Dean of Canterbury and the Moderator of the Church of Scotland joined in an appeal for a new artistic concept of Christ that would replace the meekness and sentimentality of the tradition deriving from the Primitives with a virile Christ imbued with the characteristics that appealed to the more worldly postwar generation: those of a fighting, forceful leader.

In the same week, however, after the United States Customs had been finally persuaded that two books of photographs of the Sistine Chapel ceiling were not really so obscene as they seemed to the amateur moralists and aesthetes guarding the port of entry, S. H. Kress, the merchandising magnate, was launching his collection of Italian masters of the twelfth to the seventeenth centuries on a tour of the South and Southwest, all the expenses of which were met by him. He had procured in advance the floor plan of each gallery where the collection would be shown so that he could arrange the pictures to the best advantage in each city. Simultaneously, Sir Philip Sassoon opened his London house to a charity exhibit of paintings of the reigns of Louis XIV–XVI—the first private exhibit to which the Louvre had ever lent a picture. Sassoon was also fighting Parliament to repeal the ban on lending British-owned art masterpieces to other countries.

Such important American critics as Royal Cortissoz were only reluctantly beginning to see the possibility of some worth in the modern French painters—Cortissoz cautiously congratulated André Derain for turning against "self-expression"—whose most notable American champion was Mrs. Averell Harriman, then the proprietor of the Marie Harriman Gallery. She had scheduled for the first week of March a show of thirteen paintings by Cézanne, Renoir, Derain, van Gogh, Picasso and Matisse. Henri Matisse was the subject of a new book by Dr. Albert C. Barnes, inventor of argyrol and crusty proprietor of the already legendary Barnes Collection near Philadelphia; he considered Matisse the foremost painter of the day. But to Thomas Craven, another pillar of art criticism, reviewing the book, Matisse was only "a designer of stuff to be sold by the yard" because his art "lacks significance as a human document." Yet Craven and Cortissoz represented a peak in art criticism, which at the moment, if it was not concerned with "social values," was of either the roundhouse-swing or the lyric-rhapsodic school.

On one point virtually every American connected with art shared the same view: the so-called hobby painter. At the 23rd annual exhibit of the Associated Artists of Pittsburgh, the three top prizes, to the unanimous horror of artists and critics across the country, had been taken by part-time painters: John Kane, a house painter known as the "Henri Rousseau of Pittsburgh"; Ralph Bowman, a radio-repair man; and Alfred H. Bennett, a manufacturer of trousers. It was only the capitalist, Bennett, who devoted his paintings to the Depression. One of the proletarians, Bowman, was the center of a minor scandal when it was proved that his portrait of a woman, winner of the second prize, had been copied almost entirely from a Briton's portrait of Lady Diana Manners.

While Whistler's so-called "Portrait of His Mother" was touring the United States on loan from the French government, New York's major museums were following their various bents. During that week the Metropolitan opened its new Etruscan room; the Whitney Museum of American Art was showing works by 49 Chicago artists, including Ivan Albright and Grant Wood, famous for his "American Gothic"; and the Museum of Modern Art was holding a retrospective exhibit of the paintings of Maurice Sterne, one of the first to introduce the art of Bali to Americans. John Sloan, a distinguished painter whom no school could claim, announced the 17th annual no-jury independent show, for which each exhibiting artist paid an entry fee of $9; the deficit was guaranteed by Mrs. John D. Rockefeller Jr. and Mrs. Harry Payne Whitney.

The dominant individualism of the art world of the time was exemplified in a German print exhibit at the Roerich Museum: the intensely subjective work of Paul Klee side by side with the savage social satire of Georg Grosz. And, in New York as in other cities, the unknown painter was dependent on the efforts of the College Art Association and other voluntary groups for such work as they could find for him as a maker of murals for churches or as a teacher in settlement houses.

For the sculptor such opportunities were even rarer; indeed, only three sculptors were exhibiting in New York then —and one of them was a freak of aesthetics. Besides Brenda Putnam and Paul Fiene, there was Alceo Dossena, each of whose works in the National Art Galleries was officially certified by the Italian government as a fraud. Dossena was the greatest forger of sculpture in history, having devoted his life to absorbing completely the styles of such early artists as Donatello, Verocchio, Nicola Pisano, etc. He would meticulously conceive and execute a statue in the style of one of these masters, then damage and "restore" it to give it the aura of age and authenticity. Dr. Alfred Frankfurter, the great art expert, ascribed to Dossena "the personal nature of a child and the artistic talent of a great actor, of a stupendous impersonator." Probably the outstanding example of empathy in artistic history, he felt himself into the souls as well as the styles of the men he copied and then sold "their" work for $200 a statue to dealers who did not hesitate to charge as much as $100,000 in the firm belief that Dossena's work was what he said it was.

Three other sculptors—Americans who signed their work with their own names—achieved an undesired notoriety of another kind this week. Theirs sprang from their impregnable integrity. William Zorach, Gwen Lux and Robert Laurent had been commissioned to create works for the brand-new Radio City Music Hall, as a result of designs submitted by them; but the dynamic completed sculptures were put under interdict of the Music Hall's impresario, S. H. Rothafel, who had built a kind of folksy glamour for himself around the name of Roxy. He denounced as uniformly unbeautiful and out of keeping with the spirit of his theater Zorach's "The Spirit of the Dance," Miss Lux' "Eve" and Laurent's "Goose Girl." Only the creations of Gaston Lachaise above the main doors were found suitable for the high altar of American popular entertainment.

Sculpture was little better off elsewhere. In London's exhibit by the 7 and 5 Society, dominated by "a highly individual and artistic naturalism combined with imagination," according to contemporary critics, Henry Moore's drawings won an unexpected round of praise coupled with a salvo directed at his statues. Jacob Epstein was by now accepted for what he was, and in another exhibit of the week his sculpture was praised without reservation, as were the oils, water colors and drawings of Paul and John Nash, Eric Gill and Augustus John. More typical of the traditional British attitude toward art was the success of a show titled *Beautiful Women of the 19th Century,* painted by Sargent, Watts, Holman Hunt, Rossetti and Shannon.

In contrast not only to its musical activity but to its own legend, Paris' art world was strangely quiet. An exhibition of Delacroix' Moroccan paintings was well received, but such enthusiasm as manifested itself was reserved for the sculptor Ivan Mestrovič, who was showing in Paris for the first time since 1919. His greatness was unanimously hailed, and critic after critic made the point that Mestrovič was a great European sculptor, not merely, as he claimed, a Yugoslav. The power of his work overshadowed a simultaneous exhibit of sculpture by Dégas quite different from the ballet paintings usually associated with his name.

The painter who attracted most attention in Paris that week was a Swiss, Augusto Giacometti. Working in oil, fresco, mosaic or stained glass, he combined a certain impressionism of technique and nature effects with mysticism and an almost simplist primitivism. Completely overlooked by the rest of the world, the abstractionists—Arp, the American Calder, Fischli, Moholy-Nagy, Mondrian—had only one another for audience. Each had his own concept of the nature and function of art and the value of the representational works that all considered archaic; they united in believing that art must henceforth liberate itself from representation in order to capture essence. Most of them found it necessary to verbalize as well as to exemplify their philosophy of art; and some were notably articulate. But the irrational rhetoric of others contrasted oddly with their carefully ordered meaningless designs, comparable to the arid word-patterns of the objectivists in poetry.

Those who viewed cinema as an extension of the visual arts were joyously stunned by the first apparent effect of the bank holiday on Hollywood. On March 6, the first business day after the Presidential proclamation, the heads of the major California studios met to discuss whether they should not suspend all activities. The next day some studio chiefs went even further and suggested that the industry cut off all production until the Depression should end. But panic subsided, and with it, the hopes of those who appreciated the art of the motion picture.

Among the vast welter of films on the world's screens in that first week of March, very few stood out; and of these only three were made in America. One was as much French and English as it was American: *Topaze,* directed in Hollywood by H. d'Abbadie d'Arrast, was the film version of the comedy by Marcel Pagnol, and the screen script was fashioned by Benn Levy. Frank Borzage's *A Farewell to Arms* was an unexpectedly fine rendering of Hemingway's last great book. The third Hollywood product worthy of mention was a year old, but London was seeing it for the first time—*A Bill of Divorcement*, which first brought Katharine Hepburn to the film critics' attention through the direction of George Cukor. Only one English picture of the time had real merit: *Cavalcade*, directed by Frank Lloyd from the panoramic pageant of English history written by Noel Coward, who used the fortunes of a family to form the story line for the encapsulation of a stirring half-century. *Cavalcade* drew bitterly opposing reviews from two periodicals of the same political faith: *The Nation*, in New York, dropped leftist orthodoxy long enough to appraise the film on a purely artistic basis, while in London, *The New Statesman* damned it out of hand as an apologia for British imperialism and, in afterthought, branded it mawkish.

It was characteristic of all these pictures, as it was of virtually all the French and German masterpieces on the screen that week—and it was a time of cinematic artists of high rank —that they were concerned primarily with people as individuals, except for G. W. Pabst's moving *Kameradschaft*. The creators of motion pictures were not concerned with reflecting or dissecting the transitory phenomena of the time; their art was highly subjective. Even *Kameradschaft* was not especially of the moment in its treatment of a problem: using as a dramatic base a disaster in a coal mine that extended under the French-German border, Pabst concentrated on the ludicrous artificiality of all national frontiers and the essential comradeship of all men of common background, regardless of language or citizenship.

German movies dominated a large part of the scene in that week. One of the world's few women directors, Leontine

Sagan, created that torturing drama of the inner world of a girls' school, *Mädchen in Uniform*; Fritz Lang, the brilliant creator of *Metropolis* (which was still being shown as an artistic vision of the horror of the mechanized future), probed the psyche of a murderer with his unique *M,* introducing Peter Lorre to world audiences. On a broader scale, Phil Jutzi realized the lives of many various people in *Berlin Alexanderplatz*, from Alfred Döblin's novel; Richard Oswald molded the satiric laughter of *Der Hauptmann von Köpenick*. The disillusion of pre-Hitler Germany's lost generation filtered through the lives and problems of *Drei von der Tankstelle*, from Erich Remarque's novel; *Kreuzer Emden,* directed by Louis Ralph, effectively celebrated the glorious but crushing tragedy of the Kaiser's war at sea. Though it was made by an English producing firm, *Kongress Tanzt,* which Erik Charell directed, was a typical German operetta of the first rank that found its background in the Congress of Vienna in 1815.

The greatest cinematic artist of the time was a Frenchman, René Clair. As he had already shown in *Sous les toits de Paris* and *Le Million,* Clair was an inventor in this new art, a shaper of techniques and devices to make a vignette epitomize a life or a truth, trivial or profound. Endowed with the artist's feeling for proportion that enabled him to evoke sadness without sentimentality, belly-laughs without inanity, Clair used the camera like a painter's brush and the sound track like a composer's orchestra. New York was seeing for the first time an ostensible comedy, *À Nous la Liberté,* that was a mordant yet sympathetic satire on modern society from which Chaplin was to borrow the whole essence of his *Modern Times*; an even newer Clair film, *Quatorze Juillet,* was, in the same vein, showing Paris its inner self (and at the same time winning acclaim in London).

Where Clair was sometimes interested primarily in what might be called pure cinema—using camera and sound to evoke a mood or tell a chapter of a story, sometimes without a living actor—his colleague and rival, Julien Duvivier, plunged farther into the mind of a single figure to whom all the others in a film were subordinate. *Poil de Carotte,* the vividly introspective story of an unhappy child, was at this time making a lasting artistic reputation for Duvivier, who was also represented by *Sous la Lune du Maroc,* a picture that was equally skillful if less dramatic and incisive.

Even the Soviet cinema was not untouched by lyricism. Besides Alexander Dovzhenko's technically accomplished and unfailingly dull *Ivan,* a story of the construction of the Dnieperstroi power project, and V. Pudovkin's more dramatic *Potemkin,* a nationalist Soviet analogue of the German *Kreuzer Emden,* American audiences marveled at the poetic subjectivity of Pudovkin's *Life Is Beautiful.* Virtually barren of propaganda for either the workers' state or Russia's historic glories, *Life Is Beautiful* developed still further the best of the tradition of Dovzhenko and Sergei Eisenstein, almost reveling in magnificent composition and fluid beauty. Within a mile or two of the now catatonic capitalist Stock Exchange, the thin-walleted citizens of a bourgeois democracy took delight in unashamed romanticism sprung full-grown from the fatherland of the toiling masses.

III

The day after the inauguration was a Sunday. On that day *The New York Times* Book Review devoted a long critique to the first of the "proletarian" novels that were to make American literature so dreary in the next few years: Albert Halper's *Union Square,* which centered on New York's traditional forum for radical speechmakers. But, aside from this and V. F. Calverton's *Liberation of American Literature,* reviewed the same week in *The New English Weekly* of London, the serious writer in the United States and elsewhere was still profiting by the virile individualism and experiment of the 1920's, and the outstanding characteristic of his work was its freshness and variety. Only a few astute observers like Edith Wharton, who predicted the domination of the novel by "the man with the dinner-pail," sensed the beginning of that intellectual clique that in a few years would seek to impose on the creative mind what Tocqueville had so aptly branded, 100 years earlier, "the tyranny of the majority." In the novel, the short story, poetry, drama, even in criticism, writers were concerned predominantly with people and their problems and pleasures.

The two exceptions were in a pattern that soon became a cliché. *Union Square*'s purpose was primarily to drive home the socio-political message of the malaise of bourgeois capitalism and the messianic hope of salvation through the proletariat. Calverton, a dogged Stalinist untroubled by heretical doubt and proof against Trotsky's rule that even proletarian art must be judged by artistic standards, envisaged the "liberation" of literature by way of its enlistment exclusively in the ranks of the revolution, and he declared as an article of faith that, in the art of literature, literary craftsmanship was decidedly secondary. "This is a burden," T. S. Eliot observed in *The Criterion,* "with which Mr. Calverton is not overladen."

Books sold, on the average, at $2.50 a copy; Modern Library reprints were 95 cents. The paperback experiments of the first depression years had been abandoned, but some of the "little" magazines had survived. *Story,* like most of the other expatriates, had come back from Majorca and issued its first American-published number this week; Harriet Monroe's gallant *Poetry* continued to publish every month from Chicago, though to do so it had to interlace its poems and critiques with unabashed appeals to its readers for subsidies.

The two outstanding literary weeklies—*The New York Times* Book Review and *The Saturday Review of Literature*

—were quantitatively thin but admirably rich in quality. Untainted by "cute" personality-charged columns or capsule candid colloquies with writers of high or low degree, the *Times* dealt on an adult level with important books and with literary questions; even its advertisements were predominantly concerned with serious writing rather than manuals of sexual technique or other sops to the uninvited (or uninviting). It was also a journal of literary news: of the founding of writers' seminars (the doctrinaire's jargon term, *workshop,* was unknown in this context) on East Seventeenth Street, where experiment and group criticism were emphasised, and at the uptown Barbizon Hotel for Women, where tea was served weekly; of the arrival of Walter de la Mare's first book of poetry in six years at the offices of Alfred A. Knopf; of a forthcoming Hemingway limited edition; of the election of James Truslow Adams, philosophy teacher, stockbroker, Orientalist and author of *The March of Democracy* and *The Epic of America,* as a fellow of the Royal Society of Literature; of the forthcoming publication of *The Land Reclaimed,* by a leading Soviet novelist, Mikhail Sholokhov, and of *Little Man, What Now?,* by the German, Hans Fallada; of the inception of a course in writing poetry at the College of the City of New York.

Equally sparse in pages and single-minded in purpose, the *Saturday Review* was guided by Henry Seidel Canby, who was not afflicted with messianic shingles. In early March its poetry editor, William Rose Benét, was castigating the vanity presses that were systematically victimizing the writer of even the most incompetent verse. Paradoxically, these literary confidence rackets flourished much more in the depressed economy of the time than in earlier or later periods of prosperity. The *Saturday Review,* besides catering to the collector of rare books with a special weekly article, regularly reviewed the literary situation in other countries, as did the *Times.* Both, this week, paid handsome but measured tribute to two authors who had recently died: John Galsworthy and George Moore.

The advertisements in the early March issues of these two reviews offered the reader with a bit of money (or access to a public library) a kaleidoscope of quality in books: *Mark Twain's America*, by Bernard de Voto; Winston Churchill's *Amid These Storms*; the fourth volume of Mark Sullivan's monumental history, *Our Times*; Georgette Leblanc's *Souvenirs* of her twenty years with Maurice Maeterlinck; *The Two Thieves*, somber, introspective short stories by T. F. Powys, and *A Philosophy of Solitude*, a soberly ecstatic book of reflection by his even more introverted and mystic brother, John Cowper Powys; *Human Nature*, short stories by Edith Wharton, who was not ashamed to write about the upper strata of American society; Galsworthy's last essays, *Candelabra*; D. H. Lawrence's posthumous short-story collection, *The Lovely Lady*, in which the dominant common theme of the cameolike tales was the struggle of the individual, of whatever class or education, to achieve self-recognition and self-acceptance; *Special Delivery*, a collection of essays in which James Branch Cabell remained the unregenerate poetic-ironic fantasist; a collection of introspective poems by a highly controversial Southern author, William Faulkner's *The Green Bough*, and another poetic volume, *Give Your Heart to the Hawks*, by the California poet Robinson Jeffers, whose rolling free verse was so frequently compared with the best of the Greek tragedies.

Unprofitable though poetry is to publishers in the best of times, there was more of it in that week when there was less money than ever—the Oxford University Press' *Golden Book of Italian Poetry*, which made no concessions to the unilingual; Oliver Wells' *Anthology of the Younger Poets*, introduced by Archibald MacLeish; T. S. Eliot's enigma, *Sweeney Agonistes*; the almost impressionist lyrics of *No Retreat*, by Horace Gregory, the sensitive translator of Catullus to whom the look of a poem on paper was as important as the music and the meaning of the words; *Key West* and *Collected Poems* by Hart Crane, that tragic suicide whose ecstasies and protests were equally tortured and who imposed an unswerving intellectual discipline on every emotion, personal or cosmic. There was also the *Objectivists' Anthology*; the objectivists were to literature what the abstractionists were to painting. They stressed craftsmanship above content and defined a poem as a job, a piece of work. Of them all, William Carlos Williams, the New Jersey physician, was perhaps the most intelligible, while Kenneth Rexroth anticipated the "beat" poets by a quarter-century in his rejection of both intellection and emotion, his exhaustive cataloguing of nouns and verbs without a nod to relevance.

Students of George Bernard Shaw had his new satiric novella, *The Adventures of the Black Girl in Her Search for God,* and Professor Archibald Henderson's biographical critique, *Bernard Shaw: Playboy and Prophet.* There was the lumbering lack of artistry of James T. Farrell's *Gashouse McGinty*; Thorne Smith's rollicking high comedy, *The Bishop's Jaegers*; L. A. G. Strong's perceptive short stories in *Don Juan and the Wheelbarrow*; the sentimental, sensitive, almost Kafka-esque expressionist fantasy of Leonhard Frank's evocation of his native Würzburg in *The Singers.* There was also a cluster of critical bibliographies of Hemingway, Lawrence, Katherine Mansfield.

In every country there were the esoteric quarterlies like *The Hound and Horn* and *The Virginia Quarterly* in the United States, or Eliot's *The Criterion* in England—publications that moved on the highest intellectual level of literature, criticism and philosophy. Somewhat below this snow line were the more widely read literary magazines whose essays and fiction quite accurately reflected the cultural climates of their respective countries. In *Harper's, Scribner's* and *The Atlantic* the orthodoxy of the veteran critics mingled incongruously with the short fiction of newer writers and, notably in *Scribner's,* virtually the last Hemingway stories in the pure unforced genre of his first and best period (at the same moment he was trumpeting his virility elsewhere with such documentation as he could muster and the mails would allow).

The major French literary magazines, the *Nouvelle Revue Française* and the *Mercure de France,* were not only much thicker than their English-language contemporaries but considerably more sophisticated. One of the most stimulating literary reviews in any language, the *N.R.F.* offered a collection of related excerpts from a psychoanalytic case history whose literary style reflected the essential difference between European and American preparation for the professions: the doctor could compose sentences. This was followed by a newly discovered anticlerical sketch by Stendhal and the working plan of the novel for which he had intended it. Paul Valéry told how a poet feels when he has achieved such eminence that he can attend a course on his works at the Sorbonne, and Julien Benda, reasoning like a logician and writing like a poet, called on the intellectuals of Europe to internationalize the Continent by putting aside the rivalry of national pride and the enforcement of national guilt. Appropriately, the third installment of André Malraux's great novel, *La Condition Humaine,* came next.

Ramon Fernandez, obviously influenced by that monument of the philosophy of history, José Ortega y Gasset's *The Revolt of the Masses,* and disgusted by authoritarianism, proclaimed that only the natural interplay of democratic forces could and must produce the élite that the world needed. "Fascism and Bolshevism," he wrote, "which govern the masses by adopting the vision and sentiment of the lowest, show that the contemporary élite assumes the faults of the mass it intends to govern," whereas the only genuine and acceptable élite must accept the necessary diversity of society, dedicate itself to principle, thought and the public good, and constantly depend for its tenure on forever proving its worth by its achievements within the democratic framework.

Like the *Mercure de France*—and indeed most other similar publications in Europe—the *N.R.F.* made a point of calling to its readers' attention worth-while fiction, criticism and other writing in competitive reviews. The *Mercure*, though its issue closed with a financial review, was otherwise more interested in the problems of the littérateur, the student of human behavior and the diplomat, as evidenced by the prominence it gave to a scholarly essay on Montaigne; a fascinating study of the psychology of sexual excitation, *Eros couturier*—its theme was the function of artful dress in adding to the momentary, localized sexual act the timeless, limitless dream—and a thorough study of the indoctrination of German youth that had completed the groundwork for Nazism even before Hitler was born.

Germany's own literary magazines were themselves sharply divided: those that, like *Die neue Rundschau*, recognized only the nation of the intellect; and those others, like *Die neue Literatur*, that refused to look over the walls of traditional German romanticism and persecution complex. *Die neue Literatur* was the voice of intellectual nationalism, dwelling verbosely on such themes as *Homeland* and *Ancestors* and *World Paths of German Culture*; reluctantly hailing the sixtieth birthday of Jakob Wassermann by calling him "the poet of the German tragedy of our time," the celebrator of the pure hero standing alone against a lying, sullying world. Its literary and artistic judgments were cast in a similar mold, and such little fiction and poetry as it printed clung to the murky romantic tradition.

Die neue Rundschau, in what was very nearly its last free issue, remained loyal to a deeper and broader cultural heritage, the European. The number that appeared when Hitler was already Chancellor included among its writers Heinrich and Thomas Mann, Wassermann; Jean Giono of France; Agnes Smedley, the American Communist; Stefan Zweig, Hermann Hesse and Alfred Döblin; it dared to promise for the next month Aldous Huxley, D. H. Lawrence and Heinrich Hauser. Its tribute to Wassermann was hearty and purely literary. Rather optimistically, it featured an article that concluded, after examining various German efforts to create "the total state," that this would be a "practical and political impossibility" because such a state could never control more than the physical and economic life of its citizens. Far more of this magazine than of *Die neue Literatur* was devoted to creative work: a serialized highly mystic-symbolic play by Ferdinand Bruckner, a would-be disciple of Pirandello; a short story by Giono that was a masterpiece of cynical morbidity; a translation from Shaw in which his frequently labored and self-conscious wit suffered pitiably; a forceful appeal by Döblin for concentration on truths beyond the war in Manchuria or the cabbage price in Germany; one of the first confessions of a disillusioned Communist, excerpts from Liam O'Flaherty's book on his tour to Russia.

A dichotomy somewhat similar to the German marked the Italian publications of early March, 1933; but all united in celebrating the seventieth birthday of Gabriele d'Annunzio, now almost a hermit in his feudal keep after a picturesque life as poet, flier, lover and herald of Fascism. No publication issued in Italy, of course, criticized the regime or its philosophy; on the other hand, both were ignored far more than they were mentioned by those writers who remained in Italy. Premier Mussolini considered himself one of them—and he was probably the best educated and most articulate chief of government then practicing—and had himself written the article on Fascism for the latest edition of the *Italian Encyclopedia,* which had just been published. In it the founder of Fascism told the middle class quite baldly that its destruction was one of his primary goals. Mussolini had also just published a biography of his brother, Arnaldo, and it was reviewed this week in *Pègaso,* a literary magazine of the first rank which paid somewhat more lip service to the government than did its more virile compeer, *La nuova antologia.*

Rather surprisingly, in view of Fascism's constant stridencies against the decadent democracies, *Pègaso* paid a great deal of attention to French and English books; it was also a vehicle for that outstanding novelist of the post-Mussolini period, Elio Vittorini. In the March issue a short story by Giani Stuparich, *Return of the Father,* was typical of the Italian literature of the period in its concentration on the problems of the individual divorced from politics. A beautiful exploration of the constantly shifting emotions in the relations of a father and his little boy, the story ended in a weary despair and loneliness; and the very word *loneliness* appeared in so much Italian writing, both creative and critical, at this time that it began to seem almost a code signal of distress, a disguised cry of protest at the ubiquity of the mass rule and the mass leader. Even *Pègaso*'s editorial director, Ugo Ojetti, reviewing Mussolini's biography of his brother, described loneliness as *Il Duce*'s dominant trait.

The same hunger for solitude characterized much of the writing in *La nuova antologia,* a much bigger magazine: *The Love of Solitude in Petrarch,* a critical study by Carlo Segre; *Dolphins and Islands,* a very short story made up of quick shifts of uneasy moods and restless action; a chapter from a sophisticated but sad novel by Raul Radice. In sharp contrast was an acrid selection of thirty sonnets of Giuseppe Gioacchini Belli, a nineteenth-century poet who wrote bitingly ironic verse, much of it anticlerical, in one of the numerous dialects. An incisive study, *The Collapse of Hollywood,* contrasted the vapidity and falsity of the average American film with the much higher level of French, German and Russian cinema, predicting the ultimate dominance of Italian directors.

What is perhaps most surprising in this magazine dependent for its continuance on the whim of an autocracy is the exhaustive and objective study of contemporary Soviet literature by Renato Poggioli. It is virtually the only door opened for the West at that time on what was being written in Russia. Leonid Leonov had just published a new novel, *Sot'*, that abandoned all the Dostoevskian influences of his earlier books to become an impersonal story of a construction project reading less like a novel than like a progress report, in which respect it was almost typical of Soviet fiction. Yet some Soviet writers were still genuine artists capable of creating characters that lived. One was Boris Pilniak, author of *The Volga Flows to the Caspian*. To Poggioli in 1933 the greatest Russian writer to emerge since the Revolution was the poet and novelist Boris Pasternak, who was also the translator of Rainer Maria Rilke and the author of a volume of short stories as well as two books of poetry: *Life, My Sister,* and *Themes and Variations*. Formed by a sublime and intimate law of harmony, Poggioli wrote, Pasternak's stories still epitomized the aesthetic and the spirit of a society that had made *soul* an obscene word but could not keep a great writer from exalting it with unfaltering and unique recognition.

Soul was much more explicitly emphasized in contemporary German books such as Gerhart Hauptmann's *Folk and Spirit* and Prof. Ernst Bergmann's bafflingly metaphysical treatise, *The Spirit of Experience and the Mother Spirit, Sociosophy of the Sexes*. German bookshops were crowded in this first week of March, when the politically triumphant Nazis were still only sparsely represented in print by such as Ernst Jünger, with *The Worker*, a plan for mobilizing labor to serve the State and displace the middle class, and two cries for a cultural Fascism: *Educational Experiment: National Death,* by Wilhelm Hartnacht, and Reinhold Scherer's *The Needs of the Teaching Profession,* laying down a detailed plan for integrating all schools with the camps of the misnamed *Freiwilliger Arbeitsdienst,* which contained a quarter-million iron-disciplined young Siegfrieds determined to liberate their common Brünnhilde, Germany, for the Third Reich. But what the literate German was buying in quantity was an intoxicating variety of the best (and second-best) of many countries:

The Man Without Character, a philosophical novel by Robert Musil; Ilya Ehrenburg's *Moscow Does Not Believe in Tears,* a Communist's almost lyric novel of émigrés in Paris; two studies of Rilke; books by and about Hauptmann; Schnitzler's short stories; *Brothers and Enemies,* by that great European who was incidentally an Italian, Count Carlo Sforza; Joseph Conrad, Hugo von Hofmannsthal, Giono, Antoine de St.-Exupéry, Sinclair Lewis' sorry best-seller, *Ann Vickers;* Shaw's 1879 novel, *Immaturity* (in German, *New Wine*), and Henderson's *Conversations with Bernard Shaw;* the two unrelated von Unruhs, Friedrich Franz, who studied the greatest minds of the Christian era for answers to the problems troubling a war veteran, and Fritz, who took the Monaco motor race as the basis for a harsh realist-expressionist satire on materialism that was almost banned in Frankfort; Boris Sapir's *Dostoievski and Tolstoi on the Problem of Right.*

It was also announced that on National Book Day, whose theme this year was *Folk and Book,* the Goethe Medal for Poetry would be awarded to Fernando de los Rios, Education Minister of that Spanish republic that Hitler would be instrumental in destroying a few years later—a country as poor in writers as it was in everything else. Spaniards were still debating *The Revolt of the Masses,* trying to hope that Ortega's vision of the degeneration of democracy into mass-man statism was false, and reading a new omnibus volume of his work, one sentence of which was the key to the thinking of this disciple of Miguel de Unamuno: "The European stands alone, without the living dead at his side: like Peter

Schlemihl, he has lost his shadow. That is what always happens when midday arrives." Ramón Pérez de Ayala, the ambassador to London, published an allegorical novel, *The King of Paradox*, almost simultaneously with Gabriel Miró's *Our Father San Daniel*, a long poem of a novel impregnated with melancholy.

French publishers' lists were among the smallest of the week: G. Armand's *Obscénité, pudeur,* which, in far more intellectualised fashion, covered much of the ground broken a few years earlier by D. H. Lawrence in *Pornography and Obscenity; Rabelais and Renaissance Comedy,* by Ronald de Carvalho; Gabriel Fauré's *Italian Rendezvous; L'anti-tête,* by that veteran of every artistic splinter movement of the century, Tristan Tzara; *Pipe-chien,* by Francis Jammes, a self-directed prose poet who took from many schools and adhered to none; Marshal Joffre's *Memoirs;* a biography of Richard Wagner by Guy de Pourtalès, who was accused of trying to emulate André Maurois without any of the latter's objectivity, depth or perception; François Mauriac's *The Frontenac Mystery,* in which the austere novelist for the first time abandoned his characteristic detachment to take a stand and judge his characters; and Louis-Ferdinand Céline's *Voyage au bout de la nuit,* described by Marcel Acland in the *N.R.F.* as an ultranaturalist story of physical and moral misery told in the language of guttersnipe and gourmet, pimp and poet. But Acland insisted, with the measured intelligence typical of the best French thought, on the right of the artist to choose any subject and any treatment and on the irrelevance of moral judgments in assaying a work of art.

Diversity rather than volume characterized Italian bookshops. There was Luigi Pirandello's new play, *Trovarsi*; there were also three books by military commanders—memoirs by Joffre of France and Marshal Italo Balbo and General Rodolfo Graziani of Italy—and the inevitable panegyric to Mussolini, Francesco Sapori's *L'arte e il Duce,* "a record of what Fascism has done for Italian art," as well as another apologia for Fascism, Maria Missiroli's *Italy Today.* Giovanni Papini's *Life of Christ* was in a new edition; so were Petrarch's works; and there were new translations of Shakespeare, Maeterlinck and Zweig.

By contrast, London bookshops offered a bewildering choice, though much less than that available to the American reader. In *Jocasta's Crime* Lord Raglan studied the incest taboo from a purely anthropological viewpoint, strenuously opposing attempts to explain the views and feelings of the ancients in terms of modern man and modern culture. Edward J. Dent was the author of a biography of that little-known but influential composer, Ferruccio Busoni. D. H. Lawrence, three years dead, was still a vital force with his just published fascinating study, *Etruscan Places,* and John Middleton Murry's whining, self-exonerating *Reminiscences of D. H. Lawrence.* Lawrence's staunch friend, Richard Aldington, in his new novel *All Men Are Enemies,* retreated to a degree from the incredible bitterness of his *Death of a Hero.*

Albert Schweitzer's *My Life and Thought* was much in demand; so was the classic *Works and Days* of Hesiod. C. Day Lewis' *The Magnetic Mountain* inaugurated the second series of the Hogarth Living Poets, published by Leonard and Virginia Woolf; Hugh l'Anson Fausset brought out a study of Wordsworth, *The Lost Leader,* and a reissue of his *Samuel Taylor Coleridge.* Another reissue was *The Unseen Assassins* by Sir Norman Angell, a distinguished unorthodox economist and pacifist who shared with Earl Russell the quality of articulateness so rare among social scientists. And two Americans fascinated the English reader: James Gould Cozzens with *A Cure of Flesh,* based on an imagined typhoid epidemic in Connecticut, and William Faulkner with

Light in August, his finest novel since *The Sound and the Fury.* Luigi Pirandello's short stories, *Better Think Twice About It,* embodied, according to *The Times Literary Supplement,* "that parodoxical justice that may well be called Pirandellian"—a most fitting book for this week of paradox in plethora.

CHAPTER **19**

It's Fun to Wear Bangs
This Season

IT WAS a week in an eternity of stress, bewilderment and misery; it was also a week in a time of elegance and taste that thrived on variety and individuality. Millions of people lacked the money for a night's shelter or a day's food; but thousands of dollars, pounds, francs, marks, were spent on a party, a Bugatti two-seater, a Garmisch-Partenkirchen skiing holiday, a Cartier bracelet, a Vionnet gown. American newspapers gave prizes for economy menus and *Vogue* devoted exquisitely designed pages to Cecil Beaton's *froufrou* gossip and drawings of his friends in international society.

It was a week when *Vogue* was struck particularly by the fact that *Parisiennes* would be wearing their hair back from the face, with big loose curls low on the neck; ears were, variously, completely hidden, piquantly hinted at or brazenly displayed. In New York, however, many women would "find it fun to have bangs this season." Their hats looked like hats; the hugging cloches of the 1920's, the big soft hats that half-hid, half-framed the face, and a new trend toward higher

229

Cossack caps, as well as a few hats knitted or crocheted in a Watteau mode.

The waist, by agreement between *haute couture* and nature, was anatomically defined. Dresses, suits and coats reached halfway down the calf in a graceful long line that, for once, fashion writers were correct in calling "exciting." Young girls were encased in much flouncing and ruching ($10.75 to $16.75 for an Easter dress at some of New York's finer shops); unlike *Parisiennes*, mature American women preferred some ornamentation or emphasis at the shoulders, and many dresses used capes or cowl collars. But the American modes owed their origin to the rulers of Paris: Molyneux, Agnès, Vionnet, Chanel, Schiaparelli, joined by Daché for the really chic hats. Suits were never of one color; skirts and jackets were in matching or contrasting colors, usually solid; though, as in dresses, stripes, checks, dots and plaids won great favor.

The coat-dress ensemble had many followers and it gained in effect by keeping the coat to three-quarter length. Russeks in New York was preaching the gospel of the zipper as the answer to all the problems of snaps or hooks and eyes; and many fabric makers proudly announced their use of Lastex. In Paris, the jeweled clip on dress or suit jacket was very new; chiffon was widely used on both sides of the Atlantic. The new spring coats were sometimes fur-trimmed, sometimes made of cotton, and, like the hip-length suit jackets, they were smartly but softly tailored.

There was a fashion in dogs, too: it was the Welsh or the cairn terrier. But the Westminster show gave its highest award to an airedale and the cocker spaniel was ranked as the most popular breed.

For the bachelor the smart thing was to cook dinner in his flat for his lady. *Vogue* showed a half-page photograph of the socially impeccable William Rhinelander Stewart in a dinner jacket bending over a curiously antiquated black-

enameled stove. Missing from the portrait, of course, were
the chef who prepared the repast and the butler who served
it.

In *Vogue,* as in a few other carefully chosen publications,
Cadillac bought a beautifully designed page to portray, in
a line drawing, its $7,000-plus 16-cylinder car. There were
barely two dozen words on the page: they conveyed the message that the company would build only 400 of these luxury
vehicles during the year. In England, the humbler Humber
emulated the Lautrec-like poster type of advertising favored
by Bugatti; in Germany, Daimler-Benz employed dramatic
photographs of its virile SS and 380-K Mercedes-Benz. Europe's finest coach builders continued to design bodies for
such automotive gems as Isotta-Fraschini, while New York
used-car dealers offered the same make, with equally elegant bodies, at as little as $250 for a five-year-old car.

The world's automobile names were in the hundreds. General Motors proudly announced No-Draft Ventilation, with
vertical panes that swung outward, and skirted fenders, as
if the Europeans had not already been doing it for some time;
Chrysler vaunted its floating power, achieved by means of
newly located rubber engine mountings; and Daimler in
England stressed its fluid flywheel, which made it unnecessary to use the clutch at all in changing gears while other British makers, adopting synchro-mesh transmissions, had to stop
at the claim that this device made it unnecessary to "double-
declutch" when shifting.

In America the outstanding car was the magnificently en-
gineered Duesenberg, whose unbodied chassis cost $10,000.
But the real advances were being offered in the English and
Continental markets, where Talbot and Siddeley fitted pre-
selector gearboxes, Bugatti and Hispano-Suiza used double
overhead camshafts, Adler, Citroën and Tracta built only
front-wheel-drive cars and Mercedes-Benz employed independent suspension on all four wheels. A few American

makers dared to compete, technologically and in races; the outstanding marque was Stutz. Americans knew the Auburn, too, and the Cord, the Essex, the Hudson, the Franklin, the Graham, the Hupmobile, the Lafayette, the La Salle, the Marmon, the Pierce Arrow; but Europeans had a wealth of cars, famous and reliable—Ariès, B.N.C., Chenard & Walcker, Darracq, Delage, Delahaye, Hotchkiss, Georges Irat, Lorraine Dietrich, Amilcar, Rolland-Pilain, Cottin et Desgouttes, Salmson, Tracta, Voisin, Th. Schneider, Rochet-Schneider, Mathis, Rosengart in France; F.N. and Minerva in Belgium; Adler, Audi, Dixi, Horch and Wanderer in Germany; Steyr in Austria; Itala and O.M. in Italy—that were to disappear in the next few years, like the Lanchester, Invicta and Talbot in England.

It was the heyday of the multicylinder engine: in America, the 12 and 16-cylinder Cadillac, the 12-cylinder Packard and the 16-cylinder Marmon; abroad, the 12-cylinder Voisin and Hispano. Such technological advances as hydraulic brakes, all-steel bodies and free-wheeling were, paradoxically, limited in the United States to cheaper and medium-priced cars.

Advertising in American magazines was not much utilized by the automotive industry during this week. Cosmetics—notably a new deodorant used like a lipstick—household goods, including a self-defrosting refrigerator (the Kelvinator), life insurance, toothpastes, ointments—Pepsodent Antiseptic stood out with its adaptability to internal or external use for colds, halitosis, cuts, chapped hands, dandruff, body odor, after-shave discomfort, athlete's foot and plain tired foot—and food products were the major customers of the popular publications.

These magazines were rather prosaic. An example is *The Saturday Evening Post* of March 4—a magazine intended for what its publishers considered, and probably correctly, the typical American middle-class family. A solid if not stolid publication, it made such women's magazines as *The Woman's Home Companion* seem almost flighty.

A property of the Curtis Publishing Co., which owned two outstanding newspapers, the *Public Ledger* in Philadelphia and the *Evening Post* in New York, *The Saturday Evening Post* shared the newspapers' conservatism if not their intellectual qualities. The most obvious manifestation of this antipathy to change was the uninterrupted succession of inline Cooper type that headed every article, story, serial and department in the magazine. Its name appeared on the cover in solid letters of the same old-type face followed by the notation that it had been founded by Benjamin Franklin.

The March 4 issue opened with an article by William Allen White, a well-known political journalist of the time: "Herbert Hoover—The Last of the Old Presidents or the First of the New?" Without defining either type of President or answering the question, White used several thousand words to present his thesis that if Hoover was repugnant to progressives because of his old-fashioned views, he was equally unacceptable to conservatives because of his exercise of executive power. This was followed by two short stories— "The Happy Hour" by Frederick Hazlitt Brennan, a contemporary fiction factory, which was typically popular-magazine boy-and-girl material; and "Flight from Frances," a mildly humorous, predominantly folksy story about married life by Agnes B. Hale. All fiction in *The Post* was illustrated with black and white drawings and occasional color, by artists Anton Otto Fischer, William C. Hoople, John La Gatta, Ralph Pallen Coleman and Robert W. Crowther.

Two articles followed the fiction: a picaresque true-adventure story by C. E. Scoggins, who had been a prospector in the Old West and Alaska, and an obvious potboiler about a writer's method of working by F. Scott Fitzgerald. These, like all *Post* articles, used photographs generously. Another fiction factory, Thomas Beer, contributed one of the high-life romances that were a weekly staple of the magazine.

Then there was an article by a Post stand-by, Samuel Crowther: "Breaking the Deadlock," a popularization of orthodox economics leavened with an appeal to the country to spend its way out of the Depression without either deficit financing or inflation, simply by using individual and corporate wealth. For relaxation, the reader could then turn to "Apple Time," a short story about small business and just folks by Leonard H. Nason.

The editorial page was placed uncompromisingly in the body of the magazine. Its three editorials said the same thing in different ways: the nation needed the old pioneer virtues now, when the wolf and the Indian had been replaced by the tax gatherer and the danger of insensate public and private spending loomed in every possible direction. But re-assurance lay ahead in Thomas H. Phillips' article, "Debunking Mars' Newest Toys": "As guns have improved," Phillips contended, "they have, like wars, become less deadly." He lashed scornfully at the prophets of massive aerial bombing, citing the toll of 14,000 planes in the First World War against a score of no substantial damage to any target, and he laughed most loudly at H. G. Wells' prediction of "atomic bombs" (the quotation marks are Phillips') !

Back among the full-page advertisements for Campbell's Soup and other necessities—all packed solid with type that must have discouraged any prospective reader—was the anonymous "Tale of a Bear," an exceptionally dull account of short-selling and covering in the bear market. After that came the serial, Charles Francis Coe's *Vigilante,* a set-piece based on the drama of politics, crime and the reform movement. Much farther back in the magazine, to emphasize *The Post*'s lack of intellectual pretension, was a book review page labeled *The Literary Lowbrow, Who Reads for Amusement;* but the Lowbrow rather belied his heading by his castigation of popular fiction and his praise for such books as William March's *Company K* and Gilbert Seldes' *Years of the Locust.*

The advertisements were numerous and uniformly overcrowded with type, though the selling was never hammerhard. Life insurance companies bought full pages crammed with hortatory copy urging the need for "security" for the policy-holder and his near and dear. Automotive-accessory makers were verbose about their wares (Sealed Power Piston Rings called attention also to the company's weekly radio program, *Singing Cylinders,* on the NBC network). The makers of yeast and laxatives were no more reticent, though far more euphemistic, in touting the ability of their products to relieve and then prevent constipation. That word was never mentioned, though clinical descriptions of its symptoms and consequences were considerably more offensive.

Among other words not used in newspapers and popular magazines of the time were cancer, tuberculosis, rape, gonorrhea, syphilis. These were referred to in the order named as a lingering illness, a wasting disease, assault and social diseases. In the matter of a woman who was beaten and raped, this led to peculiar sentences such as: "The assailant struck the woman on the head with a club, knocked out three of her teeth, kicked her in the ribs and then assaulted her." Somehow the message came across.

What was most notable in all the advertisements was the uniform effort to sell the product on whatever merits might be claimed for it and the complete and (retrospectively) refreshing absence of exploitation of sexual appetite to create a hunger for merchandise.

Only one advertisement utilized snob appeal, and that was subtly exploited in the relatively clean page of picture and copy devoted to La Salle automobiles. Between-The-Acts Little Cigars, on the other hand, brashly stressed economy: "When you throw away a 15-cent cigar half-smoked, you throw away 7½ cents. Repeat the process and you've thrown away the price of ten B.T.A.s." Spud, the mentholated cigarette, rhapsodized on "mouth-happiness," while Camel cigarettes continued its series labeled: *It's Fun to Be Fooled —It's More Fun to Know*." These advertisements illustrated, in color, a trick of magic, explained it, and worked into the company's theme: "The trick in cigarette making is coolness," in which Camels excelled because they burned more slowly. In odd corners *The Post* itself advertised for readers to supplement their incomes or indeed win independence by selling subscriptions. There were also a few correspondence-school advertisements, and others for corn removers, denture adhesives, pre-cut summer cottages in kit form at $165, power lawn mowers, a patent lawyer, and inexpensive articles of clothing available by mail.

The reader who had worked his way to the end of the magazine found the promise of the next issue: the first of three articles by Mark Sullivan on "Hoover and the Depression"; fiction by Sophie Kerr, a reliable romancer; Lucian Cary, whose stories centered on boxing; and Clarence Budington Kelland. There would be articles on politics, how trans-Atlantic fliers had profited from their exploits (it was less than six years since Lindbergh's pioneer flight), how the five-year-old talking movie achieved its sound effects, and the problems of a woman who married great wealth.

The Crowell Publishing Co.'s *Woman's Home Companion* was marked by an infinitely lighter and more skillful touch in both advertising and editorial content. All its fiction— five stories and two serials—was well illustrated in color, as were some of its articles. One of the illustrators, Mario Cooper, showed a surprising blend of the influence of Matisse and Modigliani. The others were Malthe Hesselriis, John Allen Maxwell, James M. Preston, John J. Gannam, Frederick Chapman, Katharine Sturges and Clayton Knight.

Virtually all the articles dealt with baby care, health, interior decoration, house renovation, cooking and serving meals, gardening and fashions. The only recognition of wider problems appeared on the editorial page, whose theme, rather astonishingly, seemed to be that perhaps it was America's own stupidity and greed that had brought on the Depression and that it was now time to make sure that everyone got the share of the national wealth to which he was entitled.

Pearl Buck was represented with a story about China, of course. Sara Haardt (who later married H. L. Mencken) was the author of "Tomboy," an excellent, sensitive and completely unsentimental story about children. James Warner Bellah, another fiction machine of the time, contributed a he-man story about aviation, and Paul Jones, a college professor, was the author of a story recounting the conflict in marriage arising from the union of an American soldier and a French working girl. One of the serials, Katharine Newlin Burt's *Beggars All,* was a mystery. The other, Samuel Jesse Warshawsky's *The Heart Compelled,* dealt with a rich woman who, when her son returns from the First World War blind and shell-shocked, devotes herself to pacifism and enters politics to fight against war. Projecting into the Presidential elections of 1936 and 1940, the author, who was not devoid of skill, showed no charity for the professional politician.

The advertising in *The Companion,* of course, dealt primarily with the same fields as the articles: the home, the family, health. But it was for the most part prepared with a light hand and a more skillful subtlety than that in *The Post.* One notable exception was the full page devoted to Jergens' Lotion (for the hands). Beside a photograph of a handsome man clutching a beautiful girl's palm to his cheek there was a block of copy:

> "Your dear little hands," he murmured, "they're wonderful." . . . Breathless—he kisses her rose-leaf palm. Could humdrum, roughened hands stir his heart this way?

The advertiser of that period was not unaware of the use of fear, especially fear of failure. A series of drawings showed what happened to a woman who, not knowing her husband was bringing a dinner guest to whom he had boasted of her cuisine, had bought some nameless cheap mustard instead of French's. Parental fear was exploited by General Foods, which warned parents that "less [sic] than 16% of children who drank coffee attained good marks in school. Over 45% of those who did not drink coffee attained good marks." The solution, of course, was the company's Postum. Even less subtle was Jergens' competitor, Hinds, the maker of a honey and almond hand cream: "She looked the lady of leisure— but her hands shrieked: 'Housework!' "

What was delicately known as "feminine hygiene" occupied other advertisers. One was the maker of "Phantom Kotex—so called because you scarcely realize you are wearing it." Another worked in an even more sensitive field, as his careful copy showed: "Can a married woman ever feel safe if her information is not complete and correct? Many women are taking risks today that are absolutely unnecessary." Security lay in the use of Zonite, either the liquid or the "forms" (suppositories).

While such products as toothpastes were offered under the seal of the American Dental Association's Council on Dental Therapeutics, the makers of cosmetics relied on less official if no less persuasive weapons. Tangee lipstick told the story of a woman who lost man after man simply because she used too much make-up; even more subtly, Helena Rubinstein filled a page with the virtues of her *Youthifying* tissue cream.

In the "pulps"—magazines specializing in "true" confessions, western stories, detective tales and the early efforts at science fiction—the advertisers catered to more primitive needs like building muscles, learning new careers by mail and becoming the life of the party by mastering some parlor trick. Science fiction was found in *Wonder Stories* and *Amazing Stories,* which shared a circulation of more than 100,000 with *Weird Tales,* a magazine concerned more with the eerie and the bizarre. *Weird Tales,* besides running more or less original horrors concocted by contemporary hacks, regularly reprinted such masters of the fantastic as Wilkie Collins, Saki and Maupassant. The others stuck more closely to true science fiction: i.e., stories based on scientific or pseudo-scientific concepts. The stories were built more on the exploitation of some technological marvel than on the reactions of the characters to it and its consequences, and dealt chiefly with space travel, time travel and interplanetary adventure. They were, in short, extraterrestrial westerns. There were already a number of science-fiction clubs throughout the country and each of these issued its own publication, which, in the jargon already coined in the fraternity by eliding syllables and joining others, were known as *fanzines,* as distinguished from the *prozines* (in English, fan magazines and professional magazines). Some of the more dedicated *prozine* writers also contributed—in the strict sense of the word—to the *fanzines;* virtually all the "literature" in the field was in periodicals rather than books.

CHAPTER 20

Trying Out the Future

SCIENCE itself, pure and applied, was notching up progress. The atom was being smashed, poked, probed and prodded, and papers made public during the week indicated that it was giving up secrets from its most private recesses. Chemistry and physics were transmuting the pure sciences to make for greater comfort and better living in the immediate future.

The most spectacular demonstration of applied physics was the infant air-conditioning industry, which this week adopted as its slogan *Any Climate Anywhere*. The project of making the insides of city buildings free from dust with controlled temperature and humidity was gaining sensational headway. The Radio City Music Hall in New York and the Sears Roebuck store in Chicago were outstanding examples of successful air conditioning that brought thousands of orders to the manufacturers. Restaurants, trains, theaters, hospitals and stores were moving swiftly to have their installations by the summer. Manufacturers were busy turning out smaller units for homes. Several enterprising dealers were installing air conditioners in automobiles. They said in the trade press: "If air delivered to our engine needs to be purified, why should not the air taken into human lungs be made dust free and germ free?" There was even talk of outdoor air conditioning. Experiments were being planned to dissipate the early-morning fog in New York's harbor with electrified sprays. If this worked, it was planned to try fog control at airports.

Aviation took a giant step forward during the week. An airplane, using instruments only, landed on an airport.

During the previous four years, blind or instrument flying had been an ordinary achievement. Regardless of weather, pilots were able to guide their craft from airport to airport, maintaining an unerring course by staying on a radio beam. But this wonderful beam could guide a plane only to a point above its destination. If the airport was hidden by fog or sleet, the plane either flew on or crashed. As a result the Government barred passenger planes from landing unless the ceiling was more than 500 feet.

For five years Colonel Clarence M. Young, Assistant Secretary of Commerce for Aeronautics, and his aide, Colonel Harry Harmon Blee, had been working on a device to supplement the long beam with a shorter, more direct beam that guided a plane from above the airport to a special runway.

When a swirling snowstorm swept the New York area, Pilot James L. Kinney of the Commerce Department was in the air several miles from Newark Airport in a Curtiss Fledgling. He pulled a hood over the cockpit and proceeded to head toward Newark by following the radio beacon. He watched a needle on a dial and listened to the dots and dashes that came over his earphones. When the needle had reached a certain point and the dots and dashes stopped suddenly, Kinney knew he had reached the blind spot directly over the airport's beacon. He swung his plane into a wide, counterclockwise turn and switched on his radio to another frequency. Immediately his radio picked up another set of signals from a localized beacon that confined its area to a special runway. Another dial told him the exact distance he was from the landing strip.

Still keeping the hood covered, aware of the snowstorm outside and below, Kinney now watched his instrument panel. Across his vertical needle he saw a horizontal needle bobbing up and down, showing him that he was either too high or too low in his approach glide. His job was to manipulate his stick so that the horizontal needle was centered on the vertical needle. Suddenly he heard a sharp *beeep* that told him to throttle down because he was now 1,000 feet from the field. Then came another beep of a lower pitch that told him he was on the edge of the field and he would have to cut the engine. By this time he was low enough to lift the mask and see the ground in any weather.

The test had been planned for February and was to have been made by Test Pilot Marshall S. (Maury) Boggs, who had an outstanding record for the number of blind landings in the worst possible weather. But Boggs went on a pleasure flight to California and crashed to his death in broad daylight.

Commercial demand for synthetics was increasing to the point where industry was putting millions of dollars into experimentation with a view to newer and greater markets. Laboratories were producing artificial rubber with elasticity and strength equal to those of the natural product. Rayon was being consumed throughout the world in enormous quantities. The United States, having produced 150 million pounds of rayon in 1932, was increasing its capacity to 233 million pounds. It was significant that Japan was the second largest producer in the world, replacing Great Britain.

The newest and most dramatic of the synthetics was plastics. An industry that had confined itself for years to the making of billiard balls and simple artifacts from Bakelite was finding that resins, air, coal and water could be treated chemically, be shaped by heat and/or pressure and retain that shape after cooling. It was discovered that beautiful color effects could be obtained. Designers found the material would lend itself easily to be made into a vast array of goods and notions from toothpicks to dinner plates, boxes, buttons, ornaments, pipestems and steering wheels, combs, and eyeglass frames in hues never before seen in these products. They were also resistant to corrosion, mildew and stain.

Perhaps the men in the laboratories were not aware of it, but they were working diligently on increased freedom for the housewife. Experiments were being conducted with low temperatures in food preservation. During the week, reports were made on a test seeking the difference in taste between meat frozen rapidly and slowly. The most fastidious experts could find no difference.

Experiments were being conducted in the quick freezing of fresh and prepared foods that could be kept under refrigeration indefinitely. Manufacturers, retailers and even the consumer were intrigued by the idea of an ever-ready food supply in home freezers. Some prepared foods were eaten months after they had been stored, and pronounced nourishing as well as tasty. Food editors talked of the future, when deep freezers in every home would contain finished foods in fancy packaging to free the housewife from the burden of cooking every day.

Food for the world was another problem being tackled in the test tube. Dr. F. Bergius of Germany announced a method of growing plants without soil, the roots being kept in chemical solution. The new science—hydroponics—was getting the attention of chemists in England and the United States, who saw in it a chance to feed land-poor countries.

The American housewife was treated to the sight of the first soapless detergent. *Drift* was packaged, marketed and received with mixed feelings of enthusiasm and suspicion.

People were not yet ready to accept the fact that something that didn't have suds could wash as well as soap powders.

Progress reports were made in the creation of better weed destruction, antiknock gasoline, vitamins and fabrics for clothing. The general trend was to take pure knowledge and apply it to the direct and immediate needs of mankind.

In the more understandable of the pure sciences Joseph Delmont, a naturalist, reported experiments on a gibbon who proved to be capable of medicating himself. The gibbon, called Bobby, had been wounded, and under observation chewed thurifer leaves into a mass and poulticed the wound. Dick, his orang-utang companion, washed the wound and also poulticed it with clay. Dick seemed to be the natural doctor of Mr. Delmont's medical menagerie. He treated other injured apes by licking their wounds and selecting only betel leaves for poulticing from several piles of other kinds of leaves. Mr. Delmont postulated the theory that animals of the higher order had some intelligence above mere instinct.

The secret of sex predetermination was explored by two Russian biologists, N. K. Koltzoff and V.N. Schroeder. They experimented on horses and rabbits, using electrical currents to isolate male and female elements in the sperm, which had opposed electric charges. Using the current on sperm in solution, they found some spermatozoids went to anode, some to cathode and some to neutral zones. The anode sperm, injected in a rabbit, produced a litter of six—all female; the cathode sperm produced four males and a female; the neuter zone produced two males and two females.

Dr. Paul Bartsch, Smithsonian Institution naturalist, reported the discovery of the greatest known fissure in the earth, a deep of 44,000 feet (8.33 miles) off the north coast of Puerto Rico not far from the Nares Deep, 27,972 feet (5.3 miles). While newspapers commented that Dr. Bartsch had found a *real* depression, he made the point that the hole was big enough to take all of Mount Everest and some smaller hills. Everest, however, was not being denigrated by comparison with the hole. Six explorers were flying this week to India to view Everest from the air. If they succeeded, they would be the first to see the summit of the world's highest protuberance.

The adventures of Dr. Roy Chapman Andrews in the Gobi Desert were recounted in a book, *The New Conquest of Central Asia,* in which the famed digger of fossils in Mongolia described speed trials he made of animals. The Gobi has a rock floor smooth enough in many places for a motorcar to travel at top speed. In clocking the animals, Dr. Andrews found that the Mongolian wild ass attains a speed of 40 m.p.h.; the wolf 36 m.p.h.; and the antelope 60 m.p.h. His assistants complained that Dr. Andrews was sometimes too eager in his researches. Once, having discovered the tops of some dinosaur eggs, they had to keep him away from the find so they could use brushes with the required delicacy. The impetuous Dr. Andrews, they said, would have been inclined to use a pickax.

In the field of atomic science, Dr. A. V. Grosse of the University of Chicago reported that not all neutrons have the same mass. Dr. Carl D. Anderson of the Pasadena Institute of Technology was confirmed in his claim of the existence of positrons—positive electrons—as opposed to normal electrons, which have negative charges. Hitherto the proton, 1,800 times the size of the electron, was the smallest known positive-charge particle. These two developments were part of a chain of discoveries in atomic science that resulted in the control of the atom. The process of confirming the work of other explorers into the nucleus was continued by Dr. L. F. Halstad of the Carnegie Institute, who smashed the atom of aluminum with alpha particles, proving an earlier experiment by Dr. M. Poe of Germany.

Learned papers published during the week were a small indication of the tremendous amount of work that was continuing and beginning in the laboratories throughout the ity toward an improved world that rested in the skill and world. It seemed as if everyone was aware of the responsibil- knowledge of the men of science.

CHAPTER **21**

Tomorrow Will Be Better

EVERYONE loves a happy ending and, as far as the bank holiday was concerned, Americans did not have long to wait for it.

Through three desolate years of adversity and privation they had been brave and patient and hopeful, waiting for better times that would bring them jobs, a modest measure of financial security and a fair chance to improve their lives. Surely they had griped and grumbled and in brief moments of utter frustration burst into violence, but somehow they had maintained a traditional expectation that something good would happen soon. They were not let down by the new Administration.

The Roosevelt charm and infectious confidence that had brought forth the necessary optimism during the money crisis were swiftly supplemented with the kind of action the people understood and appreciated. By Thursday, March 9, Roosevelt and Woodin had decided that the general orderliness of the depositors during the "holiday" warranted a positive move. Therefore Woodin invited all the banks to apply for permission to reopen. He set the following Monday as the date. It was a dramatic challenge to the experts in the twelve Federal Reserve banks and the various state banking departments, who had to examine 18,000 financial institutions by deadline. While the world watched the staggering task with wonder and admiration, the men went to work. Lights burned late and tireless fingers flew over the keys of calculating machines; cash was counted and figures were checked. It was truly a race of time and money. When countless weary men rose from their labors by Sunday midnight, the job had been finished.

On Monday more than 75 per cent of the nation's banks were back in business and the stock exchanges were resounding with the shouts of the traders. Tickers spelled out "Happy Days Are Here Again" and America's financial community moved its mighty muscles once more. Everyone stirred with renewed life. Little merchants rushed to their banks to get change, make deposits and negotiate loans. Big business moved cautiously but with increased vigor. In New York, stocks rose 15 per cent and in Chicago, the Board of Trade was strained to capacity. There were no panic queues in front of banks.

Happy days were here again indeed. The people were heartened by the reopenings. Bank doors stood wide as in other days, inviting any kind of financial transaction. Commentators of the day pointed out that this was comforting even to those who had no money in the bank. By the middle of March more than $300 million in gold had been returned by the hoarders, enough to support $750 million in Federal Reserve notes. Then came the news that the dollar would be depreciated, starting a strong surge of buying at wholesale and retail levels to anticipate higher prices. This gave a slight impetus to increased employment. More jobs meant more purchasing power. More purchasing power meant more jobs. The ambivalent cycle that had begun a downward spiral in 1929 was being unwound upward.

Light wines and 3.2 beer were made legal and Prohibition was about to be drowned in legal liquor. The brewers and distillers, distributors and retailers promised more jobs. The threat of unemployment as a result of Repeal did not worry gang leaders like Joe Adonis, Lucky Luciano, Dutch Schultz and their kind. They were retreating to previously prepared positions in such fields as management-labor relations, trucking, the water front, large-scale prostitution and narcotics. Murder, Inc., was quietly burgeoning in Brooklyn, Detroit, Chicago and Los Angeles. Prohibition, the ignoble experiment, had taught these men well. Crime was never again to be a haphazard affair of burglary or robbery. It was already organized like big business. Indeed, it *was* big business.

The all-powerful Franklin D. Roosevelt was riding the crest of his popularity, which was reflected in the actions of a Congress that denied him nothing. During the first 100 days he sought to improve conditions in every endeavor, with special emphasis on the farmer and the workingman. His measures were passed swiftly and enthusiastically. Among them were help to the banks, unemployment relief, farm relief, home-mortgage relief and the development of the Tennessee River Valley, the great experiment in government management of electric power. In each instance the proposal was directed to the common people. Roosevelt made his first Fireside Chat on March 12, when, by radio, he entered the homes of almost all Americans and in a friendly, familiar way unfolded and explained his plans for the future. He did this again and again when he had a "tough nut to crack" in Congress, and later he used the technique successfully to overcome a hostile press.

He spoke of confidence in government and in its money and he advocated *pump-priming* to restore economic vigor. He placed Secretary of the Interior Harold Ickes at the head of the Public Works Administration (PWA), which was to disburse $3.3 billion in loans and grants for the construction of highways, dams, housing, river and harbor projects, tunnels and bridges. These were regarded as vital to the needs of the country. They also gave employment—but not enough. A subsidiary, the Civil Works Administration (CWA), was created to "make jobs." These were to consist mainly of the shovel and pickax brigades, but were extended to cover a broad variety of white-collar workers. Writers were hired to put together regional histories; artists were set to painting murals in schools and post offices; actors were put on the stage to give free performances of plays and pageants. There were jokes, good-humored as well as vicious, about these things, but those who got the jobs saw in them only the dignity of paid employment.

Roosevelt tried to provide for everyone who was eligible. There were the young men just out of grammar or high school who could not find employment. For them he set aside $30 million in an organization called the Civilian Conservation Corps (CCC). By July 1, more than 300,000 youths had been mobilized and taken to their 1,450 forestry sites under the supervision of Regular Army officers, as well as some Navy, Marine and Reserve officers. This raised a clamor from both political extremes. The conservatives charged that Roosevelt was throwing away the nation's money on worthless loafers and "shovel-leaners," and the Communists screeched that he was raising a new Fascist army.

Impervious to these criticisms, Roosevelt encouraged the Government to move into the lives of all the people, making loans to the farmer, creating the Federal Deposit Insurance Corp. (which guaranteed bank deposits up to $10,000 each in bank failures) and working toward a more equitable position for labor in its dealings with industry. By no stretch of optimism could anyone say the Depression was over. But the frustration of the past three years was rapidly turning into a healthy restlessness. People were moving into new jobs. Small merchants dared to undertake new ventures as the national spirit rose. They knew that prosperity would not lunge at them from around the corner; they had to seek it out and capture it. But this time they were acquiring the means as well as the will to put "a chicken in every pot" and at least one car in every garage.

There was little concern with events in Europe and Japan. More interesting was the breath-taking race made by the New York Giants for the National League pennant. They had wound up in sixth place the year before and the experts had picked them to hold the same spot. But under Bill Terry, serving his first full year as manager, the Giants moved into first place early in April and held on through September. Then they capped their triumph by beating the Washington Senators in the World Series in five games. Here are some names to flavor nostalgia: Carl Hubbell, Gus Mancuso, Hal Schumacher, Roy Parmelee, Fred Fitzsimmons, Blondy Ryan, Travis Jackson and Mel Ott.

Europeans read with interest about the American bank holiday and then turned to their own affairs. The Italians were blissfully aware of the fact that trains were running on time; the Austrians smiled benevolently at their own *Schlamperei*; the Germans were deliriously exalted that at last they were the Master Race; the British were sure that the Empire would last forever; the cold and hungry Russians were told they were living in Utopia—and the French could not agree on anything.

The whole world was moving into a new phase where new alignments of posture and action seemed to predominate. Roosevelt, born an aristocrat, became the champion of the people. Hitler, of proletarian origin, became an autocrat. American financiers cursed Roosevelt for destroying their wealth, and their German counterparts praised Hitler for preserving theirs; yet in both countries there were the heretical rich who, in one case, threw their support to Roosevelt and, in the other, turned their resources against Hitler.

Everywhere there was the feeling that the bottom had been reached; that the only direction was up. The week was one that brought to an initial climax two revolutions that had their origins in completely opposite philosophies and ethics, yet for a period ran roughly parallel, each centered on a single strong leader without whom it could not have survived but who owed his own supremacy nonetheless to a fateful combination of circumstance and personality. One of the revolutions has outlived the man who made it, to the general benefit not only of the country in which it began but of the world at large. The other, it is hoped, collapsed with the disappearance of its protagonist after it had almost mortally wounded civilization.

It was a week to remember.

ACKNOWLEDGMENTS

THE authors wish to record their thanks for the valuable assistance rendered to their researches by:

János Almási, lecturer in modern history, Loránd Eötvös University, Budapest.

Peter Dinella, librarian, the New York *Post*.

István Diöszegi, lecturer in modern history, Loránd Eötvös University, Budapest.

Dr. Filippo Donini, director, Istituto italiano di cultura, New York.

N. Dyakonov, press department, Embassy of the U.S.S.R., Washington.

The late Harold E. Fellows, president of the National Association of Broadcasters, Washington.

Sidney Garfield, Columbia Broadcasting System.

John W. Hoines, National Broadcasting Co., New York.

Dr. Arno Huth, New York.

H. V. Kaltenborn, New York.

André Leveillé, Food & Agriculture Organization, Rome.

Mrs. Alice Lewitin, assistant director, Radiodiffusion-télévision française, New York.

Dr. Karl E. Lichtenecker, press attaché, Austrian Embassy, Washington.

B. O. McAnney, New York *World-Telegram & Sun*.

Mavis McIntosh, McIntosh-McKee, New York.

Marion Moss, British Broadcasting Corp., New York.

Doris L. Muller, Barnard College.

William F. Murphy, M.D., Boston, Mass.

Robert Parrella, New York *Herald Tribune.*

Mrs. Henrietta T. Perkins, assistant librarian, Yale Medical Library, New Haven.

Margaret Ratcliffe, British Information Services, New York.

Alexander Rylander, National Broadcasting Co.

Marie-Cecile Schulte Strathaus, press secretary, Embassy of the Federal Republic of Germany, Washington.

G. K. Seleznyov, scientific worker of the U.S.S.R. Academy of Sciences, Moscow.

M. H. Shapiro, Broadcast Music, Inc., New York.

Mary Sherwin, New York.

Dr. Tibor Szamuely, professor of modern history, Loránd Eötvös University, Budapest.

G. Takacs, Jr., secretary, Hungarian Legation, Washington.

Hon. Ludwig Teller, New York.

A. E. Ulmann, New York.

Roger Vaurs, director, Press and Information Service, Embassy of France, New York.

Herman Weiler, the New York *Post* library.